LOST'S
BURIED TREASURES
2ND EDITION

THE UNOFFICIAL GUIDE TO EVERYTHING
LOST FANS NEED TO KNOW

**LYNNETTE PORTER, DAVID LAVERY,
& HILLARY ROBSON**

SOURCEBOOKS, INC.®
NAPERVILLE, ILLINOIS

Published by Sourcebooks, Inc.
P.O. Box 4410, Naperville, Illinois 60567-4410
(630) 961-3900
Fax: (630) 961-2168
www.sourcebooks.com

Library of Congress Cataloging-in-Publication Data
Porter, Lynnette R.
  Lost's buried treasures : the unofficial guide to everything Lost
fans need to know / Lynnette Porter, David Lavery, Hillary
Robson.
    p. cm.
  Includes bibliographical references and index.
  1. Lost (Television program) I. Lavery, David II. Robson,
Hillary. III. Title.
PN1992.77.L67P66 2007
791.45'72—dc22

                         2007039523

     Printed and bound in the United States of America.
            VP 10 9 8 7 6 5 4 3 2 1

CONTENTS

Is There an (Ancestor) Text on This Island?

Books on the Island: *After All These Years* | *Are You There, God? It's Me, Margaret* | *Bad Twin* | The Bible | Book of Law | *A Brief History of Time* | *The Brothers Karamazov* | *Carrie* | *Catch-22* | *Dirty Work* | *Evil Under the Sun* | *The Fountainhead* | *The Gunslinger* | *Hindsight* | *The Invention of Morel* | *Lancelot* | *Laughter in the Dark* | *Left Behind* | "An Occurrence at Owl Creek Bridge" | *Our Mutual Friend* | *Rainbow Six* | *The Third Policeman* | *The Turn of the Screw* | *VALIS* | *Watership Down* | *A Wrinkle in Time*

Ancestor Texts: *Alice's Adventures in Wonderland* | "The Damned Thing" | *Death and the Maiden* | *Gilgamesh* | *Lord of the Flies* | *The Mysterious Island* | *The Odyssey* | *Of Mice and Men* | *The Outsiders* | "A Psychological Shipwreck" | *Robinson Crusoe* | *Solaris* | *The Songlines* | *The Stand* | *Stranger in a Strange Land* | *Walden Two*

Must-See TV and Essential Movies: *The Adventures of Brisco County, Jr.* | *Alias* | *Buffy the Vampire Slayer/Angel/ Firefly* | *Cast Away* | *Crossing Jordan* | Disaster Movies |

ACKNOWLEDGMENTS

Thanks to my friends in Hawaii who "found" me and taught me about aloha spirit. Leilani, Malia, Pat, Jean, Jill, and Maile—thank you for sharing your insights and being such excellent tour guides! Thank you, too, to everyone in Tol Andûne for your friendship and support.

As always, my thanks to David and Hillary, the best collaborators I could imagine in this or any parallel universe. Thanks, too, to Uwe Stender for his continuing guidance and, at Sourcebooks, Peter Lynch, our excellent and supportive editor.

Deepest thanks to my family, who I hope will share my flashforwards, as well as my flashbacks, for many years to come. I dedicate my work to you, Bart, Nancy, and Heather.

—Lynnette Porter

Thanks, of course, to Lynnette and Hillary, most excellent friends and collaborators. I am indebted as well to all those students who have listened to me go on about *Lost*. I especially want to express my gratitude to my amazing family, Sarah, Rachel, and Joyce, all of whom watch *Lost* avidly (wish we could visit the island together more often). When my life "flashes before my eyes," it is their achievements I see.

—David Lavery

A very special thanks for the always enjoyable experience of working with my brilliant collaborators, David and Lynnette. I'd gladly live a life on Mystery Island if the two of you were my co-conspira—er—survivors.

In the years I've watched and loved *Lost*, I've had the good fortune of sharing my thoughts about the series with some people near and dear to me: our discussions about various theories, hypotheses, and plot have been truly inspirational. To you, I raise my (margarita) glass and salute.

I also would like to second Lynnette's appreciation for the guidance of Peter Lynch and the support of Sourcebooks. There's no greater pleasure than working with a publisher that truly knows and understands the import of your work. And to my family and friends, thank you for your support, love, and guidance. You mean the world to me, and have my heart.

—Hillary Robson

Nota bene: The authors offer special thanks to Tyler Hall and Sarah Caitlin Lavery, both of whom penned entries in the "*Lost* Reading and Viewing" sections.

INTRODUCTION

"The fans have helped this show to be like no other. The ways we interact with the show have been groundbreaking and the passion can be seen in the frustration and celebration after each show, especially if you peek into the world of *Lost* Internet postings and podcasts."[1] So said Dean Shull, Chief Executive Officer of Los Angeles-Catchphrase Entertainment, and one of the directors of an upcoming documentary about *Lost* and its fandom. As long-time *Lost* fans (four seasons and interest dating back to March 2004, when rumors of the pilot episode surfaced on the Internet, count as a long time in TV-land), we heartily agree with Shull. *Lost* fans are intelligent, vocal critics who are helping to change the face of network television by forcing television producers and network executives to look at the many ways people "watch television" online, via mobile phones, on DVD, and during weekly TV broadcasts. They interact with other fans and the creative talent behind *Lost*, and they spend valuable time dissecting the series and putting it back together in personally meaningful ways.

My co-authors and I are long-time *Lost* fans. Individually and together, we have spoken at conferences and taught classes about what *Lost* means and how and why its popularity says a lot about television and fandom; academics, fans at public presentations, students learning more about television, and the media capturing the *Lost* phenomenon are among those seriously studying *Lost* and recognizing it as more than just a fad. In the past two years, I've been fortunate to visit Oahu three times. During each visit I meet more people who work behind the scenes or in front of the camera, watched *Lost* being filmed, met the cast, or just are pleased that the series is being filmed locally. Seeing the many former filming locations around the island gives me a better appreciation of the care and dedication of everyone involved in *Lost*'s production. The people of Oahu, as well as the temporary residents who create the series, seem genuinely proud of *Lost*. Being part of *Lost*'s legion of fans led us to write this book.

Lost fandom is large and inclusive; when conducting interviews for the documentary, Shull noted that he and his colleagues talked with "academics, *Lost* tour guides, mega fans, actors, and people involved with the show."[2] *Lost* fans come from diverse backgrounds and have different reasons for watching the series, but they are united in their continuing interest. What surprised Shull most about *Lost* fans? "The communal experience of the show."

Lost fans revel in their ownership of the series and its fandom. They often like insider information (but sometimes protest the ways spoilers are leaked, as occurred in May 2007 when details of the "snake in the mailbox" ending to Season Three somehow wriggled onto fan sites; a similar problem occurred in May 2008 when Lostfan108 struck again with detailed information about the Season Four finale, dubbed "frozen donkey wheel" by series' creators/writers Damon Lindelof and Carlton Cuse). Fans share just about everything they know about the show, debate it, and want to know more. They gather to watch episodes and immediately post online their kudos and criticisms of each episode. They develop websites—a May 2008 search of "*Lost* fan sites" pulls more than five million English-language sites dealing with the series (up three million since last year). Fans buy *Lost* merchandise and become immersed in ARGs that unravel clues to international conspiracies. This isn't your parents' fandom— *Lost* creates a global community whose diverse members express their interest in hundreds of different ways but are linked by their interest in and evaluation of the series.

What do *Lost* fans need to know *beyond* the facts of the series to enhance their viewing pleasure? Which songs, books, TV programs, movies, or even places should be understood and, we hope, (re)visited and enjoyed to attain even greater ownership of their series? That's where this book comes in—a guide to the buried treasure only glimpsed in episodes, the gems just waiting to be picked up and admired. New fans needing to catch up with the best of *Lost* or long-time fans looking for more ways to "get *Lost*" can find where to go and what to read, watch, or listen to as part of the complete *Lost* experience. Before going back to the island (if you can find it) or catching up with the Oceanic 6, discover even more *Lost* treasures.

*Lost*lore is steeped in published works, and during the first four seasons the creative staff and characters lead us into the world of literary masterpieces, some well known, some more obscure. The first chapter, *Lost* Reading and Viewing, leads us into the *Lost* library to uncover literary clues to the island's mysteries. Like any good popular culture icon, *Lost* offers much more than the traditional library; after all, the hatch enticed us not only with its bookshelf but an eclectic collection of videos and vinyl. Must-See TV and Movies brings us up to date on the essentials from television and film history.

Music deserves special attention, and the *Lost* Playlist features the greatest hits of Geronimo Jackson and DriveShaft, hits from the past forty years, as well as a guide to composer Michael Giacchino's soundtrack for the series.

"Sawyerisms" have become a mainstay on the island and in TV culture, and Between the Lines: *Lost* and Popular Culture not only lists what Sawyer says but discusses our favorite con man's knowledge of television, film, and literature. Of course, Sawyer isn't the only one to name drop people and places from popular culture, as a second list illustrates. What makes *Lost* an important part of our popular culture? This chapter also explains how being *Lost* has changed the nature of television and become part of global culture.

Lost frequently asks us to understand science, even if it's questionable science that goes against the way we think the world should work. Since the surprise appearance of Locke's body in a coffin at the conclusion of Season Four, fans wonder if reanimation is possible on that movable island. An ongoing question, whether posed for scientific or supernatural consideration, is *Are the dead really dead*? Characters like Christian Shephard, or the more recently deceased Charlie Pace, seem to have a very active afterlife. Like M. Night Shyamalan, we see dead people on *Lost*, and theories about their purpose and existence abound in fandom. "Waking the Dead" is a popular *Lost* storytelling device that deserves to be unearthed for closer examination.

"Guys, where are we?" The different answers to that question have led to many destinations and theories, and Season Four adds more locations to our itinerary. The Significance of Place offers a global triptych to places important to characters, and a special section at the end of the chapter highlights where fans might go if they want to become *Lost* on Oahu.

Those fans who, like Ben Linus, enjoy playing mind games might find a new game or strategy in Playing Games. From puzzles and board games to e-games and real-world role playing, *Lost* offers plenty of entertainment choices for those down times between island crises (or the long hiatuses between new episodes).

Behind the Scenes provides a Who's Who of the talented individuals in front of and behind the cameras. Finally, a series of Top 10 lists gives a checklist of the best of the best—what every fan should read, watch, listen to, or do for the definitive *Lost* experience.

Season Four introduced great change in the *Lost* storyline, both in response to a lengthy writers' strike and the need to complete a story all too quickly heading toward a Season Six climax. The most recent season featured both flashforwards and flashbacks, time travel, messages from beyond the grave, the arrival of new characters (and the return of Michael), the deaths of familiar characters, rescue and loss, and the biggest shock of all—a movable island. The shape-shifting plot answers some questions but leaves fans wanting more.

Because so much changes from season to season, *Lost* offers new directions to explore as we meet new characters and travel through time and space. We've completely revised each chapter to provide insights and investigations into each episode through the Season Four finale, "There's No Place Like Home." We've also included a new chapter to analyze the increasingly important role of the dead in *Lost*'s mystery.

Lost offers us a wealth of treasures, but we have to dig into the story to find them. In the following pages, we provide a map to our favorites and hope you'll also be intrigued to find some buried treasures that help you understand *Lost* a little better and, along the way, enjoy some unexplored facets of the *Lost*verse.

—Lynnette Porter

## CHAPTER ONE

LOST READING AND VIEWING

IS THERE AN (ANCESTOR) TEXT ON THIS ISLAND?

Even before the library in the Swan hatch, entered for the first time in "Man of Science, Man of Faith" (2.1, the initial episode of Season Two), and that Bible Mr. Eko finds in the Arrow hatch, the one the Tailies stumble upon in "...and Found" (2.5), made Mystery Island more bookish, tomes were common enough on *Lost*—not as common as miniature liquor bottles, but not exactly rare either.

Throughout Season One, we find the unlikely avid reader Sawyer page-turning a variety of books, from Richard Adams' *Watership Down* (a book he re-reads in "Left Behind," 3.15) to Madeline L'Engle's *A Wrinkle in Time*. In Season Two, he continues to read from his word horde: Judy Blume's *Are You There, God? It's Me, Margaret* and Walker Percy's *Lancelot*. In the Swan even more books have screen time: James' *The Turn of the Screw*, Bierce's *An Occurrence at Owl Creek Bridge*, and, most notoriously, O'Brien's *The Third Policeman*, an obscure Irish novel that became a surprise bestseller due to its unintentional product placement cameo. And speaking of product placement, in "The Long Con" (2.13) we find Hurley reading the manuscript of *Bad Twin*, a Lost tie-in novel written by the late Oceanic 815 passenger Gary Troup, later released by Hyperion, the publisher of official *Lost* books. Season Three continued to be bookish. The opening scene of the first episode ("A Tale of Two Cities," 3.1) shows a book club—the assigned book Stephen King's *Carrie*. Later, in "Every Man for Himself" (3.4), Ben evokes Steinbeck's *Of Mice and Men* in his humbling of Sawyer, and in "Not in Portland" (3.7), Aldo is seen reading Stephen Hawking's *A Brief History of Time*.

To paraphrase a question literary critic Stanley Fish once famously asked in the title of a book: "Is there a text on this island?" Many, many texts is the answer. Astonishingly, given that *Lost* is the story of the aftermath of a plane crash, not a single John Grisham novel has been found.

Not all the "texts" are literary, of course. Cinema ancestors— disaster films, *Cast Away*, *Jurassic Park*—and television series—*The Adventures of Brisco County, Jr.*, *Buffy the Vampire Slayer*, *Gilligan's Island*, *Survivor*, *The Twilight Zone*, *Twin Peaks*, *The X-Files*—have all influenced *Lost*'s themes, its mise-en-scene, its characterization, its narrative style. The postmodern, as Umberto Eco has noted, is the age of the "already said." Books, films, and television have all had their say on *Lost*.

Each time a new *Lost* text opens for perusal, the fans go wild and speculation runs rampant as the *Lost*-fixated begin to read, backward and forward, an extraordinarily complex, still unfolding, still entangling narrative. The threads of a text, a "kind of halfway house between past and future," the critic Wolfgang Iser would write, always exist in "a state of suspended validity" (370), and such threads are particularly well-suited for today's avidly conjecturing, anxious to conspire "fan-scholar."

"Quality" television series, according to Robert Thompson's authoritative delineation, are "literary and writer-based" (15), and most readily, proudly, acknowledge their ancestors and their influences. When *Twin Peaks*' Black Lodge turned out to be in Glastonbury Grove and Windom Earle and Leo Johnson cozied up in their Verdant Bower, the Arthurian legends and Spenser's *Faerie Queene* were born again in a new medium. When Tony Soprano sobbed uncontrollably at the ministrations of Tom Powers' loving mother in *Public Enemy* (as seen on TV), televised and filmic mobsters became brothers in the same gang—and genre.

Books, film, music, television, as well as other manifestations of both low and high culture—to borrow the witty formulation of film scholar Robert Stam—are governed by the same principle as sexually transmitted diseases. To have sex with another is to have had sex with all of his or her other sexual partners, and every "text"—every new novel or short story, song, or movie, or television series—is far from innocent; each potentially carries the "contagion" of every other text it, and its creators, have "slept with."

Lost is highly promiscuous, sleeping around with a wide variety of textual "partners." We divide these partners, one form of buried treasures, into three sections: **Books on the Island** considers texts which have actually put in an appearance on/in the beach, the hatches, the barracks. **Ancestor Texts**,[3] offers accounts of *Lost*'s literary predecessors. **Must-See TV and Movies** provides a guide to the series' film and television ancestors.

Books on the Island

After All These Years—Susan Isaac's 2004 novel is one of several books Sawyer reads while convalescing in the Swan in "Everybody Hates Hugo" (2.4). It concerns Rosie Meyers, a Long Island English teacher suspected of murdering her husband on their 25th wedding anniversary after she learns he has deserted her for a younger woman. Escaping the authorities, she sets out to discover the real killer.

Are You There, God? It's Me, Margaret—When caught reading Judy Blume's novel *Are You There, God? It's Me, Margaret* ("The Whole Truth," 2.16), Sawyer downplays his interest in the pre-teen drama by calling it "predictable" and with "not nearly enough sex." Though *Margaret* is often referred to as the quintessential teen novel, with its focus on the title character's experiences with menstruation and buying her first bra, the novel is just as much about struggling with spiritual development. Margaret grows up with a mixed religious heritage—one Christian and one Jewish parent—and the novel follows her efforts to come to grips with her own beliefs. Menstruation and training bras aside, it is a story of religious quest.

Though Sawyer belittles the book for its lack of sex, *Margaret* is (according to the American Library Association) among the top 100 frequently challenged books in libraries because of its frank treatment of sexuality and religion. Needless to say, it is certainly more than a simple, pre-teen drama.

Lost often delves into the importance of faith, of good vs. evil, of scientific vs. spiritual. Like Margaret, the *Lost*ies have trouble deciding if they buy into spiritual mumbo-jumbo, and, like Margaret, they receive many mixed messages about faith—at once bringing people back from the dead and pitilessly killing off members of the group.

Perhaps it would seem more fitting for a character like Locke, who frequently stresses the importance of faith and, even more frequently as of late, battles with his own ability to believe in the island's spiritual properties, to be seeking answers in Judy Blume. Perhaps Margaret would have taught him that it's okay to not be sure about every facet of spiritual experience—that it's okay to question a higher power.

Instead, it is Sawyer, the island's resident literati and bad-boy, who finds himself reading the coming-of-age novel, who has not yet had much affiliation with the island's spiritual properties, though he often struggles to find a balance between what is right and wrong. Even more, Sawyer's proclamation that the novel doesn't have enough sex further brands him as the most hormonally driven of the *Lost*-clan (he is the one, after all, who regularly engages in extra-marital sexual activity—with Ana Lucia and Kate—on the island).

When Margaret and her friends are desperate to increase their bra size, they chant, "I must, I must, I must increase my bust," a catch-phrase that has surely raised the eyebrows of overprotective mothers across the world. But to Sawyer, of all people, Margaret's spiritual journey is predictable and the book's lust-factor dismal.—**Sarah Caitlin Lavery**

Bad Twin—Hurley introduces the audience to the "original" *Bad Twin* manuscript in "The Long Con" (2.13) before it later ends up in Sawyer's hands. Sawyer's reading is spoiled when Jack burns it in "Two for the Road" (2.20)—before Sawyer can finish the final ten pages. Damon Lindelof and Carlton Cuse affirm that within the series, author "Gary Troup" (an anagram for "purgatory" and pseudonym for ghostwriter Laurence Shames) survived the crash but was the first to die when sucked into the turbine engine. *Bad Twin*'s storyline focuses on small-time P.I. Paul Artisan's investigation of Clifford Widmore's missing twin, Alexander ("Zander"). The book is largely standard detective-fiction fare, with a storyline that peripherally mentions some minor characters and entities that are part of the *Lost* universe, mainly those that involve the wealthy Widmore family and their corporation, the Hanso Foundation, Paik Industries, Oceanic Airlines, and Mr. Cluck's Chicken Shack.

For all intents and purposes, *Bad Twin* is a tie-in text that throws *Lost* fans a few familiar nibbles in its pages, primarily involving the numbers (for example, Cliff Widmore was born on 8/15). Other references include literary texts like *Gilgamesh*, *Lord of the Flies*, the *Odyssey*, and *The Turn of the Screw*. The most important component of *Bad Twin* is its significance in the 2006 *Lost* Alternate Reality Game (ARG) launched near the end of Season Two. Print ads for the ARG included a "Don't Believe *Bad Twin*" ad campaign hosted on the Hanso Foundation website (hansofoundation.org) that accused the book of committing libel, with threats to sue publisher Hyperion.

Fans and Lindelof and Cuse alike were largely disappointed with the bestselling text, perhaps because the creative team had given Shames a wealth of elements to include in the text and the author instead picked and chose only those he wished to include. Cuse went so far as to admit in a *Hollywood Reporter* article that the book had not met their expectations and that "Gary Troup" met a fitting demise.

The Bible—Within the first three episodes a character with a prophetic name—Christian Shephard—had been introduced. Since then, *Lost*'s ever-interlocking characters and multiple-meaninged events have created a mythology of biblical proportions. How appropriate, then, that the Bible is one of, if not *the* most important ancestor text for this evolving series.

Popular names with biblical origins abound in the *Lost*verse: Aaron, Adam, Benjamin, Daniel, David, Elizabeth, Isaac, Jacob, James, John, Mark, Mary, Naomi, Ruth, Samuel, Sarah, Stephen, Thomas. Some names or their variants, such as Daniel/Danny/Danielle and Thomas/Tom/Tommy, are used many times in the first four seasons.

Christianity seems to be the dominant religion of those Oceanic 815 survivors expressing their faith. Mr. Eko carves the chapter and verse numbers of scripture he wants to remember, although his memory sometimes is faulty. He changes the words to the 23rd Psalm, for example, and writes the wrong scripture beneath John 3:05, although perhaps "John" refers to John Locke, who reads "Lift up your eyes and look north" as a divine sign ("I Do," 3.6).

Both Old and New Testament references have made their way into *Lost*. Series' creators and frequent episode writers Damon Lindelof (a Jew) and Carlton Cuse (a Catholic) have said that they sometimes infuse their philosophical and religious perspectives and questions into the story. To illustrate the number and variety of biblical references, here are only a few from the first four seasons:

- In "Catch-22" (3.17), two women seem to know Desmond: Ruth (seen in the backstory) is Desmond's former fiancé, and Naomi (on the island) recognizes him from the picture of Desmond and Penny she carries with her. In the Book of Ruth, Naomi is Ruth's mother-in-law. After both are widowed, Naomi suggests that Ruth return to her own homeland, but she refuses, preferring to accompany Naomi and join her people. A connection between Desmond's Ruth and Naomi, if it exists, hasn't been revealed, but the Bible's story of Ruth often is used to illustrate loyalty and great love, which Penny certainly seems to show for Desmond.

- Also in this episode's flashback, novice monk Desmond has difficulty understanding why God would test Abraham by requiring him to sacrifice his son, Isaac, a story recorded in Genesis. Although Brother Campbell explains the nature of sacrifice, Desmond still questions God's act. On the island, however, Desmond finds himself in a similar predicament; he, like Abraham, lures the unaware potential sacrifice into the wilderness. When the time comes to sacrifice Charlie, Desmond can't stand idly by; he saves Charlie and thus sacrifices a future in which he will be reunited with Penelope. Desmond may well feel, as Abraham did, that God tested him by asking him to sacrifice his greatest love (Penny).

- The life of John the Baptist, as described in the Gospels, plays prominent visual and symbolic roles in "Fire + Water" (2.12). In flashback, a portrait of John the Baptist hangs in young Charlie Pace's home; adult Charlie dreams of his mother, Claire, and Hurley dressed and placed similarly to the background figures in the painting. This dream motivates Charlie to have Aaron baptized, at whatever cost. By the episode's end, Mr. Eko baptizes both Claire and her baby.

- Mr. Eko tells Locke the story of Josiah and the way he rebuilt the temple. He explains that Josiah relied on the Book of

Law (knowledge), instead of gold, to rebuild it correctly and suggests that the book he found in another DHARMA Initiative station may help Locke "rebuild" the hatch to its correct purpose ("What Kate Did," 2.9). The story of Josiah is recorded in Second Kings.

- "Exodus" is both a *Lost* episode title (the Season One finale) and a book in the Bible. Moses' older brother Aaron becomes an eloquent spokesman for his brother and is known as a gentle peacemaker, unlike stern Moses. Aaron leads the Israelites into the Promised Land. Fans wonder if Claire's Aaron might one day grow up to be such a leader of a new generation of island dwellers, leading them off the island or to their own Promised Land. (Although Season Four revealed that at least some castaways get off the island long before Aaron becomes a man, fans still speculate that this baby is special in some way.)

- The 23rd Psalm is both the best known of all Psalms and another *Lost* episode title (2.10). Mr. Eko and Charlie recite this prayer (although they invert some key phrases) in memory of Eko's brother, the priest Yemi, and in re-dedication of their spiritual lives.

- Alex tells Jack that the Others base their law on the biblical concept of "an eye for an eye," noting that they punish people quite strictly in accordance to their law. The law of retribution traces its legal roots to several Old Testament books, although the often quoted "an eye for an eye, a tooth for a tooth, a hand for a hand" comes from Exodus; according to the Gospel of Matthew in the New Testament, Jesus didn't refute the premise of this law but taught that people should look beyond it to be more compassionate in their daily lives and to avoid invoking the law for personal revenge.

• Perhaps the most widely discussed *Lost* biblical name is Jacob. The mysterious leader of the Others, a (mostly) unseen but powerful healer, has become the foundation of their cult-like devotion. (Although Jacob is "revealed" to Locke as a shadowy image and disembodied voice during "The Man Behind the Curtain" [3.20], his hold over the Others is still a mystery.) The Others often ask WWJD (What Would Jacob Do?), and Jacob's teaching becomes a key part of the brainwashing film to which Karl is subjected ("Not in Portland," 3.7). Jacob is also important because he is Isaac's son and Abraham's grandson, which peripherally ties him to the previously mentioned story of sacrifice. Furthermore, Jacob is a deceiver; he disguises himself as his slightly older twin brother Esau in order to gain his father's blessing and inheritance as firstborn son (which leads to further specula-tion about whether either Ben or Locke can see the "real" Jacob). Christian Shephard claims to speak on Jacob's behalf ("Cabin Fever," 4.11), but so far the writers haven't revealed exactly who or what Jacob is. The Biblical Jacob becomes father to Benjamin (and the ephemeral Jacob seems to be a father figure to Ben Linus), a favored son used to test his older brothers' loyalty. (Like the Biblical Benjamin, Ben wants to stay in Jacob's good graces and acts jealous when Locke hears what Jacob says. When Locke seems to have won Jacob's favor and replaced him, Ben turns over the job of running the island—and doing Jacob's bidding—to Locke.) Finally, Jacob is recorded as having seen the face of God and lived—certainly a mark of a special prophet.

Whatever marks the island's Jacob as special, he certainly controls his followers.

Lost's writers add weight to their story when they invoke biblical precedents, whether through plot details or character names. *Lost* provides a modern context for biblical themes and spiritual dilemmas important in human development throughout history.

Book of Law—Mr. Eko uses this name for the Bible's Old Testament as he tells Locke the story of Josiah ("What Kate Did," 2.9). He then explains the parallel between the story of Josiah and the castaways' recent experiences.

A Brief History of Time—Stephen Hawking's bestselling *A Brief History of Time* showed up twice in Season Three of *Lost*. In "Not in Portland" (3.7) Aldo is reading it while standing guard at the Hydra while Karl is being brainwashed in Room 23. Later, in "The Man from Tallahassee" (3.13), the book can be glimpsed in Ben's living quarters in the Barracks. First published in 1988, *BHT* was intended to be the famous astrophysicist's explanation of everything "From the Big Bang to Black Holes" (the book's subtitle) for the layman. Writing, in an accessible prose style, almost devoid of mathematical formula, about the nature of space and time, the expansion of the universe, the uncertainty principles, elementary particles, the fate of the universe, and the hope for a unification of physics, as well as providing brief capsules biographies of Einstein, Galileo, and Newton, Hawking largely succeeds at his goal.

Given that *Lost*'s creative team has indicated that they have been reading books on physics and string theory, fans have found it significant that Hawking's *BHT* would appear on the island. Interestingly, the woman in "Flashes Before Your Eyes" (3.8) who refuses to sell Desmond a wedding ring and can apparently foretell the future also shares a surname with the famed physicist.

BHT also makes pop culture appearances in such films as *Harry Potter and the Sorcerer's Stone*, *Harry Potter and the Prisoner of Azkaban*, *Donnie Darko*, and *Legally Blonde*.

The Brothers Karamazov—In a Season Two episode of *Lost*, "Maternity Leave" (2.15), a new character, Henry Gale (later revealed to be Benjamin Linus), suspected of being one of the infamous "Others" and bearing the surname name of Dorothy from *The Wizard of Oz*, is given a copy of Dostoevsky's *The Brothers Karamazov* to entertain him during his captivity in the Swan's armory. This leads to Locke's comments to Jack about Ernest Hemingway's inferiority complex about his Russian literary predecessor, a bookish digression seemingly inconsequential until the episode's end, when a clearly scheming Ben uses it to provoke Locke's second-banana anger against Jack.

Brothers is often considered to be the finest novel of the Russian writer Fyodor Dostoevsky (1821–1881), author as well of such important books as *Notes from the Underground* (1864), *Crime and Punishment* (1866), *The Possessed* (1866), and *The Idiot* (1869), who died only months after its publication. The influential critic Mikhail Bakhtin (not to be confused with Mikhail Bakunin) once praised Dostoevsky as superior to his contemporary literary titan Leo Tolstoy because of his ability to give expression—in a process Bakhtin deemed "dialogism"—to a wide variety of voices in the culture of the day without "authorizing" a single point of view as the "Truth" (in Bakhtin's terminology "monologism"). *Brothers* is a near-perfect example of Dostoevsky's art. Primarily concerned with the murder of the patriarch of the Karamazov family, the novel never fully establishes the culprit, but along the way it does explore, in depth, not only the psyches of the major characters:

- Fyodor Pavlovich Karamazov, the father;
- Dmitri Fyodorovich Karamazov, the spendthrift and hedonistic oldest son, who is ultimately tried for parricide;
- Ivan Fyodorovich Karamazov, a rationalist and atheist, obsessed by the world's suffering (his poem "The Grand Inquisitor" is one of the book's most famous sections);
- Alexei (Alyosha) Fyodorovich Karamazov, the hero (or so the narrator claims), a deeply religious visionary;

but profound questions of faith, reason, redemption, guilt, justice, suffering, and happiness.

Lost shares *Brothers'* (and Dostoevsky's) dialogism. No one voice, no single point of view, no solitary backstory to date can be established as authoritative. It is fascinated, too, with many of the same themes. And *Lost* shares an interest in the figure of the patriarch: Mr. Paik (Sun's ruthless father), Christian Shephard (Jack's alcoholic, womanizing fellow surgeon), Charles Widmore (Penny's tyrant of a dad), Wayne (Kate's loathsome stepdad), Anthony Cooper (Locke's cruelly manipulative con-man parent). Wayne is already dead when our story begins, and Cooper is murdered, at Locke's behest, by Sawyer in "The Brig" (3.19). Should Benjamin Linus, yet another patriarch, end up murdered before *Lost* comes to an end, like the father in the novel he read on-screen, no doubt the suspects will be innumerable, but perhaps Ben is not the true father figure. Perhaps the barely glimpsed Jacob will turn out to be the father of *Lost*.

Carrie—In the opening scene of Season Three ("A Tale of Two Cities," 3.1), Juliet hosts a book club meeting in her cottage. Being the host, it's her turn to pick the book and chooses *Carrie* by Stephen King. It's a curious choice—not typical book club material. It was King's first published novel (1974) and tells the story of Carrie White, a sixteen-year-old girl with telekinetic powers raised by a fanatical, fundamentalist, Christian mother, who is teased and humiliated constantly at school. The climax of the story is a cruel plan hatched by one of Carrie's classmates to rig the vote and have Carrie crowned queen of the prom. Then, when she is on stage, a bucket of pig's blood can be dumped on her head. The plan succeeds and pushes Carrie over the edge. Rage fills her and she uses her powers to set fire to the dance burning nearly everyone alive.

During the book club meeting, Juliet tells the other members that *Carrie* is her "favorite book." While a horrific story, it's not an unsurprising choice. Juliet can identify with Carrie. Both consider themselves outsiders living in an isolated, self-sustaining environment full of social and political tension. Juliet is a prisoner on the island, unable to return home. She lacks the unquestioning faith in the island Ben and the other Others possess. Carrie is trapped in high school. She's naïve, unsophisticated, and the constant butt of jokes.

Lost viewers familiar with King's novel might notice additional similarities between the two women. While ultimately strong female characters, our first impressions find both in vulnerable situations at the mercy of their peers. In the opening scene of *Carrie*, she is naked, showering after gym class when she begins to menstruate for the first time. She panics. The other girls realize what's going on and chant "Plug it up!" while pelting her with tampons and sanitary napkins. Juliet is caught off-guard when her doorbell rings and burns her hand in the oven. Injured, but looking forward to the book club, she's accosted by other members for choosing *Carrie*. One man says, "It's not even literature. It's popcorn," and alludes to Ben's disapproval, too. If not for Oceanic 815's catastrophe overhead, the argument would have continued.

Taking a step back and looking at the structure of *Carrie*, we see that it's broken up into a third-person narrative mixed with newspaper articles, eyewitness accounts, and letters detailing the events unfolding within the story. Nearly fifty percent of the novel is written this way. King uses these pieces to add additional details that might not have fit naturally in the narrative. They help solidify Carrie's story by providing multiple points of view. This technique works well for *Lost*'s producers also. While each episode furthers the overall storyline, there is typically a backstory told through flashbacks, and more recently, flash-forwards. These extra scenes create a complex web of coincidence and crossed paths in the lives of the castaways.—**Tyler Hall**

Catch-22—The 17th episode of *Lost*'s third season, offering the second Desmond backstory in less than two months, owes its title to Joseph Heller's 1961 book, one of the greatest anti-war novels ever written, a novel so influential its title has become part of the language.

Set on an island off the west coast of Italy, *Catch-22* tells with the blackest of humor the story of an American bomber squadron toward the end of World War II. Paranoically but accurately convinced that the enemy is trying to kill him, Heller's hero,

Captain John Yossarian, wants out of the war and hopes to do so by having himself declared insane, but his path to freedom is blocked by "Catch-22." The desire to get out of war—to no longer, in Yossarian's case, insanely pilot a flimsy B-24 bomber through the flak and fighter interceptor-filled skies over enemy cities—is, of course, perfect proof of his sanity. Hence, by the strictures imposed by the impossible, absurd Catch-22, he cannot escape by reason of insanity.

The mysterious, Portuguese-speaking parachutist Naomi who arrives in "Catch-22" (knifed in the back by Locke in the Season Three finale, her identity and allegiance remained unknown)—in the final episode—is carrying with her a copy of a Portuguese translation (*Ardil-22*) of *Catch-22* (a copy of the photo of Penny and Desmond is found therein). Soon after finding the book, Desmond opts to save Charlie's life by pulling him out of the way of a Rousseau arrow that had proved fatal in his earlier vision of the incident, leaving both Desmond and the audience to wonder whether in so doing he has altered the course of events—in his vision, after all, the parachutist appears to have been Penny herself. Desmond's dilemma—to stretch the point, Desmond's "catch"—may very well change the future course of events on the island.

Director Mike Nichols completed an all-star-cast film version of *Catch-22* in 1970.

Dirty Work—Stuart Woods' 2003 novel actually makes two appearances on *Lost*, first in "Orientation" (2.3), where it shows up in the Swan library, and later on a shelf in Jack's office in "A Tale of Two Cities" (3.1). The book is the ninth in the Stone Barrington series, whose hero is a former police detective who has metamorphized into a lawyer. While investigating a case of marital infidelity on the behalf of his employer, a prestigious law firm for whom he does the more unsavory cases, Stone finds himself involved with the beautiful assassin Carpenter (a recurring Woods' character) and caught up in a world of espionage where the good guys and the bad guys are hard to distinguish.

Evil Under the Sun—Sawyer is reading this 1940 Hercule Poirot novel by the famed British crime fiction writer Agatha Christie (1890–1976) when he is interrupted by Nikki in "Exposé" (3.14). In what would became a cliché of the genre, a woman is murdered at the Jolly Roger hotel in Cornwall on the English Channel, and Poirot must discover the culprit (and of course does) out of a group of vacationers, all of whom become suspects.

A perfect choice of reading material, given that "Exposé" is a mystery as well. But none of the islanders is a Poirot, and the "murders" of Paolo and Nikki are never solved. In fact, the castaways themselves are the actual killers since they bury the two diamond thieves alive.

The Fountainhead—In Season Three's "Par Avion" (3.12) Sawyer is seen on the beach reading Ayn Rand's novel *The Fountainhead*. First published in 1943, Rand's story of a New York architect, Howard Roark, who refuses to compromise his principles for mere monetary gain, stands as a manifesto of its notorious author's philosophy of "objectivism," her absolute faith in what she would call "the virtue of selfishness." The title refers to the Russian émigré Rand's bedrock principle that "man's ego is the fountainhead of human progress." Although Rand struggled for some time to find a publisher, the book became a bestseller and was made into a movie in 1949, with Gary Cooper playing Rand's mouthpiece hero Roark.

Throughout the novel, Roark must do battle—often in court, where he has plenty of opportunities to spout his creator's philosophy—with those who would, through their sinister machinations, bring him down to their lower level. His genius triumphs, of course, and at the book's end he is building the world's tallest skyscraper as a symbol of his triumph over lesser souls.

Other than Sawyer's unphilosophical selfishness, no close connection between Rand's novel and the world of *Lost* immediately presents itself, and Sawyer's egocentricity has its limits: does he not ask that his reward in "Every Man for Himself" (3.4)—a Randish title, undercut by the end of the episode—be put in trust for his daughter-to-be? Does not Kate bring out the willing-to-sacrifice hero in him?

The article on *The Fountainhead* in Wikipedia[4] details numerous other appearances the novel has made in popular culture, including the films *Dirty Dancing* and *Heaven Can Wait* and the television shows *Barney Miller*, *Desperate Housewives*, and *Gilmore Girls*.

The Gunslinger—When Locke confronts Ben in "The Man From Tallahassee" (3.13) a copy of Stephen King's *The Gunslinger* is sitting on Ben's bookshelf. While not the first King novel featured in *Lost* (*Carrie* and *Hearts in Atlantis* in "A Tale of Two Cities" [3.1]), this is the first connection to his *Dark Tower* series. Spanning seven volumes, *The Dark Tower* is King's magnum opus—a sprawling epic that connects all of King's other novels together into a common plotline. It is the story of Roland, the last gunslinger, and his quest to save the Dark Tower. The Tower is said to stand at the center of all worlds—a place where all of space and time converge at a single point. If the Tower should fall, then all of existence will fall with it. It's fortunate that *The Gunslinger* remains tucked away safely on Ben's bookshelf rather than in the eager hands of Sawyer. If the castaways on *Lost* were to learn about Roland's world, they might notice eerie similarities with their own.

King tells us that Roland and his companions are traveling through a world that has "moved on." The disease spreading through the Tower has caused the fabric between worlds to grow thin, allowing artifacts from one world to pass through. They pass ancient, half-working machines created by a lost race simply referred to as the "old people." The lush prosperous world that Roland remembers from his youth has worn down and dried up. As he searches for the Dark Tower, he sees the same rot and deterioration present in every world he visits. It's a symptom the castaways would find familiar. As they trek across the island, they come across the technological leavings of the DHARMA Initiative. They know very little about who these people were or the purpose of the things they left behind.

As the mystery unfolds, Locke becomes the group's chief inquisitor—communing with the island and divining its secrets. When the lights go out in the hatch in "Lockdown" (2.17), Locke sees a mural drawn on the blast door. It depicts each DHARMA station on the island arranged in a circle around a question mark. In "The Cost of Living" (3.05) we find out that the question mark location is a hatch called "the Pearl," which is connected to every other station by video cameras. In *The Dark Tower* Roland often talks of how the Tower is circled by twelve portals like the numbers on a clock. Each portal is said to be a gateway between worlds and connected to the Tower by six beams—one portal at the end of each. As a child, Roland was taught the names of each portal in his nursery rhymes: Bear, Turtle, Eagle, Lion, etc. It's a naming scheme similar to that picked by DHARMA for its stations: Pearl, Swan, Arrow, Flame, etc. Each is a simple, singular noun.

Physical similarities aside, perhaps the most striking connection between *Lost* and *The Dark Tower* is the driving presence of fate throughout their storylines. Roland believes wholeheartedly in fate—a force King calls Ka. No matter how much one may rail against it, Roland says time and time again that there is no escaping the life Ka has planned. It's such a strong factor in the Tower that the ultimate conflict becomes Roland fighting against a destiny he knows he cannot escape. In *Lost*, Locke places a similar faith in the island itself. He sees events on the island happening for a reason. The other characters may not agree with him, but the viewer sees how dependent each person is on fate as backstories cross paths and intertwine in ways that can't be explained away as merely coincidence.—**Tyler Hall**

Hindsight—Yet another book Sawyer reads while recovering from his wound in "Everybody Hates Hugo" (2.4) is Peter Wright's self-published 2005 science fiction novel.

Hindsight tells the story of a Cambridge scientist and Cal Tech grad student who create a device that will allow them to become spectators of events out of the past (they want to see da Vinci painting, Newton doing physics). Their work is paid for by a mysterious wealthy sponsor—not to the best of our knowledge Alvar Hanso or Charles Widmore. Of course their scheme meets with strong opposition from those who fear it will somehow destabilize reality, and their attempt to acquire "hindsight," like any good mad scientist scheme, begins to go "horribly wrong."

How a book published in 2005 found its way onto the island in 2004 is not explained.

The Invention of Morel—In "Eggtown" (4.4), Sawyer is immersed in Adolfo Bioy Casares' 1940 novella during his time in the Barracks, an exceedingly strange Argentinean fiction by a countryman, close friend, and frequent collaborator of the polymathic genius Jorge Luis Borges that would seem to be the product of a very *Lost*-like epistemological mindset. On an uncharted Polynesian island (imagine that!), a fugitive Venezuelan writer condemned to life in prison for, apparently, political crimes, keeps a diary that records the strange arrival of a group of tourists. The fugitive/diarist falls in love with one of the tourists, a woman called Faustine, who may or may not be in love with a tennis player named Morel, but he is unable to interact with any of the visitors, weird anomalies begin to take place (for example, the sky now has two suns and two moons), and they eventually vanish entirely, only to reappear soon after. The fugitive/diarist's speculation about the island's riddles fills many pages, but eventually he discovers that Morel is in possession of a device of his own invention that reproduces reality, captures souls, and makes possible a repetition of time in an endless loop, which will allow his love for a certain woman, presumably Faustine, to remain eternal but brings about the death of its subjects. After Morel flees the island in anger, the fugitive/diarist steps into his role and sets about using the device to reconstruct reality with Faustine now *his* love.

Like Bierce's "A Psychological Shipwreck" and O'Brien's *The Last Policemen* (both available on the island), *The Invention of Morel* offers no simple resolution and no real closure. We are as confused—and mesmerized—at its end as we have been throughout. Like *Lost*, it interweaves profound questions about time, space, and reality with themes of love and loss in a science fictional narrative. If, however, *Lost* ends as inconclusively in May 2010 as *Morel* does at the end of its barely one hundred pages of rich text, millions of fans may well be gravely disappointed.

Lancelot—In "Maternity Leave" (2.15) the always-reading Sawyer has his head buried in (for him) a new book, Walker Percy's 1977 novel *Lancelot*. When he opened it to the title page he would have found the following epigraph (a quote from Dante's *Purgatorio*):

He sank so low that all means
for his salvation were gone,
except showing him the lost people.
For this I visited the region of the dead…

If Sawyer had been a fan of *Lost* rather than himself a *Lost*away, he might well have taken this epigraph to be yet another invitation to read the series, contrary to the repeated denials of Carlton Cuse and Damon Lindelof, as a story of a kind of purgatory.

The fourth of only six novels by the Louisiana-born physician (trained as a brain surgeon) Percy (1916–1990), *Lancelot* is the story, related in a series of monologues, of lawyer Lance Lamar, told in a mental hospital where he has come for a rest cure, to his childhood friend Percival, now a minister. His wife has been burned alive in their palatial home, and his daughter, he discovers, is not his. Obsessed with the nature of evil, he seeks to indulge in it (blowing up his house and killing his unfaithful wife).

We don't know, of course, if Sawyer ever finished *Lancelot*, but if he did *and* if he knew (and he did not, despite half-hearing her incoherent soliloquy beside his sick bed in "What Kate Did") that Kate had murdered her stepfather; and if he knew (and he did not, despite running into his car door and drinking with him in a Sydney bar) that Christian Shephard was Claire's real but secret father; and if he knew (and he did not, despite Hurley's several near revelations) that one of his fellow survivors had spent a good amount of time in an institution, he might well have found *Lancelot* a relevant book to be stuck with on this particular desert island. (Why, had he not himself fathered a child without being at first aware of it?) And surely its investigation into the nature of evil would have kept a man whose parents had been brutally murdered and who had himself committed a murder while seeking revenge turning the pages.

Laughter in the Dark—In "Flashes Before Your Eyes" (3.8) we see Hurley on the beach reading Vladimir Nabokov's 1932 *Laughter in the Dark*. (When first translated into English in 1936 its title was *Camera Obscura*.) Not the most famous book by the great Russian-American writer (1899–1977)—his notorious *Lolita* (1955) and the brilliant *Pale Fire* (1962) are better known, *Laughter* seems unlikely reading material for Hurley, but then again, the selection of books on the island is fairly limited.

Like *Lolita*, *Laughter* is the darkly humorous story of a middle-aged man (Albinus), an art critic in Berlin, seduced by a very young woman (Margot), who aspires to be a movie star. With an old lover, Margot betrays Albinus, attempting to rob him of his wealth. Over the course of the novel, Albinus degenerates into a blind shell of his former self.

In Nikki's seduction (and eventual murder) of Howard Zuckerman in "Exposé" (3.14) we can detect an echo, conscious or not, of Margot and Albinus' relationship in *Laughter*.

Reportedly, *Laughter* was a major influence on American writer Joseph Heller, author of the book that supplied the title of Season Three's 17th episode, "Catch-22."

Laughter in the Dark was made into a film by British director Tony Richardson in 1969. The film starred Nicol Williamson and Anna Karina.

Left Behind—A series of thirteen books penned by collaborators Tim F. Lahaye and Jerry B. Jenkins details the fate of those "left behind" after the Christian rapture (the ascension of living and dead souls to heaven before the return of Jesus Christ) as detailed in the Book of Revelations in the Bible. The first book in the series follows the trials and tribulations of 747 pilot Rayford Steele. While flying and contemplating committing adultery, he is informed that some of the passengers on the plane have disappeared—the rapture has begun and the rise of the Antichrist is just beginning.

The book is mentioned twice in *Lost*, both in the episode that shares the same title (3.15). Kate, Jack, and Sayid are "left behind" by the Others, who disappear in a cloud of gas and smoke without warning or explanation. Prior to the vanishing act, Locke informs Kate that she will not be accompanying the Others in their Exodus because of what she has done—a theme similar to those souls taken during the rapture (and the Others philosophy of who is good enough to make the "list"). The other mention is made by Sayid, who comments on how the others seemingly disappeared.

Left Behind—primarily the first in the series—has some comparisons to the ambiguous idea of "good" that plays out in the *Lost* characters. While the Others don't see *Lost*aways like Sawyer and Kate as "good people," we, the audience, know otherwise, and see their capacity for redemption. This theme is one that plays out throughout the text of *Left Behind*.

"An Occurrence at Owl Creek Bridge"—In "The Long Con" (2.13), Locke discovers and briefly handles a copy of *An Occurrence at Owl Creek Bridge* by Ambrose Bierce (1842–1914?). This collection of stories by the notorious 19th Century American cynic and man of mystery (he disappeared in Mexico, never to be seen again), best known for his wonderfully dark *The Devil's Dictionary*, immediately fed fan interest and why not?

Although at least two other stories in the collection ("A Psychological Shipwreck" and "The Damned Thing," both discussed in this guide) are worth reading by *Lost* fans, the titular tale, an account of the hanging of a southern plantation owner by Union soldiers during the Civil War, seems the most relevant. Though the victim escapes the noose and flees, we learn in the end, having fallen for Bierce's mislead, that his reprieve is all in his mind and his getaway transpires in the split second before the rope snaps his neck. The story's famous ending:

Doubtless, despite his suffering, he had fallen asleep while walking, for now he sees another scene—perhaps he has merely recovered from a delirium. He stands at the gate of his own home. All is as he left it, and all bright and beautiful in the morning sunshine. He must have traveled the entire night. As he pushes open the gate and passes up the wide white walk, he sees a flutter of female garments; his wife, looking fresh and cool and sweet, steps down from the veranda to meet him. At the bottom of the steps she stands waiting, with a smile of ineffable joy, an attitude of matchless grace and dignity. Ah, how beautiful she is! He springs forwards with extended arms. As he is about to clasp her he feels a stunning blow upon the back of the neck; a blinding white light blazes all about him with a sound like the shock of a cannon—then all is darkness and silence!

Peyton Farquhar was dead; his body, with a broken neck, swung gently from side to side beneath the timbers of the Owl Creek bridge.

For *Lost* fans already wondering if the frequently proffered conjecture that all the *Lost*aways are in fact dead and that the island is a kind of purgatory—a supposition repeatedly, ardently denied by *Lost's* creative team (despite their obvious shout outs in that *Purgatorio/Lancelot* epigraph [see *Lancelot*] and in the name of *Bad Twin* author Gary Troup), the occurrence of *Occurrence* seemed irresistible evidence.

Several film adaptations of "Occurrence" exist, including a 1962 movie by Robert Enrico—available for viewing online[5]—as well as *Alfred Hitchcock Presents* (1959), *Twilight Zone* (1964), and *Masters of Horror* (2005) versions.

Our Mutual Friend—Charles Dickens' final completed novel is a literary tome that Desmond carries with him at all times with the intention to read it before he dies (literally—right before he dies, no sooner, no later). Desmond's true love, Penelope, hid a letter within the book's pages with the intention of Desmond's reading while in prison, but he does not find it until much later, after contemplating suicide after spending three years in the hatch.

The novel follows protagonist John Harmon, son of a wealthy tycoon destined to marry a woman he has never met—Bella Wilfer—in order to inherit his father's fortune. When the body of a drowned man is found and identified as Harmon, John takes up a new identity as secretary John Rokesmith and, in the years that follow, works to earn his own fortune and marry.

Dickens is an important author for the *Lost* fan to consider, primarily for the similarities between Dickens' body of work and *Lost* as serialized drama. Dickens put out chapter-length installments of *Our Mutual Friend* over a year and a half and was known for playing into the desires of his fans, not unlike the way that the creative team behind *Lost* considers the fans when sculpting storylines. The creative team admits to admiring Dickens' ability to produce quality material on a tight schedule—a demand that often results in a decline in creative quality in the output. Dickens also includes a wealth of primary and secondary characters in *Our Mutual Friend*, a trait mirrored in the multitude of characters in every episode of *Lost*. But the most significant parallels are those that exist between the storyline of the protagonist, John, and his desire to gain approval based on his own means (not unlike the efforts made by Desmond to win acceptance of Penelope Widmore's father).

Cuse and Lindelof got the idea of including the book in the storyline as homage to novelist John Irving—who claimed *Our Mutual Friend* was the last book he wanted to read before he died.

Rainbow Six—Briefly visible on a Swan bookshelf in "Orientation" (2.3), *Rainbow Six* is a typical, action-filled Tom Clancy, his 10th. In it, the recurrent Clancy character John Clark, about to retire from service in the CIA, is asked by President Jack Ryan to head up Rainbow, a special, multi-national anti-terrorism unit based in England (Rainbow Six is Clark's call sign). Basque and Iranian terror schemes are foiled, but the core of the book concerns Clark and his team's struggle to stop a group of eco-terrorists out to prevent environmental degradation with a plot that will also kills millions.

The Third Policeman—When Desmond hurriedly packs a few belongings before he bolts from his underground home ("Orientation," 2.3), the camera briefly shows a copy of Flann O'Brien's novel, *The Third Policeman.* Prior to this episode, rumors circulated that the book is important to understanding what is happening on *Lost*. Fans rushed to order the novel, a good read on its own, to discern any similarities between O'Brien's dark tale of life after death and the castaways' fate. The sudden increase in the book's popularity surprised publisher Dalkey Archive Press, which had to publish more copies, and illustrated the buying power of *Lost* fandom.

In O'Brien's novel, the narrator's journey involves a strange visit with two policemen at their station and on their rounds. Along the way, the student-turned-writer-turned-thief-turned-murder-victim learns about the absurd nature of the world he now inhabits. Bicycles, for example, not only meld with their owners physically and emotionally after they spend so much time riding together, but they also have a mind of their own. (A penny-farthing bicycle is the Village's logo in *The Prisoner*, forming yet another link among *Lost* and several ancestor "texts." See *The Prisoner* in the film and TV section.) Bicycles are an excellent example of the way "atomic theory" works; the atoms of humans and machines interact and eventually merge. Even more interesting, a mysterious vault contains whatever riches the policemen and the narrator can imagine; whatever they desire is provided. However, there is one catch: The goods cannot be taken above ground.

By the end of O'Brien's novel, the narrator finally meets the third policeman, who reveals to him the strange nature of time and space. They are not what living people presume, and the narrator discovers that what seems to have taken place only moments or hours before actually occurred in "real time" several years ago. He now can travel through walls or even back to his old home to visit with the partner who did him in for his share of pilfered wealth. O'Brien does more than create a good ghost story; he develops a "real" surreal world that plays with readers' notions of space and time, life and death.

Lost, however, may not imitate an important part of the book. O'Brien's main character, the story's narrator, is dead, although he fails to understand that for most of the novel. *Lost*'s creators persistently deny this is true of the castaways. Nevertheless, Claire's "transformation" that leads her to abandon her baby and join her dead father, Christian Shephard, in Jacob's cabin ("Cabin Fever," 4.11) makes us question whether she is alive or dead. The dead, like Charlie and Christian, seem to lead active lives, just as O'Brien's characters do.

What is a more direct link to the novel is the mysterious "box" Ben Linus introduces during Locke's second Season-Three backstory ("The Man from Tallahassee," 3.13). To keep Locke in line, Ben tells Tom Friendly to bring the man from Tallahassee to the Barracks. Ben explains to Locke that whatever he wants can be provided by the "box." At the end of the episode, Locke discovers that the box has produced, to his shock and horror, the one person who could turn his island paradise into Hell—his father. Although Ben insists that Locke is the one who has brought Anthony Cooper to the island to work out their unresolved issues, Locke denies ever wanting to see his father again ("The Brig," 3.19). Apparently, whatever Ben desires, such as a way to motivate Locke to share his inside connection with the island and to keep control of his followers, is manifested in the "magic box," just as it is in *The Third Policeman*.

The Turn of the Screw—As Locke looks for the DHARMA Initiative "Orientation" video just where Desmond told him it would be—"top shelf, right behind *The Turn of the Screw*," for just a moment the Dover edition of the classic Henry James' ghost story fills the left half of the screen. Set in a country house called Bly, not on a desert island, James' story is really the diary of a young governess who has become convinced the two small children she cares for, Miles and Flora, are demonically controlled by their former governess, Miss Jessel, and her lover, a servant named Peter Quint. The book has inspired a variety of readings since its publication in 1898, with some critics taking it to be a true tale of the supernatural and others convinced everything is in the mind of the young governess, who has "projected" the haunting out of her own repressed sexuality.

Other than serving (like *The Third Policeman*) as Desmond's reading material, is *Turn of the Screw* a *Lost* ancestor text? Mysterious children under the thrall of "Others"; the presence of ghosts—or are they?; an indecipherable text, capable of multiple interpretations. These factors make *Turn of the Screw* a must for the hatch bookshelf, but it is clearly not a major source.

VALIS—In "Eggtown" (4.4), Locke brings an imprisoned Ben reading material with his food, *VALIS* by Philip K. Dick (1928–1982). The choice disappoints Ben, however, who has already read it. Locke suggests his nemesis read the book again: "You might catch something you missed the second time around"—and indeed, we do find Ben perusing it once more two episodes later in "The Other Woman" (4.6). The moment was the first time the Dickverse and the *Lost*verse intersected, but given that illusion and reality was the late, prolific American master of science fiction's preeminent subject and a *Lost*ian major theme as well, the crossover seems in retrospect almost inevitable.

In *The Dreams Our Stuff Is Made Of: How Science Fiction Conquered the World*, the late Thomas Disch wondered why it had to be that the one religion created by a science fiction writer had to be the work of perhaps the worse practitioner of the genre of all time. Instead of L. Ron Hubbard's risible Scientology, Disch asks, why could we not have had a religion founded by the likes of a master such as Dick, who, if he had lived a bit longer, might well have given us a new faith. At the time of his too, too premature death, he was well on his way to outlining his theology in *VALIS*, an odd amalgam of fiction, autobiography, and philosophical reflection.

A "plot" summary of *VALIS*, a book that almost demands a second read, is a virtual impossibility, but philipkdick.com offers the following reasonable facsimile:

A coterie of religious seekers forms to explore the revelatory visions of one Horselover Fat; a semi-autobiographical dialogue of PKD. The groups [sic] hermeneutical research leads to a rock musician's estate where they confront the Messiah: a two-year old named Sophia. She confirms their suspicions that an ancient, mechanical intelligence orbiting the earth has been guiding their discoveries.

That eponymous "intelligence" is, of course, "VALIS"—an acronym for "Vast Active Living Intelligence System."

VALIS' presence as a *Lost* text of course fueled already-in-progress speculation about the island as living entity and enriched the popular hypothesis that the series' narrative might be some kind of Dickian simulation or illusion. The entry on *VALIS* in the online Lostpedia[6] offers a good comparison of shared themes and ideas.

Watership Down—As Sawyer puts it in "Confidence Man" (1.8), Richard Adams' *Watership Down* is a nice little story about bunnies. Just like *Lost*, the story isn't quite that simple or benign. Beneath the "nice bunny story" or "crash survivor story" lurk dangers and monsters in a world neither story's characters could have anticipated.

Lost fans quickly picked up on *Watership Down* as a possible ancestor text that could provide clues about the series' subplots. The rabbits face danger in their familiar world and escape toward what they hope will be a safer place. Although *Lost's* castaways are forced to live on the island instead of choosing to leave their homes, their encounters with dangerous monsters, human and otherworldly, force them to find new homes from time to time. The Tailies, for example, agree to travel to the other side of the island to merge with another group of survivors primarily because the Others keep attacking them. The hatch becomes a bomb that implodes/explodes and forces Locke and Desmond to return to beach living. Kate, Jack, and Sawyer rebel against their new "home" with the Others and manage to escape to their little society on the beach. When the beach camp is attacked at the end of Season Three, two now-antagonistic groups of survivors hike in different directions to find what they hope will be a safer new home, a split that has major consequences by the end of Season

Four. The Oceanic 6 are rescued and begin their post-island lives, while the islanders they leave behind are relocated somewhere unknown in space and time.

For the first three seasons, the castaways' journeys require them to follow different leaders, depending upon the situation, but Jack and Locke lead them most often. *Watership Down*'s Hazel, the rabbit leader, finds a "paradise" with plenty of food, friendly rabbits, and few predators. Just as the Oceanic 815 survivors find threats within their Eden, such as Rousseau's and the Others' deadly traps, snares, and fences, Hazel discovers that his paradise hides wire snares. Cowslip, a spokesrabbit for the group already ensnared in this environment, knows about the deadly traps. He not only fails to share this information with the newcomers but refuses to help free a trapped rabbit. It seems that a few casualties are expected as a fair trade for food and relative safety from birds and dogs. A few *Lost* characters may be "Cowslips": Rousseau knows enough about the Others to fear them, but she doesn't share information easily. Kelvin saves Desmond from his wrecked boat and introduces him to the joys of underground living—with a price tag of personal freedom. Desmond has plenty of food and a relatively comfortable shelter, but he must stay in the hatch and push a button every 108 minutes. As soon as he can escape, he imposes this fate on Locke and other castaways, leaving them to push the button.

The rabbits face many monsters and dangers on their trek to a new home, just as the castaways discover ever more perils await them as they explore the island. Not everyone survives, but those who do are stronger for their struggles. As the rabbits band together during their journey, they develop a new society, with leaders and visionaries to guide the way and help them fend off rival groups. The castaways do the same.

Watership Down's Fiver seems to have a sixth sense; his dreams often provide knowledge of current or future events. Several *Lost* characters act like Fiver at times: Locke follows his visions, which lead him to the hatch and, after its destruction, to his captured friends living in the Others' camp; Charlie becomes motivated by his dreams to "save" other castaways; after his death, Charlie even becomes a specter haunting Hurley, who claims he talks with the dead and delivers their messages; Eko acts in accordance with visions of his deceased brother, Yemi. Desmond, however, becomes a true "Fiver" in Season Three when he glimpses pieces of the future and modifies his actions either to prevent or ensure predicted events. His visions and their repercussions help return him to his true love, Penny, by the end of Season Four.

Part of the enjoyment of reading *Watership Down* is understanding the larger world from a rabbit's eye view. When Bigwig is nearly run down by a car one afternoon, he glories in the feel of wind rushing through his fur. He isn't afraid of the monster when it drives past. Bigwig believes the car can't hurt him during daylight. When the other rabbits point out roadkill, Bigwig explains that the monster only kills at night. Then its large, bright eyes lure animals into its path of destruction.

In a similar way, Locke tempts fate by allowing the monster to drag him toward and down a hole ("Exodus," 1.24). Locke tells Jack that he'll be all right, but Jack insists that Kate blow up the monster in order to free Locke. As Locke regains his faith in the island during Season Three, he seems to develop a divinely inspired understanding of the way some things work on the island. Ben Linus, however, tells Locke that his understanding is limited, a problem that Ben begins to remedy in "The Man Behind the Curtain" (3.22). Locke may have limited knowledge, based only on his experiences with the island; Ben is more like *Watership Down* readers, who understand how the greater world operates and might chuckle at Bigwig's interpretation. As Locke's and the Oceanic 6's understanding of the island and its importance to men like Ben Linus and Charles Widmore increases, their (and our) initial ideas about the island seem humorously naïve.

A Wrinkle in Time—Madeline L'Engle's Newbery Award-winning young adult science fiction action-adventure was published in 1962 and is widely considered a classic. The book focuses on the Murry family, primarily Meg, who goes on a journey across space, time, and alternate dimensions to find her missing father, a physicist named Alex. Alex had been working on a theory involving a tesseract as a way to travel through time, and one day had gone missing mysteriously, effectively abandoning his family.

Early in Season One, Sawyer is seen reading the book on the beach, his follow-up choice to *Watership Down*. *A Wrinkle in Time* is an ancestor text not only due to its appearance in the series, but also because of interesting parallel connections between central characters and themes throughout the book. Meg's youngest brother, Charles Wallace, is described to readers as "different"— a difference not unlike Walt's. Both Charles Wallace and Walt, extremely perceptive if not psychic, appear to know things before they happen.

Meg encounters Ms. Whatsit, an interesting figure who informs both her, Charles Wallace, and her mother that there "is such a thing as a tesseract." Meg and Charles Wallace pair up with Calvin O'Keefe, one of Meg's classmates, and travel to another dimension with the help of Ms. Whatsit and her two equally eccentric sisters, Mrs. Who and Mrs. Which. They utilize the tesseract to "wrinkle," or travel across dimensions, so that they can overcome a mysterious darkness—a shadow—that is described in *A Wrinkle in Time* as "not even as tangible as a cloud," a cloud that seems similar in description to the shadowy black *thing* seen over the exploding engine in the Pilot (1.1) and again in "Exodus" (1.24).

Since tesseracts make travel to other dimensions possible, the idea proved convenient for fans seeking a "scientific" explanation for the castaways' appearance on an uncharted island in Season One. Other parallels exist: Ms. Whatsit loans the children her magical glasses to help them see the "reality" of their situation, not unlike the glasses that are crafted for Sawyer so he can be relieved of headaches caused by his farsightedness. Charles Wallace is even abducted in the course of the novel by the sinister force behind the ominous CENTRAL Central intelligence—IT, a being whose thirst for control and domination had resulted in populating the universe, in the name of science, with emotionless, thoughtless creatures. The similarities between *Wrinkle's* IT and the Others are obvious. When Charles Wallace, under IT's control, states "Perhaps you do not realize that on Camazotz we have conquered all illness, all deformity"—we cannot help but think of the Hanso foundation, whose mission statement includes its goal "to further the evolution of the human race and provide technological solutions to the most pressing problems of our time."

ANCESTOR TEXTS

Alice's Adventures in Wonderland—A strange literary ancestor of *Lost* is Lewis Carroll's 1865 *Alice's Adventures in Wonderland* (shortened to *Alice in Wonderland* for many filmed versions of the story, including Disney's animated movie; Disney is a parent company producing *Lost*). Early in the series, writers borrowed a *Wonderland* character for the episode "White Rabbit" (1.5), a reference inspiring multiple interpretations, both literary and musical.

"White Rabbit" is Jack's first backstory, in which viewers see the frazzled doctor reach a breaking point. Although he has saved many lives since the plane crash, he also has lost a few, most notably the marshal and, at the beginning of this episode, a young woman caught in a rip current. In his peripheral vision, Jack begins seeing a man in a black suit, but when he turns to get a closer look, the man disappears. Viewers, and Jack, don't know if the vision is real or imagined. Locke later convinces Jack it doesn't really matter if the vision is real or not. What is important is what Jack does when he sees the vision.

As in Carroll's Wonderland, *Lost*'s jungle is full of hidden marvels and dangers. Jack's introduction to the surreal nature of the island comes from the vision of, it turns out, his father. This White Rabbit guides Jack into the jungle and over a cliff, instead of down a rabbit hole. Instead of a pocket watch, Christian Shephard carries a nearly empty drink in his hand, clinking the ice cubes against the glass as he walks. This aural cue reminds Jack of a dominant image from his childhood and a recurring theme in his father's life—alcohol. Like Carroll's White Rabbit, the apparition of Jack's father appears and disappears suddenly to get the story (flashbacks) moving again. During this episode, Jack confronts his troubled memories of his father and follows the apparition/hallucination through the jungle until he finally discovers caves with a limitless supply of fresh water. There Jack's awe-filled entry into this wonderland ends.

At times, Jack seems like a White Rabbit, too. Alice's White Rabbit is often nervous and flighty, rushing from task to task with a never-ending fear of being late. Immediately after the plane crash, Jack rushes from person to person, crisis to crisis, in his fear that he won't be in time to save the wounded. In later episodes, Jack acts like the White Rabbit, the character who stands up to the king and demands that Alice be allowed to testify at her trial. In flashback (during "All the Best Cowboys Have Daddy Issues," 1.11), Jack stands up to his father during a medical inquiry into Christian Shephard's actions during a botched operation. Jack's testimony leads to his father's dismissal as chief of surgery. The court in *Alice in Wonderland* parallels the board of inquiry in "All the Best Cowboys Have Daddy Issues." Jack also stands up for Juliet during her murder trial ("Stranger in a Strange Land," 3.9). He confronts Ben, forcing him to intercede on Juliet's behalf to lessen her punishment. Perhaps most important, Jack's testimony at Kate's trial ("Eggtown," 4.4) helps lead to her plea bargain. Kate is free but must live in California for the next ten years. Jack's sincerity convinces the judge to trust Kate. Although these actions take place long after "White Rabbit," they are still Jack's White Rabbit moments.

Christian Shephard further haunts Jack in the Season Three finale, "Through the Looking Glass" (3.23). This title is a shortened version (usually used for film and borrowed by other TV series, such as *Angel* and *Farscape*) of Carroll's 1871 follow-up to *Alice's Adventures in Wonderland*. The novel's complete title is *Through the Looking-Glass and What Alice Found There*. Alice willingly steps through the looking glass into an alternate world, in which flowers speak and the poem "Jabberwocky" makes sense. On the island, hypothesized multiple timelines and parallel worlds seem to exist. Although Jack knows his father died in Australia, Christian Shephard seems to "live" again on the island, as well as in a possible alternate timeline or universe, as revealed in the Season Three finale. When Charlie stops the jamming signal inside the island's Looking Glass station, clear communication is opened between the island and the outside world. The convoluted sequence of events leading to the Oceanic 6's rescue propels them into a new world—a version of home very different "through the Looking Glass" than they remember from their pre-crash lives.

In this new world, when Kate and Jack set up house together, Jack reads Aaron a bedtime story: *Alice in Wonderland.* He tells Kate that his father used to read the book to him. Perhaps in this way *Lost*'s writers remind us that the next generation also will see life from a very different perspective—or travel into strange new worlds again.

"White Rabbit" and "Through the Looking Glass" have popular counterparts in music, as well as literature. Jefferson Airplane's Grace Slick wrote "White Rabbit in Wonderland" in 1967, with trippy lyrics echoing not only Carroll's Wonderland but Jack's as well. Several artists named albums after "Through the Looking Glass"; Toto (another *Wizard of Oz* link) used this title for their eleventh album. Whether in literature or music, Carroll's stories inspire the creative use of altered states of mind or worlds peripherally linked to our own, in which anything can happen. *Lost* is only one of the latest creative endeavors inspired by this ancestor text.

"The Damned Thing"—One of three relevant stories in Ambrose Bierce's *An Occurrence at Owl Creek Bridge*—we discuss the title story from this collection, as well as the equally relevant tale "A Psychological Shipwreck," elsewhere in this guide—"The

Damned Thing" is a terrifying account of an invisible monster. In a fashion made popular by Edgar Allan Poe, the story is told via a mysterious diary and a too-incredible-to-be-true story-within-a-story read at an inquest. With the horribly mangled corpse of Hugh Morgan front and center before the coroner and assembled jury, William Harker, a reporter and friend of the deceased, tells the tale under oath.

Morgan, whose rural way of life Harker has come to study as research for a novel, had, it seems, for some time been aware of an anomalous "damned thing" prowling his property. Although it is, apparently, invisible, its presence can be detected, as Harker himself explains:

"I was about to speak further, when I observed the wild oats near the place of the disturbance moving in the most inexplicable way. I can hardly describe it. It seemed as if stirred by a streak of wind, which not only bent it, but pressed it down—crushed it so that it did not rise; and this movement was slowly prolonging itself directly toward us."

Though not initially terrified himself, Harker looks on in alarm as his host fires both barrels of his shotgun at the spot, a blast that evidently hits home, for it produces an agonized cry.

Brushed aside by something he can feel but not see, Harker then looks on astonished at a terrible struggle:

"All this must have occurred within a few seconds, yet in that time Morgan assumed all the postures of a determined wrestler vanquished by superior weight and strength. I saw nothing but him and not always distinctly. During the entire incident his shouts and curses were heard, as

if through an enveloping uproar of such sounds of rage and fury as I had never heard from the throat of man or brute!"

By the time he reaches his host, Morgan is dead.

The jurors don't believe a word of Harker's account and find that Morgan died from an attack by a mountain lion, but in the diary he left behind (which the coroner is reading in the story's opening scene) we are given an explanation "from beyond the grave" of the killer's real identity.

The monster, so large that it can blot out the stars—

> "*Sept. 2.*—Looking at the stars last night as they rose above the crest of the ridge east of the house, I observed them successively disappear—from left to right. Each was eclipsed but an instant, and only a few at a time, but along the entire length of the ridge all that were within a degree or two of the crest were blotted out. It was as if something had passed along between me and them; but I could not see it, and the stars were not thick enough to define its outline."

—like those sounds we cannot hear because they are beyond the capacity of the ear to discern, is of a "colour" not visible to human sight.

Not exactly Smokezilla, to be sure, but in size, lethal power, and inscrutability, alike enough to be an imaginative ancestor/relation of the island's own Damned Thing.

Death and the Maiden—In the Season Three episode "Enter 77" (3.11) flashbacks reveal that, while working as a chef in Paris sometime after he had left Iraq and his time as a Republican Guard interrogator, Sayid was taken captive by Sami, whose wife, Amira, had been one of his torture victims. Sayid eventually shows true contrition for his deeds and is freed.

The episode bears more than a passing resemblance to the 1991 play *Death and the Maiden* (*La muerte y la doncella*) by Chilean writer Ariel Dorfman. Inspired by events in his native land during the reign of dictator Augusto Pinochet—put into power thanks to a CIA-backed coup against the popularly elected communist Salvator Allende—*Death* tells the story of a sadistic prison doctor, Roberto Miranda, who by happenstance falls into the clutches of one of his victims, Paulina Escobar. At the end of the play it is not entirely clear whether or not Paulina has killed her tormenter.

The play was adapted for the screen in 1994, directed by Roman Polanski and starring Sigourney Weaver as Paulina and Ben Kingsley as Dr. Miranda.

Gilgamesh—*Gilgamesh* appears as the answer to #42 down in a crossword puzzle Locke works in "Collision" (2.8). *Gilgamesh*, a Sumerian epic poem describing the friendship between a king of the same name and the wild half-man Enkidu, is recognized as one of the earliest literary works. Divided into twelve tablets (or books) the narrative guides human understanding about the nature and worship of deities, provides the purpose of death and suffering, and offers insight on how to be a good person and live a fruitful life. *Gilgamesh* includes the myth of the great flood (which appears in several other literary and religious texts, including the Epic of Atrahasis and the Bible).

While *Gilgamesh* is most certainly ideal reading material for anyone given its historical significance and overall literary merit and influence on countless other important literary texts, the *Lost* fan has even more incentive to read this ancient myth. Since appearing late in Season Two, many have asked why *Gilgamesh* was such an important crossword clue? Some theorize that Mr. Eko is a character based off the wild and unruly Enkidu, citing the character's bizarre prophetic dreams and his journey with the ruler Gilgamesh, a character that may or may not remind readers of Locke. There's also a door that Gilgamesh fashions for the Gods, not unlike the blast door Locke discovers during "Lockdown" (2.17). But the main reason that every *Lost* fan should read *Gilgamesh* is that most literary scholars have noticed startling parallels between *Gilgamesh* and *The Odyssey*—another must-read literary text.

Lord of the Flies—Because *Lord of the Flies* (1954) has been one of the most often-read books in American secondary schools for more than thirty years, it would be surprising if it had not influenced the creators of an American television series about the survivors of a plane crash on a desert island. Indeed, the novel is evoked at least twice on the series, once by Sawyer in "…in Translation" (1.17): "Folks down on the beach might have been doctors and accountants a month ago, but it's *Lord of the Flies* time now"; and later by Charlie in "What Kate Did" (2.9), when he observes that the Tailies went "all *Lord of the Flies*."

Written by British novelist and Nobel Laureate (1983) William Golding (1911–1993), *Lord of the Flies*, of course, had its own ancestor text. Golding's novel can be read as a revision/repudiation of R. M. Ballantyne's popular Victorian novel, *The Coral Island* (1857), in which shipwrecked proper little subjects of the Queen build themselves the very model of a modern British society on a desert island. Golding, whose next novel, *The Inheritors* (1955), would tell the story of the eradication of Neanderthals by early *homo sapiens*, would take a much darker view of how the marooned might behave.

As every reader of *Lord of the Flies* (or its CliffsNotes) knows, Golding's English schoolboys don't fare quite as well as *The Coral Island*-ers. Survivors of a plane crash and of some distant war they appear to be fleeing (Golding quite intentionally never makes the context clear), the boys must choose between two possible leaders: the quiet and serious Ralph, who would establish—with the advice and counsel of pudgy, thoughtful, bookish, bespectacled, asthmatic Piggy—a fledgling democracy on the island; and the aggressive, cruel, and hedonistic Jack. Lured by the attraction of becoming boys-run-wild—painting their faces, hunting wild boar, enjoying the pleasures of the tribe—Jack and his followers triumph. The only thing they need from Ralph and Piggy is the occasional use of the latter's glasses in order to focus the sun's rays to start a fire.

Early on, fear spreads that there is a "Beast" on the loose, and even though the fabled monster is only an air force pilot who crashed and died on the island, Jack finds it convenient to keep the myth alive in order to maintain control over his subjects. (The image of the dead pilot in Peter Brook's 1963 film version of *Lord of the Flies* is evoked in the image of Naomi hanging from a tree in "Catch-22" [3.17].) A final encounter between Jack and his hunters and Ralph and Piggy over their common future should they never be rescued results in Piggy's murder with a deliberately toppled boulder. As the forces of Jack stalk Ralph, all are saved by the deus ex machina of the British Navy. At the end, a naval officer inquires whether the boys have put on a "Jolly good show. Like the Coral Island."

A few micro-similarities between *LoF* and *Lost* exist (though hardly as many as *Gilligan's Island/Lost*). Both islands have an asthmatic inhabitant: *LoF's* Piggy ("Sucks to your ass-mar," repeated by friend and foe alike, is one of the book's most familiar lines) and *Lost*'s dearly-departed Shannon. Glasses play a role on each: Piggy's broken, then stolen, lenses not only mark his character but help to drive the plot; and, on *Lost*, Jack (with an assist from Sayid), provides glasses for the headache-afflicted but constantly reading Sawyer (who, if he had been on *LoF*'s island, would have been one of the first to belittle Piggy). Both in *LoF* and on *Lost*, the desert islanders hunt boar for food. Both narratives have a resident "Monster" (the real nature of which on *Lost* remains, at the time of this writing, unknown).

In its approach to the formation of a new society apart from civilization, however, *Lost* follows a middle road between *The Coral Island* and *Lord of the Flies*. By the end of Season Three, the *Lost*aways have not reverted to barbarism, but they have not yet exactly built a stable social order either. For much of Season One, after all, they lived apart as two enclaves, those who remained on the beach and those who had moved to the caves. Though we have yet to see a severance anything like that of Ralph/Jack, we have seen oppositions developing between several pairs: Jack/ Sawyer, Michael/Jin (over Sun), Kate/Sawyer (they fought over a briefcase and a place on the raft long before they felt caged heat), Sayid/Sawyer, Locke vs. Boone/Jack/Charlie/Eko/Sayid, Ana Lucia/Sawyer.... And they have done their share of killing: Boone (indirectly by Locke), Ethan Rom (by Charlie), Goodwin and Shannon (by Ana Lucia), Libby and Ana Lucia (by Michael), Colleen (by Sun), Paolo and Nikki (by everyone), Anthony Cooper (by Sawyer), Ryan Price (by Hurley), Jason (by Sayid), Tom (by Sawyer), Naomi (presumably, by Locke). With the emergence of the Others in Season Three and their manipulation and cruel physical mistreatment of the *Lost*aways, the likelihood of a *Lord of* *the Flies*-like rending of the island's social fabric seems all the more likely, though which are to be followers of (*LoF*'s) Jack and which Ralph remains to be seen.

Lost Horizon—See the entry in Must-See Television and Movies.

The Mysterious Island—Like *Lord of the Flies, Robinson Crusoe*, and *Lost Horizon*, Jules Verne's 1874 novel about a group of five Northern POWs escaping by balloon from the American Civil War who crash land on a mysterious island in the South Pacific (2500 kilometers east of New Zealand) is a no brainer *Lost* ancestor text, as even dim bulb Shannon, who refers to the castaways' new home as "mystery frickin' island" in "Whatever the Case May Be" (1.12), seems to realize. Though hardly a rival of *Lost*'s island in mysteriousness, Verne's nevertheless offers its fair share of odd goings-on. One of the balloon's passengers impossibly survives a fall; guns and ammunition and a cure for malaria appear out of nowhere; a menacing pirate ship blows up and its crew is slaughtered. The mysteries, however, are all explained when the novel turns out to be a chronologically impossible sequel to *20,000 Leagues Under the Sea* and the island the last sanctuary of Verne's scientific genius, Captain Nemo. The builder and master of the Nautilus dies of old age and the ballooniacs escape a volcanic eruption that destroys Lincoln Island and make it back to civilization.

Verne's enigmatic atoll has no monster, no unexplained numbers, no ghosts, no creepy whispers, no time dislocation. But the two narratives do share arrivals by a balloon (recall the late Henry Gale from Minnesota?), pirates, dogs, the baffling arrival of supplies. These coincidences could be mere chance, but a shared orangutan named Joop—domesticated by the Union soldiers in

Mysterious Island; the subject of controversial experimentation by the Hanso Foundation in *Lost*—confirm that *Lost*'s makers were familiar with Verne's book.

The Odyssey—The second of the great epic poems by the Greek bard known as Homer—a sequel, if you will, to *The Iliad*, the story of the Trojan War, *The Odyssey*, written sometime between 800 and 600 B.C., tells the story of Greek hero Odysseus' long (ten-year), arduous return home from Troy after a total of twenty years away to his beloved Ithaca, his son Telemachus, and his long-suffering wife Penelope.

Prior to the final episode of Season Two of *Lost* ("Live Together, Die Alone"), *The Odyssey* had shown no sign, other than being one of the foundational works of all western literature, of being a *Lost* ancestor text. The *Lost*aways have met many adversaries, fought polar bears, monsters, and human killers, but no deity like Poseidon or witch like Calypso, no Scylla and Charybdis or Cyclops (we hadn't met Mikhail/Patchy yet) or Siren, have threatened their lives or offered supernatural temptations.

But then, in the Season Two finale, we meet Penelope (Penny), the love of Desmond's life, the woman he had deserted in order to embark on a round-the-world sailing race sponsored by her father Charles Widmore (using a boat given to him by Libby), in order to impress him, in order (as we learn in "Flashes Before Your Eyes" [3.8]) that he might fulfill his destiny as laid out for him by the psychic Mrs. Hawking: to crash on the island, input, for years, the numbers in the hatch, and be the one to turn the failsafe key and save the world.

Penelope Widmore, it is true, has not been required to fend off, as her Homeric namesake had to do, a score of suitors seeking her hand in the absence of her great love, but she has not been idle. As we learn in the "What the x&#*&?" final moment of Season Two, she has used her fortune to find her Odysseus by identifying the geo-synchronous location of electromagnetic anomalies, as tracked by her Portuguese researchers Mathias and Henrik. How it is that she knew Desmond would be found where such an irregularity is detected—that we still don't know. Had Penny been talking to Mrs. Hawking? Why did Naomi—about whom Penelope knew nothing (as she told Charlie)—carry a photo of Desmond and Penny.

Des and Penny were reunited in Season Four's final episode (an end to their odyssey set up in brilliant and poignant "The Constant" [4.5]) though we do not know what will come after. After all, a time traveling Ben had promised Charles Widmore (in "The Shape of Things to Come," [4.9]) to seek revenge for Keamy's murder of his daughter Danielle by finding and killing the daughter of his nemesis—Penny. Will Desmond be her heroic protector against the former leader of the Others? We do not yet know, but with Penelope Widmore firmly established as one of *Lost's* major players and with Desmond's odyssey elevated from minor tale to epic status, *The Odyssey* must now be considered as a prime *Lost* ancestor text.

Of Mice and Men—John Steinbeck's *Of Mice and Men* must have made a big impression on Sawyer. He reads it in prison, which helps when he later uses literary metaphors to spar with Ben Linus. In "The Brig" (3.19), Sawyer later wonders if Locke, like Ben a few weeks earlier, may be leading him to an isolated spot to trick or attempt to kill him; the con man tells Locke that he remembers the bunny. Sawyer's connection with the book seems to haunt him;

he might pride himself on being as manipulative as George, but he could secretly fear being Lennie.

In the novel, friends George and Lennie begin work on a new ranch; they had to move on because large, strong, child-like Lennie unintentionally assaulted a woman, who pressed charges. As a manifestation of his child-like demeanor, Lennie likes to pet animals, but because he is mentally challenged, he does not realize that his touch is too forceful. He often kills the animals as he pets them. Nevertheless, he hopes one day to tend rabbits on his own farm. After all, rabbits are larger and might withstand his loving care.

In a fateful encounter with the flirtatious wife of his new boss' son, Lennie accidentally snaps her neck. Once more George and Lennie escape, but this time the friends cannot simply slip away. With a mob close behind them, George takes Lennie to a quiet spot where he tells him once more about their rabbit farm. Just before George kills him to "save" him from the mob, Lennie asks again if he can pet the bunnies. They become his last sweet thought.

During "Every Man for Himself" (3.4), Ben Linus tortures Sawyer with the idea that an implanted pacemaker can easily kill him if his heart rate becomes elevated. Ben even shakes to death a test bunny, also with a pacemaker, to prove his point. Although he later reveals that the bunny is fine, ever-skeptical Sawyer knows that this might be the second Bunny #8. (A similarly marked rabbit is mentioned in "On Writing," part of Stephen King's memoir; King is a *Lost* fan, and his books, such as *Carrie*, are mentioned in or are ancestor texts for the series.) Like the rabbit, Sawyer is a replaceable test subject.

Ben repeats lines from *Of Mice and Men*, which Sawyer recognizes. He asks if Ben/George has brought him on a long hike just to kill him. Sawyer, like Lennie, may not know his own cruel power over people; his words and actions kill relationships just as surely as his gun kills his enemies. Ben assures Sawyer that murder is not his intention, but he swiftly kills Sawyer's hope for escape when he explains that the Others live on a second island.

The Outsiders—Published in 1967 and written by the then-fifteen-year-old S.E. Hinton, *The Outsiders* makes an appearance in *Lost* by a casual comment made by Hurley's friend Johnny in "Tricia Tanaka Is Dead" (3.10). This coming-of-age fiction is a well-known classic and is often required reading for high school students. Over the forty years since its initial publication the novel has been both revered and protested against for its portrayal of drug and alcohol use and violence among teenagers.

The Outsiders portrays divisions of social class among teenagers during the late 1960s. The plot focuses on the rivalry between the upper-class Socials, or "Socs" that rule over the lower class "Greasers" in a Tulsa, Oklahoma, high school, a rift similar to that between the island's "hostiles" and the DHARMA Initiative, or even between the Others and the survivors of Oceanic 815.

There's also a striking similarity between Hinton's Ponyboy and *Lost*'s Sawyer. A bookworm with a smoking habit and a preoccupation with his overall physical appearance, especially his hair, Ponyboy may seem dumb to others—just as Sawyer may be thought a stupid redneck, but he is acutely aware of the divisions of class and the inner-motivations of others.

"A Psychological Shipwreck"—As we point out elsewhere, the appearance of a collection of stories by the nineteenth-century American writer Ambrose Bierce in the Swan invites investigation of several of the tales contained within as *Lost* ancestor texts (see also "An Occurrence at Owl Creek Bridge" and "The Damned Thing"). One such candidate is "A Psychological Shipwreck." As Jeff Jensen has suggested in his comprehensive, controversial *Lost* theorizing in *Entertainment Weekly*, this enigmatic tale about an ocean voyage, a love affair, and a transportation calamity that may or may not have happened is clearly worthy of our attention.

"Shipwreck" is narrated by an American merchant sojourning (in 1874) in Liverpool after the collapse of his business, who books a return home on a sailing vessel called, significantly, *The Morrow*. *The Morrow* carries only two other passengers, a young South Carolina woman and her Black maid, traveling suspiciously alone after her traveling companions, a married couple, had both died in Devonshire. In a bizarre coincidence, the husband had the same name, William Jarrett, as the narrator.

The narrator finds himself attracted to his fellow passenger, Janette Harford, but reassures himself that it is not love he feels. One night, on the eve of the 4th of July, he is overwhelmed by a bizarre notion:

It seemed as if she were looking at me, not with, but through, those eyes—from an immeasurable distance behind them—and that a number of other persons, men, women and children, upon whose faces I caught strangely familiar evanescent expressions, clustered about her, struggling with gentle eagerness to look at me through the same orbs. Ship, ocean, sky—all had vanished. I was conscious of nothing but the figures in this extraordinary and fantastic scene.

At the moment this strange inversion takes place, a book, Denneker's *Meditations*, lies in the lady's lap, and the narrator takes note of a perplexing passage suggesting the possibility of consciousness switching bodies.

A terrible calamity, not fully explained, ensues, and the ship goes down. Later, the narrator finds himself on a steamer, *The City of Prague*, stranded because of a mechanical breakdown, on which he has apparently been traveling all along, accompanied by his friend Gordon Doyle, whose fiancé, Janette Hartford, is likewise on her way to America—on board the sailing vessel *The Morrow*.

Doyle is, of course, reading Denneker's *Meditations* as well (his fiancé had a second copy). Leafing through it, the narrator's attention is directed to the same passage—marked by Doyle—about swapping consciousness with another. At this point the story abruptly ends with these words:

A week later we were towed into the port of New York. But The Morrow *was never heard from.*

Needless to say, "A Psychological Shipwreck," considered as a *Lost* Ancestor Text, lends fuel to the fire not only of that tiny band of "Two Plane Theory"[7] advocates (Bierce's tale, after all, has *two ships*), but all those fans who want to read the events of the series as in some way unreal/delusional/in-the-mind. The temptation to see the entirety of *Lost* as a "psychological shipwreck" begins with its opening shot (in the Pilot) of Jack's eye. Is everything that then ensues, some have wondered, in Dr. Shephard's mind? It is safe to say that, when *Lost* finally reaches port (aka when the series ends), if it turns out it has all been somehow an illusion, we, and a huge majority of viewers who have completed the entire journey, will be mighty disappointed.

Robinson Crusoe—Daniel Defoe's 1719 book about a man shipwrecked for twenty-eight years on an island is an obvious ancestor text for *Lost*. The original story has been popular for nearly three hundred years and so is the ancestor of several films and television shows. In October 2008, *Crusoe*, a TV series version of the tale obviously inspired as much by *Lost*'s success as Defoe's novel, began airing on NBC.

Defoe's hero may have written the survival handbook for the *Lost* castaways' behavior during Season One. These characters seem determined to survive after a wreck, whether by ship or plane, and they approach life on the island in remarkably similar ways. Crusoe is the only survivor from his ship and must rely only on himself for several years, until he saves the man he dubs Friday from cannibals and thus gains a companion for the remainder of his stay on the island. Although the *Lost* castaways share the workload among more people, they, too, gain new companions, such as the Tailies (after Season Two's "The Other 48 Days" and its aftermath) and Desmond, who officially joins beach society in Season Three. Instead of fearing cannibals, the castaways fear the Others, who favor abducting children and pregnant women, although they are also known to take other adults prisoner.

Crusoe's initial plan, one the modern castaways share, includes salvaging goods from the wreck, finding food and water, building a shelter, and setting up camp for the long haul. Both Crusoe and Michael build rafts, although Michael wants to use his to leave the island instead of hauling supplies from the wreck, as Crusoe does. Crusoe easily finds a pure water source and soon begins to hunt birds and fish. Jack eventually finds fresh water in the caves, Locke hunts boar, and Jin fishes.

Robinson Crusoe shares other minor plot points with characters from *Lost*:

- Crusoe thankfully has scavenged goods from the ship before the wreckage is washed to sea. The castaways abandon the fuselage, after it has been stripped of usable parts and supplies, because a rapidly rising tide begins to wash away the wreckage.
- Crusoe's masted wooden ship may have looked similar to the *Black Rock* beached miles inland on *Lost*'s mysterious island.
- Like Crusoe, whose family name originally is Kreutznaer, Sawyer abandons his family name (Ford).
- "Father issues" come into play in both stories. Crusoe fails to take his father's advice and live a comfortable, safe, middle-class life in England. Instead, he goes against his father's wishes and takes up a life of adventuring. The senior Crusoe warns his son that he will live a miserable life if he insists on going to sea, but Robinson disregards this warning. Later stranded on the island, Robinson remembers his father's words and wonders if God is punishing him, a question that Sun also asks herself. Several *Lost* characters disagree with their fathers or father figures and, on the island, ponder their troubled relationships. More specifically like Crusoe, Desmond vows to prove his love Penelope's father wrong about her suitor's worth and goes to sea to win an around-the-world race; Charlie follows his interest in music, despite his father's objection, and often suffers because of his career and life choices; Claire disregards the prediction of the psychic (a possible father figure) who says she must be the one to raise her baby, or something bad will happen.

- Crusoe keeps a journal of his island life, as does Claire.
- While on the island, Crusoe talks to God and becomes more spiritual. Locke finds that the island provides him with a miracle; he establishes his own dialogue with the island, his deity. Eko and Charlie also periodically "find religion" on the island.
- Crusoe is rescued from the island by the mutinying crew of a passing ship, similar to the inhabitants of *Lost*'s mysterious island being found by the freighter folk. When Charles Widmore's mercenary leader, Martin Keamy, becomes too vicious for the freighter's captain and crew to abide, they turn against him. Helicopter pilot Frank Lapidus helps rescue the Oceanic 6 plus Desmond, a direct violation of Widmore's orders.

Defoe's *Robinson Crusoe* became a popular novel in its time and succeeding centuries because it offered an escapist story that allowed readers to wonder what they might do in a similar situation. It put readers in an exotic location very different from their homeland and gave them the vicarious freedom to do exactly as they pleased. *Lost* provides similar escapist fare in an exotic location, but its themes more often illustrate how people must work together to survive.

Those who have never lived through such an ordeal tend to romanticize it as an "adventure" and don't understand just how traumatic the experience can be. The readers of *Robinson Crusoe* might have longed for their own escape to a remote island to do as they pleased, but they probably didn't understand the magnitude of Crusoe's life-or-death experiences, just as Hurley's parents, happily throwing their newly returned son an island-themed birthday party ("There's No Place Like Home," 4.13), have no idea of all that occurred before the rescue.

Solaris—Almost from the beginning, *Lost* fan speculation has been fanned by the frequent appearance on the island of figures from the *Lost*aways' past. Early in Season One ("White Rabbit," 1.5), Christian Shephard appears to his son Jack. Dave, Hurley's imaginative friend from "the institute," arrives, challenges his sanity, and nearly lures him to his death ("Dave," 2.18). Mister Eko's brother Yemi appears to him in dreams and does lure him to his death at the hands of The Monster ("The Cost of Living," 3.5). A cat from Sayid's *Death and the Maiden*ish encounter with a woman he tortured in Iraq appears at Mikhail Bakunin/Patchy's in "Enter 77" (3.11). Locke's dastardly father shows up as "The Man from Tallahassee" (3.13). Is the island, or perhaps the magic box Ben speaks of ("The Man from Tallahassee") somehow able to materialize beings from the characters' memories?

In Stanislaw Lem's science fiction novel *Solaris* (1961), and in two film adaptations, Andrei Tarkovsky's 1972 Russian version and Steven Soderburg's 2002 American one (starring George Clooney), a distant planet, covered almost entirely by a vast ocean which seems to be a living sentient organism, is capable of reproducing, out of the minds and memories of all those humans who venture near it, almost exact, biologically functional replicas of individuals dear to them, and, although its motives in doing so are never fully understood, it seems to offer them as gifts and as experiments in understanding, despite the disastrous effects which result. Among its replications is the ex-wife of the novel's narrator, Kris Kelvin, a woman he helped drive to suicide years before.

The externalization of the internal lives of its visitors is not the only result of this thinking ocean's "consciousness." (Both film adaptations pretty much ignore these other aspects of the planet's life, preferring to concentrate on the human story.) The ocean is able to create periodically a panoply of formations as part of its very texture, which thousands of Solarian scientists during years of extensive study of the mysterious planet have classified variously as "tree-mountains," "extensors," "fungoids," "symmetroids," "assymetroids," and "mimoids." It is the last of these on which Lem's own imagination concentrates.

Mimoids are wave formations of hundred of thousands of tons of water, lasting in duration from a day to a month, in which objects external to the ocean are imitated within its textures. Viewed from above, we are told, "the mimoid resembles a town, an illusion produced by our compulsion to superimpose analogies with what we know." The mimoids are awakened out of the ocean commonly by a cloud passing overhead, an object that the mimoid's original seed crystal—a large, flat disc beneath the surface of the ocean—then seeks to reproduce. The mimoids, Lem informs us, have a particular fondness for all human artifacts, producing facsimiles of machines and other objects within a radius of eight or nine miles with great facility. A mimoid, which lives in slow motion, pulsates at a rate of one beat every two hours, thus allowing explorers to enter and examine it closely. In addition, mimoids have what are termed "gala days," on which each of them goes into hyperproduction and performs with wild flights of fancy, playing "variations on the theme of a given object" and embroidering "formal extensions" that entertain it for hours, "to the delight of the nonfigurative artist and the despair of the scientist, who is at a loss to grasp any common theme in the performance" (122–24).

At the novel's close, after enduring the agonizing second loss of his wife's double, Kelvin confides to Snow, the Solaris station's expert on cybernetics, that he has come, after a futile effort at comprehending Solaris' mysteries, to think of the planet-ocean as an aspect of an evolving ego, which in an early stage of development approached "the divine state," but "turned back into itself too soon," and became, instead of a god, an "anchorite, a hermit of the cosmos," completely under the sway of repetition, as witnessed in the endless formations gestated by its waters.

If we were to replace the name of Kelvin in the above account with that of John Locke (or perhaps Benjamin Linus), exchanging, too, "the island" for each mention of "Solaris" or "the ocean," would we not be well on our way to transforming Lem's mind-boggling SF into something more *Lost*-like?

The Songlines—In the penultimate flashback sequence of "S.O.S." (2.19), Bernard takes Rose to Australia (a journey that would put them on their return on Oceanic 815), where he has secretly arranged for her to see the faith healer Isaac of Uluru, who, with the aid of powerful energies in the earth, seeks to heal his patients. Reading Rose's aura, he quickly determines that he cannot help her, though he does not rule out that another place on the planet might be able to. She resolves to lie to Bernard—to tell him that she has been cured, and indeed, like Locke, a paraplegic before the crash (and whose secret she knows), Rose is later cured—by the island.

In 1987's *The Songlines*, a book part memoir, part travel book, part philosophical/anthropological meditation, the late British writer Bruce Chatwin (1940–1989) explores the theory of the aboriginal people of Australia that powerful electromagnetic forces in the continent, created by and creating the landscape in the "dreamtime," inseparable ultimately from human consciousness, part poetry and part geology, are, under the right circumstances, in an art/science known as geomancy, capable of magical healing.

The Stand—The writers and creators of *Lost* have specifically stated on several occasions that Stephen King's 1977 novel *The Stand* never leaves the writers' room. On podcasts and in interviews, Abrams, Lindelof, and Cuse repeatedly hint at the importance of the book, its characters, and storyline. "We took *The Stand*," Cuse would insist, for example, "and put it on an island." The parallels are indeed remarkable.

King's novel opens with an outbreak of a weapons-grade influenza virus in a secret government weapons facility in the California desert. When the quarantine protocol fails, one man is able to escape along with his wife and child, effectively exposing the rest of the United States population to a super flu popularly known as "Captain Tripps" that kills off 99 percent of the population. The novel chronicles the virus' effects and the plight of the immune as they struggle to find potable water and uncontaminated food in a post-flu world. They are involved in a deeper battle as well—one of good versus evil, God versus Satan, as survivors are divided into two distinct camps based on dreams and their inherent goodness (or evilness) as they travel to either Mother Abigail's camp in Boulder, Colorado (the "Free Zone") or Randall Flagg's in Las Vegas, Nevada.

The threat of disease exists in both *The Stand* and *Lost*: in King's work, disease is the catalyst for all the novel's action. In *Lost* we first hear of its presence on the island when mentioned by Rousseau in "Solitary." The presence of disease reappears when Kate stamps "Quarantine" on the inner hull of the hatch ("Man of Science, Man of Faith," 2.1), Desmond daily inoculates himself, and the mural on the Swan station hatch wall pictorially depicts a deadly sickness. Whatever the disease is, Rousseau explicitly defines it as dangerous—dangerous enough to cause her to kill a crew of researchers that included her husband.

The most obvious parallels between *The Stand* and *Lost* exist in the characters. Several share similar traits and attitudes.

- **Frannie Goldsmith and Claire Littleton.** The first and most apparent is King's Francis "Frannie" Goldsmith and Claire Littleton. Both women are young and pregnant and struggle with the realities of their pregnancy in less than optimal conditions. Both keep a diary, exhibit similar fears about motherhood and raising their children, and have psychic experiences through dreams. Frannie repeatedly dreams of Mother Abigail, the emissary of goodness who beckons the survivors first to her old homestead in Nebraska and later to Boulder, Colorado. Claire dreams of the *Black Rock* and fuzzy details of her capture. Both are carrying children that have extreme significance: Frannie's child will be the first born in a post-flu world and will let the survivors know if the human race can hope for long term survival, and Claire's child is born on an island that is in quarantine for an unknown disease. Eventually, both Frannie and Claire give birth to male children that do survive: Frannie's Peter fights off Captain Tripps, and Claire's Aaron survives a kidnapping initiated by Rousseau.

- **Larry Underwood, Harold Lauder, and Charlie Pace.** Charlie can be seen as a combination of two characters in *The Stand*: Larry Underwood and Harold Emery Lauder. Larry is a one-hit-wonder guitarist and singer with a history of cocaine use and has never been an all-around nice guy. He has let several people down in his life, including his religiously pious mother. At the novel's beginning, as Captain Tripps claims its first victims, Larry is on the run from California after blowing his advance from the record company and owing debt collectors forty thousand dollars. He journeys to New York to hide out with his mother. Larry's quasi-hit, "Baby Can You Dig Your Man," appears throughout the novel, sung by Larry and other characters as an ephemeral thread between the characters and the old world, not unlike DriveShaft's "You All Everybody." Selfish and self-absorbed before the flu, he only gradually achieves redemption, mostly acquired through witnessing the horrific deaths of his mother and a traveling companion. Charlie, of course, mirrors Larry in his rock-star status and his drug use, but he calls to mind King's Harold Lauder as well, an inveterate loser devoted to Frannie Goldsmith.

When the two are the only survivors in Quantagnut, Maine, Harold positions himself in the role of protector for Frannie in a way similar to Charlie's desire to protect Claire. Mild-mannered and apparently harmless, Harold exhibits a streak of violence that is unexpected and uncontrollable— much like Charlie when he takes revenge on Ethan Rom for kidnapping Claire. In addition, both Harold and Charlie read their beloved's diaries.

- **Stuart Redman and Jack Shephard.** Stuart, or "Stu," Redman is a rough-and-tumble East Texan who escapes from the disease control center in Stovington, Vermont. Despite their obvious difference in education and a country drawl that might remind some of Sawyer, Stu most resembles Jack. Like him, Stu becomes a reluctant leader, forced into his role because no one else is there to do it. He uses deadly force only when necessary, a policy Jack also follows. And both serve as "shepherds" for their wayward "flocks," placed in control of the group without requesting the position. When Stu's traveling party is joined by a man with an appendicitis, Stu finds a medical textbook and attempts to save the man by performing an impromptu appendectomy—a surgery that mirrors Jack's futile effort to save Boone. Stu exhibits the same degree of stubborn control that Jack aspires to have, and does not want to give up—even after his patient has died from blood loss.

Named Marshal of the Free Zone following Mother Abigail's death, Stu becomes a psychic superconductor, receiving prophetic visions from the beyond. Jack takes on the role of the island's only doctor and its unconventional leader, delegating responsibilities such as burial of the dead, finding a water source, and ushering the survivors to the caves, and eventually warming to his role as protector and leader. But Stu and Jack are both coaxed into this role by others, Glen Bateman and John Locke, respectively, who suggest that good, strong leadership is central to the continuity of the new society that they hope to form.

- **Glen Bateman, Trashcan Man, and John Locke.** Locke's character can be understood as an interesting (and conflicting) combination of King's Glen Bateman and the "Trashcan Man." Glen Bateman is a retired sociologist, painter, and all-around philosophical good guy. Accompanied by a Irish Setter (named Kojak) that he found post-flu, Bateman is both practical and realistic: he sees the promise in the social and psychological realities brought about by the flu—the capacity to build a new world in place of the old—predicts the coming order of things, attempts to explain away the supernatural elements all the survivors are experiencing, and remains benevolent throughout the course of the novel. Like Glen, Locke contemplates the needs of their new society long before the other survivors. Like him, he is a counselor and spiritual facilitator for others (see Chapter Four below). Unlike Locke, however, Glen is not a firm believer in the spiritual elements of the survivor's experiences. Locke's profound and unblinking faith in the island does resemble the strange religiosity of *The Stand's* Trashcan Man, who, while manic and unquestionably insane, believes in the spiritual dimension 100 percent.

- **Rita Blakemoore and Shannon Rutherford.** King's Rita Blakemoore is rich and insufferable, and it is only through Larry Underwood's help that she is able to make it outside of New York City alive. Rita is accustomed to the finer things in life, has a frivolous attitude, and has no idea how to take care of herself—all characteristics shared by Shannon Rutherford. Rita tries to hike in stylish heeled boots, pops a Valium when reality is too much, and is constantly nostalgic about the life she once had; Shannon sunbathes in a bikini and gives herself a pedicure while others seek to recover from the crash. And both Shannon and Rita prove themselves to be extraneous to their stories: Rita kills herself (a drug overdose); Shannon is shot by Ana Lucia.

- **Lloyd Henreid, Nadine Cross, and Kate.** In the pre-crash world, Kate Austen is a fugitive. She stands accused of murdering her biological father, Wayne, organizing a bank robbery, and bringing about the death of her high school sweetheart Tom. The character most similar to Kate is Lloyd Henreid, a criminal by nature who survives on the body of the man in the adjourning cell and a rat for weeks following the flu outbreak, before Flagg offers him redemption. Lloyd is Flagg's "soldier," his right-hand man, and experiences a redemption based on accepting the special status Flagg offers him.

From the moment the marshal is knocked unconscious as the plane goes down, Kate proactively works to secure her own survival. Unlike Lloyd, however, Kate does not appear to intend to serve (or desire to serve) evil, but she does struggle with the concept of goodness. In "What Kate Did," she desperately longs to be good, condemning Jack for his goodness and her mother's bad choices as the reason that, forever tarnished and marked with badness, she can never be *truly* good.

Nadine Cross in *The Stand* struggles with the teeter-totter of good versus evil. She tries to make good by joining up with Larry Underwood, for she sees the capacity for transformation in him and knows he is a "good" man. But, Nadine is drawn inexplicably to the west and Randall Flagg. She is to be his bride, his intended, and in that respect believes herself to be evil. Nadine is attracted to both Larry and Randall in a way that mirrors Kate's attraction for both Jack and Sawyer. As much as Kate wants goodness for herself, and possibly believes that Jack's good nature might finally redeem her, she is drawn to Sawyer. Ultimately Nadine chooses Flagg and regrets her choice, eventually killing herself in a final attempt to repent.

- **Mother Abigail, Mr. Eko, and Rose.** Mother Abigail is the penultimate "good" character in *The Stand*. She is 108 years old, communicates with the other survivors through psychic dreams, and has pipeline access to the word of God. She is benevolent and warm and good—all qualities that inspire others to travel across the country to join her. The African American Mother Abigail has traits similar to both Rose and Mr. Eko on *Lost*. Rose, after all, is spiritual and has unwavering faith in her husband's survival, despite his being in the tail section. She prefers to dry her laundry on a clothesline (as does Mother Abigail), and appears to exhibit certain psychic tendencies similar to Mother Abigail's.

  In the first half of Season Two, Mr. Eko appears to be religious or spiritual to some extent. He pays penance for those that perished in the crash and the Others he killed on their first night on the island by observing forty days of silence. He carries a stick that he carves as he makes his journey across the island. And he tells Locke an obscure Old Testament story about the long forgotten King Josiah. Eko's references to scripture are similar to Mother Abigail's—the elderly mother often references scripture in the course of the book, occasionally as hidden clues.

- **Joe/Leo and Walt Lloyd Porter.** Nadine Cross and "Joe" find Larry following the death of Rita Blakemoore, and Larry spends a great deal of time helping to care for the two. Nadine found Joe in a grocery store, abandoned, mute, and feral. The child cannot communicate and often reacts with a predatory anger toward those that try to touch or confine him, and it is only with careful provocation that he emerges from his silent shell. When the boy finally becomes comfortable with Nadine and Larry, he informs them that his name is Leo, and from that moment on, Leo acts as a psychic conductor, knowing things about people that no ordinary child would know. Leo is first to notice Harold's deceit, and perceives Nadine's darkness as soon as she commits herself to her "destiny" as the Dark Man's bride. Leo's psychic ability is similar to Walt's on *Lost*: Both boys are able to perceive the thoughts and feelings of others, and both can "read" the goodness or badness inherent in others. The boys also share an interesting vengeful streak: Leo attempts to stab Larry several times as he sleeps; Walt burns down his father's first raft so they cannot leave the island. Seeking mentors, they both form relationships with men other than their father: Leo seeks out and bonds with Larry, and Walt grows close to Locke.

- **The Black Rock.** A "black rock" exists in both the novel and *Lost*. Randall Flagg's symbol, worn by his followers, is a black stone marked with a red flaw, on more than one occasion referred to as "the Black Rock." The Black Rock in *The Stand* is able to change shape and meaning—Flagg turns it into a key on more than one occasion—the key to the demonic kingdom that all his followers are promised.

  The *Black Rock* in *Lost*, first mentioned in the paranoid mumblings of Rousseau, is a marked location on her map and a place on the island that she avoids. By the end of Season One, we learn that the *Black Rock* is a run-aground, masted slave ship of unknown age and origin that, among other things, houses some very old dynamite. Rousseau's hesitation to go on board the ship indicates that the place is more frightening and sinister than she is willing to say.

The ambiguity of the ship's name (and unanswered questions about its meaning or how it got on the island) closely parallel the ephemeral concept of the black rock that Randall Flagg's followers wear.

- **Animals.** Animals appear as symbolic in both *The Stand* and *Lost*: Randall Flagg often appears as a crow or sends out packs of gray wolves to do his bidding and spying. Rats swarm the corn fields in front of Mother Abigail's homestead, and she attributes the rodents to "The Devil's Imp"—Randall Flagg.

   On the island, the Others have sharks and polar bears that appear to display significance—especially that shark emblazoned with a DHARMA logo. A black horse may be the animal embodiment of Kate's dead father, and Charlie is inspired to break his heroin addiction thanks to a magnificent Moth.

   Kojak in *The Stand* and Vincent on *Lost* are both extraordinary dogs. Kojak survives a few encounters with the Dark Man's wolves and tracks across the country looking for his owner, Glen Bateman. Vincent goes missing on several occasions in Seasons One and Two, most notably his disappearance and reappearance following the crash. Kojak is even the point-of-view character for a passage in the course of *The Stand*, a dog's-eye-view of his journey and all the perils encountered along the way. Damon Lindelof admits that he had initially hoped to close out the first season with an episode from Vincent's perspective, but discarded the idea after news of the concept leaked out onto the Internet.

- **Spies and Spying.** Spying is pivotal to the narrative of *The Stand*, as the Free Zone elects to send out three spies to explore the west and learn more about Randall Flagg. The

Others in *Lost* have also used at least one spy, Goodwin, to ascertain the "good" and "bad" survivors from Oceanic Flight 815 before he is killed by Ana Lucia. Although the writers have never established Ethan Rom or Nathan as Others, the audience has collectively assumed them to be spies.

- ***The Stand* Miniseries.** The filmed version of *The Stand* was a network television miniseries event in 1994, starring Rob Lowe, Molly Ringwald, and Gary Sinese. Some notable additions to the filmic text appear to have influenced *Lost*. The dog Kojak is a yellow Labrador Retriever, in the miniseries, not an Irish Setter, and truly resembles Vincent. The black rock necklace Flagg's followers wear is completely black, without the "red flaw" described in the book.

  In the miniseries Harold delivers two lines that are not in the book but echo with *Lost* significance. He says to Frannie that their survival of the flu is as lucky as winning the "Megabucks Lottery." Hurley's winning lottery ticket on *Lost* was from none other than Megabucks. When Harold turns against the committee in the Free Zone and makes a bomb with dynamite, he explains that dynamite sweats nitroglycerin—a line that Arzt echoes prior to his death in "Exodus" (1.23).

Until the end of the series, it is impossible to know every parallel between *The Stand* and *Lost*. Several characters, most notably Sawyer, Ana Lucia, and Michael, have no clear ancestors in *The Stand*. In time, these connections may appear, as well as even greater resonance between the two texts.

Stranger in a Strange Land—The ninth episode of *Lost*'s third season, the almost completely forgettable "Stranger in a Strange Land," owes its title to a 1961 novel of the same name by the controversial American science fiction writer Robert Heinlein (1907–1988). His four decades of prolific authorship earned Heinlein a variety of labels: "a conservative, a militarist, a Calvinist, a sexist, a libertarian, a solipsist, and even a fascist," and none of his books seems harder to classify than *Stranger*, an epic novel about a young man, raised by Martians on the Red Planet, named Valentine Michael Smith, who becomes upon his return to Earth the founder of a new religion centered on "grokking," a philosophy of oneness and love with all people and things. In the psychedelic Sixties, *Stranger* became a campus bestseller. In his short life, Smith has many adventures and may have changed the nature of human history through his influence, but he does not go to Thailand and engage in outlaw tattooing. *Stranger* is an ancestor text in name only.

Walden Two—Even if unaware that *Lost* co-creator Damon Lindelof has been interested in B.F. Skinner since an undergraduate at New York University, the attentive *Lost* viewer might well have concluded that the pioneer behavioral psychologist was a presence on the island.

In the "Orientation" film, after all, Marvin Candle actually evokes his name:

The DHARMA Initiative was created in 1970, and it is the brain-child of Gerald and Karen DeGroot—two doctoral candidates at the University of Michigan. Following in the footsteps of visionaries such as B.F. Skinner [there is a jump cut/splice here] imagined a large scale communal research compound where scientists and free thinkers from around the globe could pursue research in meteorology, psychology, parapsychology, zoology, electromagnetism, and utopian social [splice] Danish industrialist and munitions magnate Alvar Hanso whose financial backing made their dream of a multi-purpose social science research facility a reality.

And although Lindelof and Cuse deny they had Skinner in mind in creating Sawyer's cage in the Season Three "miniseries," the temptation to see the enclosure as a "Skinner box" and its push-the-right-combination-of-buttons-and-win-a-fish-biscuit as a classic example of Skinnerian "operant conditioning" is hard to deny.

Skinner's most important book is probably *Beyond Freedom and Dignity* (1971), but his utopian "novel" *Walden Two* (1948) is the most likely candidate as a *Lost* ancestor text. Hardly a novel at all, *Walden Two* is more of a Socratic dialogue between Frazier, the founder of the eponymous utopian community of the book, and Burris and Castle, two visitors to Walden Two. Set just after World War II, the book was supposedly inspired by Skinner's contemplation of the social problems caused by returning war veterans.

Since we do not yet know exactly what the Others, presumably heirs to the DHARMA Initiative research agenda, are really up to—why were they so interested in Walt? Claire's pregnancy? taking children captive?—we have no way of knowing to what degree life in the Barracks was Walden Twoish. Judging by the pettiness and rancor of the book club meeting which opened Season Three and Ben's scheming to maintain his power in later episodes, we can be fairly certain that the Barracks' society was/is anything but Utopian.

MUST-SEE TV AND ESSENTIAL MOVIES

The Adventures of Brisco County, Jr.—One of Carlton Cuse's early (1993–1994) ventures in television as an executive producer was with *The Adventures of Brisco County, Jr.*, a Fox series scheduled in the Friday night slot preceding *The X-Files* and later relegated by TNT to Saturday morning reruns. However, *Brisco* was far from a typical Western or a children's show. Part comedy, part science fiction, part drama, and part buddy series, its snappy dialogue defied the "Thank you, ma'am" and "This town ain't big enough for the both of us" school of Western dialogue. Double entendres and comments on nineties' culture (that's 1990s, not 1890s) permeated the episodes. For example, an Elvis impersonator becomes a recurring character, and a slab of beef placed on a bun is eternally saved from being known as a "cow patty" by Lord Bowler's timely comment.

Cuse, who created *Brisco* with Jeffrey Boam, also wrote the teleplay or story for seven episodes spanning different genres and playing with popular culture icons. "The Orb Scholar," the second episode in the series, begins the mythology of the mysterious orbs. Episode 20, "Bye Bly," concludes the orb saga with a time-traveler denouement, as thief-from-the-future John Bly is stopped and the orbs returned to their rightful place in time.

Playing with timelines during a multi-episode story arc is perhaps the clearest link between *Brisco* and *Lost*. During the latter's Season Three, Desmond sees flashes of the future. His present-time actions revolve around these glimpses of another timeline; he tries, usually in vain, to change or preserve the "future that was," depending on what seems to benefit him or his friends the most.

Desmond frequently saves Charlie from his "future" death: being electrocuted by lightning, drowning, breaking his neck, becoming impaled by an arrow. Although Desmond one time decides to let Charlie die, he saves him at the last second ("Catch-22," 3.17). (It seems that Charlie has to decide to die—as he does in "Through the Looking Glass," 2.23—before Desmond can't save him or "bring him back.") Brisco, too, has the power of life or death over pal Bowler, who dies helping Brisco during a shootout. Because Brisco has been honorable in stopping Bly and then returning the orbs to their rightful owners from the future, he is allowed to travel back in time a few minutes to try to save Bowler. Brisco succeeds, and Bowler lives.

Lost also shares other story elements with *Brisco*. The concept of killing main characters—or teasing viewers with that idea—is nothing new to *Lost*. *Brisco*'s last episodes portrayed Brisco's and Bowler's deaths by firing squad. Viewers later find out that the duo faked their demise. Cuse and Lindelof staged similar "fake" deaths for Charlie and Shannon during Season One (although later in the series the death scenes became real).

Plays on words also grace both series. *Brisco* features a lawyer named Socrates; *Lost*'s characters include John Locke, Rousseau, Edmund Burke, and (Desmond) David Hume. *Brisco*'s "chapter" or segment titles include "The Blast Supper" and "Spur of the Moment" (from the pilot); an episode about Dixie Cousins is entitled "Deep in the Heart of Dixie." *Lost*'s first-season episode titles often refer to song titles or lyrics, such as "Born to Run" (1.22), or play with the theme of the episode, such as "Whatever the Case May Be" (1.12), about the marshal's briefcase. Although this pattern becomes less noticeable in later episodes, it periodically resurfaces, as in the *Alice in Wonderland* allusion in the third-season finale, "Through the Looking Glass," and the Henry Gale (Ben Linus) *Wizard of Oz*-themed "The Man Behind the Curtain."

Brisco County, Jr., and Jack Shephard share similar "daddy issues." Jack, like Brisco, fails to gain his father's approval and support while his father is alive. Like Brisco's father, Jack's dad dies before father and son work out their differences. Jack, like Brisco, sees his father's ghost (or hallucinates the visions) and gains insights from seeing the apparition.

Cuse demonstrates an attraction for a "buddy" theme in *Brisco*, later echoed in *Nash Bridges* and *Lost*. (Cuse worked with Daniel Roebuck on both *Nash Bridges* and *Lost*.) Brisco's and Bowler's sometimes prickly but strong friendship evolves during the season as the two share adventures: Charlie and Hurley similarly bond on the island. As in all series in which Cuse is involved, a wide variety of often quirky characters come together to pool their disparate knowledge and skills for the greater good in plots occasionally otherworldly. Although Cuse doesn't blatantly steal from his previous work, supernatural or mystical elements, father/son relationships, and the themes of friendship frequently turn up in a Cuse series.

Alias—J.J. Abrams' spy drama, *Alias* (2001–2006) has whisked its audience to a thousand and one exotic locations with main character and series heroine, Sydney Bristow (Jennifer Garner), in an array of flashy (and often revealing) costumes and disguises. But the premise of *Alias* isn't just about the couture: Abrams has said the original concept came from his WB network semi-hit *Felicity*, which inspired him to concoct a storyline that centered around a college student who just happened to be a spy. (*Alias*, according to Abrams, "was the result of wanting to do something with dramatic stakes a few notches higher than the romantic turmoil of a college coed.") Add a mythos concerning prophetic Renaissance inventor Rambaldi, who created devices that can destroy the world, and a dysfunctional father-daughter relationship, and a new cult hit was born.

The series was initially dependent on standard cliff-hanger endings that prevailed through much of the first season, while Sydney tried to keep her secret lives secret: She juggled working as a double agent both for the CIA and against the nefarious SD-6, which she'd previously thought was a black ops division of the CIA. Her best friends, roommate Francie (Merrin Dungey) and reporter Will (Bradley Cooper), were kept in the dark, thinking that she worked for an international bank, Credit Dauphine. Her boss at SD-6, Arvin Sloane (Ron Rifkin), functioned as Sydney's prime nemesis for the duration of the series (in the finale becoming immortal, though buried alive), and her relationship with her father, fellow Season One double agent Jack Bristow (Victor Garber), traveled through a dizzying array of up and down emotionality.

Sydney endures the loss of her fiancé, Danny, in the pilot episode after revealing her spy status to him (he is killed by SD-6). She witnesses her best friends, Will and Francie, destroyed as a result of her secret lives—Francie is killed and cloned by the second and third season baddie, the Covenant, and Will is put into the Witness Protection Program. She learns that her mother (Lena Ollin) was a traitor—a spy for the Russians against the U.S.—and that her death when Sydney was a child was a lie told to protect her. In the five seasons of *Alias*, Sydney found out her dead mother was actually alive; lost her memory; worked as an assassin for the government; saved the world—repeatedly; fell in love with her CIA handler; took down SD-6, the Alliance of Twelve, and the Covenant; discovered a long-lost pair of aunts (one evil, one semi-evil); and had all of her eggs stolen. Add to the mix that she's a key figure in the apocalypse predicted by Rambaldi, whose creepy inventions and even creepier designs on the future world somehow always managed to figure into each season's story arc.

The connections between *Alias* and *Lost* are manifold. Despite the action-packed drama on each series, both are primarily character driven. In both *Alias* and *Lost*, intrigue and mystery imbue the characters. The taciturn and occasionally brutal Jack Bristow may remind viewers of both shows of the hard-edged but tender Sayid. The quirky techno-hip-geek Marshall (Kevin Weisman) might be seen as a (slightly smaller) mirror image of the funny (yet cursed) Hurley, or maybe even Charlie Pace. The characters of both J.J. Abrams series share depths unusual for these kind of shows. Without their inner turmoil, neither show would have much of a life expectancy.

Sydney's emotional trials and tribulations are often set against the backdrop of life-or-death situations not unlike the challenges the castaways of *Lost* face. Sydney had to MacGyver herself out of many situations while in "spy mode," requiring the audience to suspend disbelief in a way occasionally required by *Lost* as well. The mythology of *Alias* enlists fans to become experts on all things CIA, spy or black ops, and the existence of a prophecy involving the series' heroine has engaged more than one fan on wild goose chases, solving the Rambaldi prophecy—futile quests well known to the zealous *Lost* fan. Other tie-ins between the two series include the destination city of Sydney, Australia, and the number 47—a prominent fixture in *Alias* that makes a brief appearance on *Lost* in the pilot episode (a tally of the number of survivors). Terry O'Quinn (John Locke) spent two seasons on *Alias* as FBI Assistant Director Kendall, and *Alias* regular Greg Grunberg made an appearance as the short-lived, pulled-out-of-the-cockpit-by-the Monster pilot in the series pilot. (He's very briefly visible in "Exodus" as well.)

Never a big success in the ratings, *Alias* benefited greatly in its fourth season from having the more successful *Lost* as its lead-in. *Alias'* better Season Four numbers were in part the result of viewers who tuned in for the new Abrams series and stuck around for the older one. If they didn't budge from their seats, even at the end of each show, they got to see twice that rapidly moving, red cartoon automaton and hear the children's voices scold "Bad Robot"—the name of J.J. Abrams' production company, responsible for both shows. Even without that signature the careful viewer might well have guessed *Lost*'s and *Alias'* shared genesis.

Talking about his two Bad Robots with *Cinefantastique*, Abrams had a lot to say about his more successful younger child:

If 8 or 9 million people are watching Alias *and 16 or 17 million people are watching* Lost, *then it says that* Lost *is doing better than* Alias. *But if a show is doing well enough to stay on the air, the experience from my point of view is fairly the same on both shows. As long as you're on the air and doing well enough to sustain, you don't really experience an enormous difference in the creation or the reception of the show.*

In fact, from Abrams' perspective as executive producer, "The job is exactly the same. The numbers are different, but you're still trying to do a good show. I've always been really proud of *Alias* and of the viewership of the show. There's something special about it being a cult show."

Buffy the Vampire Slayer, Angel, Firefly—Episodic television in the first decade of the 21st century owes a substantial debt to the critically acclaimed series created by Joss Whedon. *Buffy the Vampire Slayer* (1997–2003), *Angel* (1999–2004), and *Firefly* (2003–2004), though never big Nielsen successes, nevertheless made possible multi-genre, character-driven shows with fantastic themes. *Lost* cannot be said to be directly under the influence of the Whedonverse; so far, *Lost* has given us no chosen ones, no demons, no vampires, no spaceships.

Still, its credits are studded with the names of key writers and directors who came to the series with the experience of working for Whedon still fresh in their minds. Major Whedon collaborator David Grossman, director of 21 episodes of *Buffy* and *Angel*, did *Lost*'s "The Greater Good" (1.21). *Buffy* director (and television veteran) Tucker Gates directed "Confidence Man" (1.8), "…In Translation" (1.17), "Born to Run" (1.22), and "I Do" (3.6). Marita Grabiak, who worked on all three Whedon series, directed "Raised by Another" (1.10). Daniel Attias, who helmed two Season Five episodes of *Buffy*, directed the pivotal episode "Numbers" (1.18), co-written by David Fury—another key Whedon collaborator, both as a writer and director, on *Buffy* and *Angel*—and Brent Fletcher, who had written a Season Five *Angel*. Fury also authored "Walkabout" (1.4), "Solitary" (1.9), and "Special" (1.14). Drew Goddard, author of three episodes of *Buffy's* final season, has written/co-written "Outlaws" (1.16), "The Glass Ballerina" (3.2), "Flashes Before Your Eyes" (3.8)," "The Man from Tallahassee" (3.13), and "One of Us" (3.16) for *Lost*.

No single episode better exemplifies the Whedon touch than "Numbers," both written and directed by Whedon alums. Its comic attention to detail (the chicken on Hurley's fast-food work shirt in the first flashback, for example), its dark, absurdist humor (the dispassionate death of his grandfather during Hurley's appearance on TV as the lottery winner), its mixing of pathos and humor in the same scene, its self-referentiality (Hurley complains to Rousseau about the island's perplexing mysteries, especially the Monster, with a kind of impatience that suggests he might just be a regular watcher of the series in which he appears: "I want some freakin' answers!")—all of these are Whedon signatures.

Cast Away—*Cast Away* (2000) must have played a role in the chain-of-inspiration for *Lost*. An Oceanic Airlines plane (Fed Ex plane) crashes after a terrifying in-flight incident on (nearby) an island in the South Pacific; the story then tracks the struggles of the survivors (the only survivor) of the disaster to survive on the island. Was Lloyd Braun's bare-bones idea for the series in fact a case of what is now sometimes called "kleptonesia," a conveniently forgetful "borrowing," from the Zemeckis/Hanks film? Perhaps, but the basic idea, in whatever form, is not exactly high concept nor terribly innovative.

Tom Hanks—who purportedly brought the idea for the film to Robert Zemeckis—plays Chuck Noland (No-land), a Fed Ex efficiency expert, whose life is ruled by the clock. Jetting all over the world to spread the company gospel of on-time delivery (the film opens in Moscow in what *Slate* critic David Edelstein has deemed "an overture that plays like an especially grandiose Federal Express commercial"), Noland is sent off to Asia on Christmas day to deal with an emergency but never arrives. The air cargo plane on which he's the only passenger goes down over the ocean in what Edelstein rightly describes as "the most harrowing plane crash ever filmed (or computer-generated)," and he makes it, thanks to a life raft, to a nearby island where he will spend four years. Except for a volleyball, a fellow survivor he names Wilson (he gives it a face painted with his own blood), Noland goes it alone, and the film follows his solitary struggles: to crack coconuts, make fire, stay sane, build a raft. He makes it to sea and is rescued. The film's ineffective final act shows Noland trying to re-enter a world where the love of his life (Helen Hunt) has married another man and he is now an alien.

By multiplying the number of survivors by 48 (with 14 the center of focus)—a move that was a necessity for an ongoing series, *Lost*, of course, radically alters *Cast Away*'s subject matter. In just over 100 days of *Lost* time, exponentially more has happened to the *Lost*aways than transpired in Noland's four years. With no fellow survivors, nor Others, on his island, Noland's interactions can only be with the contents of washed-ashore Fed Ex parcels (including the one containing his Fridayish volleyball), nature (like *Lost*, *Cast Away* is full of beautiful seascapes), and, most importantly, himself. *Cast Away* is more *Robinson Crusoe* than *Lost* or *Lord of the Flies*.

Watching *Cast Away* again after *Lost*, we can't help but remark how much better Darlton and company are doing with the return of the *Lost*aways to civilization. *Cast Away* is at its best when Hanks goes solo, but director Robert Zemeckis is "out of his depth" in the scenes of human interaction, particularly those that follow Noland's return to Memphis. *Lost*, for all its wonderful, tantalizing mysteries, is at its best in its human interactions, but both the very human struggles of its characters and the island's enigmas (What killed Locke? How can the island still control Michael back in New York?) have followed them home.

Crossing Jordan—A long-running American television series on NBC, a drama, set in Boston, about a psychologically troubled, crime-solving medical examiner named Jordan Cavanaugh (Jill

Hennessy), *Crossing Jordan* is one of the least well-known successful series of the last twenty years. In over 120 episodes in its six season run (2001–2007), it attracted little buzz and almost no academic interest and was treated rather shabbily by NBC, which has routinely moved it all over its schedule. Its creator, Tim Kring, has gained tremendous notoriety with his new series *Heroes*, as has *Jordan* alum Damon Lindelof (who wrote nine episodes, 2001–2004) as one of *Lost*'s co-creators. Other *Lost* directors—Michael Zinberg, Steven Williams, Karen Gaviola, Roxann Dawson—and writers—Lynne E. Litt, Liz Sarnoff—likewise worked on *Crossing Jordan*.

Like the better known *CSI* franchise, *Jordan* offers plenty of considerably-less-graphic procedure, but unlike *CSI* becomes deeply involved in the personal lives and loves of an ensemble of characters in and around the medical examiner's office: Jordan's boss, Dr. Garret Macy (Miguel Ferrer); Mahesh "Bug" Vijayaraghavensatyanaryanamurthy (Ravi Kapoor); a British-born forensic entomologist from Liverpool; a grief counselor, Lily Lebowski (Kathryn Hahn); a British, possibly gay, criminologist, Nigel Townsend (Steve Valentine); Woody Hoyt (Jerry O'Connell), a police detective; and a dozen other recurring characters.

Jordan has undertaken cross-over episodes with the NBC series *Las Vegas*, most famously in Season Four's "What Happens in Vegas Dies in Boston" (4.7). Despite Lindelof and Kring's close friendship and their playful suggestion they might merge the *Lost* and *Heroes* verses, it seems less likely we should expect a *Lost-Jordan* crossover anytime soon.

Lost fans wanting to at least imagine such crossovers will have difficulty viewing *Jordan* episodes to which Lindelof, et al contributed. Copyright issues concerning the series' always interesting soundtrack music have so far precluded its release on DVD.

Disaster Movies—As a producer, writer, and director, one of J.J. Abrams' mission statements has long been "Take a B-genre and do it A." One clear and distinct "B" *Lost* ancestor is the disaster movie. Both Abrams and Lindelof espouse their great love of movies like *Airport* (1970), *The Poseidon Adventure* (1972), *Earthquake* (1974), *Towering Inferno* (1974), all from the disaster movie's Golden Age, the Seventies. Whether the star "vehicle" is a severely damaged jumbo jet, a capsized cruise ship, a city devastated by a 7-on-the-Richter-Scale-tremor, or a huge skyscraper on fire, the formula is the same. An incongruously diverse assemblage of people, usually walking stereotypes, more often than not played by a conglomeration of not quite A-list stars, mouthing clichéd dialogue and bearing complex, usually troubled personal histories, are thrown together in some kind of catastrophic situation and must, despite their tendency to clash, overcome their selfish concerns and strive heroically for the common good. *Lost* elevates this blueprint to A by making its characters, largely played by unknowns, anything-but-stereotypes, "goosing" the challenges the survivors face, and resolutely resisting the cliché in word and deed.

Forbidden Planet—We won't know for sure whether the 1956 science fiction classic *Forbidden Planet* is or is not a *Lost* ancestor text and may not until the mystery of the island's Monster (aka Smokezilla) is solved once and for all. *Forbidden Planet*, directed by Fred M. Wilcox from a screenplay by Cyril Hume (no relation, we presume, to Desmond), from a story by Irving Block and Allen Adler, tells the story of the arrival of United Planets Cruiser C-57D, captained by Commander John J. Adams (Leslie Nielsen before he got his comic genius on) on Altair 4, a distant planet formerly the destination of the *Bellerephon* expedition, which hasn't been heard from in twenty years. The previous explorers, we learn, have all mysteriously died, leaving only the ship's philologist, Dr. Morbius (Walter Pigeon), and his daughter Altaira (Anne Francis).

Morbius introduces the visitors to the amazing world of the Krell, a highly advanced but now extinct civilization on Altair 4, whose miraculous machines beneath the planet still function after thousands of year. Morbius reveals that he has been using their magical technology to boost his own brain power. Soon after arrival (and soon after the all-male crew begins lusting after Altaira) a mysterious, invisible monster attacks C-57D and kills several members of the crew, triggering Morbius' fear that the force that wiped out the *Bellerephon*'s crew, and apparently exterminated the Krell as well, may have returned. On its next attack, C-57D's forces manage to make the beast visible using an electrical grid and discover that it is a powerful being of pure energy.

In a final showdown at Morbius' home, the monster is revealed to be a "creature from the Id"—Morbius' id to be precise—a Freudian nightmare writ large and all powerful, and it is only when the Doctor, in keeping with Shakespeare's *The Tempest*, a key inspiration for the filmmakers, acknowledges his Calibanish monster as his and dies in the process, that all are safe.

Since we know that *Forbidden Planet* influenced such major figures as *Star Trek* creator Gene Roddenberry ("Requiem for Methuselah" was also a *Tempest* wannabe) and Joss Whedon (in the movie *Serenity*, C-57D appears several times on the planet Miranda—the name of sorcerer Prospero's daughter in *The Tempest*, the point of origin for the Reavers); since echoes of *Forbidden Planet* appear too in *Babylon 5*, *Rocky Horror Picture Show*, and *Halloween*, it seems only natural to wonder if Abrams, Lindelof, and Cuse might have borrowed their conception of the Monster from it as well.

Might Smokezilla—a security system as Rousseau deemed it, and yet able to be stopped by the Others' own Maginot Line in "Left Behind" (3.14)—be the manifestation of previous weird/bad science, the brainchild—literally perhaps—of a scientific genius on the island we may or may not have yet met?

We should note, too, that *Lost*'s Rousseau, like Morbius the survivor of a scientific expedition mysteriously wiped out, stands as another *Forbidden* echo.

Fringe—As we write, *Fringe* (FOX, 2008–) has only aired five episodes, but a show hailed as "the next *Lost*" (Salem) and co-created by J.J. Abrams (this time with Roberto Orci and Alex Kurtzman), has already announced itself as must-see for *Lost* fans. Produced by Abrams' Bad Robot, *Fringe* is a kind of *X-Files* for the 21st century in which a team made up of eccentric/brilliant scientist Walter Bishop (John Noble), his son Peter (Joshua Jackson), and FBI agent Olivia Dunham (Anna Torv), assembled by Homeland Security's Philip Broyles (Lance Reddick) investigates/does battle with the Pattern, an emerging series of incidents, perfectly suited to episodic television, involving "out there"/occult/cutting edge/ fringe science, from reanimation to telepathy.

As if inviting a linking of the two series' audiences, *Fringe*'s pilot, which broke *Lost*'s record as most expensive ever, began with a horrifying in-flight incident on a passenger jet. Other *Lost/ Fringe* intersects come to mind: *Fringe*'s showrunner, Jeff Pinkner, worked on *Lost* as a writer and producer, and Bryan Burk produced for both series; Reddick is on both shows (he plays the mysterious Matthew Abaddon on *Lost*); Michael Giacchino has written the original music for both; in the first episode of *Fringe*, a character holds a airline ticket for seat 108—the sum of, 4, 8, 15, 16, 23, and

42, *Lost's* mysterious numbers. Several characters or places share names with *Lost* characters: Charlie (Pace and Francis), Walter (Lloyd/Porter and Bishop), John (Locke and Scott), Claire as a character and St. Claire's Hospital where Walter Bishop lived for 17 years. In addition, *Fringe* science takes to the next level disciplines in science and pseudo science studied by the DHARMA Initiative and Hanso Foundation on *Lost*.

Fringe is already generating an Internet fan blitz. Check out the Fringe wiki at fringepedia.net. Not surprisingly, fans of both series salivate online at the possibility, to-date not even contemplated, of a crossover of the two 'verses.

Gilligan's Island—Imagine, if you will, a television series in which the following events transpire:

- Marooned on a Pacific island, castaways try to retool a radio into a transmitter.
- One of the island's new residents is fabulously wealthy. Another is certain he has won millions in a sweepstakes.
- An airplane is discovered in the jungle.
- The new residents are besieged by recurring strange dreams.
- The islanders construct a golf course.
- The newcomers discover that the island is already inhabited by another castaway from a foreign land.
- The island turns out to be inhabited by mysterious others.
- One of the survivors is afflicted with amnesia.
- Another survivor is expected to perform surgery under primitive conditions.
- Plans are made to build a vessel in order to escape.
- A member of a rock group is on the island.

- One of the castaways is believed to be a criminal, perhaps a murderer.
- The islanders discover that their paths have crossed before their fateful journey.
- A mystery attaché case is found.

As a reader of a book on *Lost*, no doubt you are rolling your eyes at such belaboring of the obvious. The series in which these events take place is, of course, the one that inspired you to read these pages. Even an honorable mention winner in a *Lost* trivia contest can probably identify each of them, chapter and verse. But they were not original with *Lost*. Each of these narrative events can be found as well in a series often considered to be one of the most idiotic in the history of television: *Gilligan's Island*, a half-hour sitcom about a seven-member sight-seeing party on the charter boat *S. S. Minnow* shipwrecked on a South Pacific island.

Running on CBS from 1964 to 1967, *Gilligan's* cast included The Skipper (Alan Hale), a burly, usually jovial, former Navy officer; Thurston Howell III (Jim Backus), a supercilious billionaire, who made his fortune on Wall Street; Lovey Howell (Natalie Schafer), his snobbish wife; Ginger Grant (Tina Louise), a beautiful, flirtatious, self-important, and vapid actress; Mary Ann Summers (Dawn Wells), a beautiful, honest, down-to-earth girl-next-door from Kansas; the Professor (Roy Hinkley), a high school teacher with a Ph.D., who possessed an extraordinary breadth of scientific knowledge and was fluent in multiple languages as well; and, of course, Gilligan (Bob Denver), the *Minnow*'s second mate, the Skipper's "Little Buddy" and all purpose screw-up (his comedy of errors deep-sixes every possibility of rescue), who finds himself quite happy in his new home.

Some of the *Gilligan* Seven likewise share traits in common with the *Lost* Fourteen. When the *Gilligan's Island* Fan Club website describes one of the characters as "display[ing] little tact, blam[ing] the Skipper for the shipwreck, and…always trying to break the castaways' laws and bribe others…sneaky, untrustworthy, conniving, greedy and corrupt," the *Lost* fan might well think, if we substitute Sayid for the Skipper as the recipient of blame, that it is (all together now!) Sawyer being described. The Professor certainly reappears in *Lost* as well, although his functions are divided among several different characters: Jack and Leslie Arzt (however briefly) exhibit some of his scientific knowledge, Sayid and Locke inherit his Mr. Fix-it-ness and Locke his survival skills, and at least a trace of his felicity for language emerges in Shannon. The Howells' wealth is passed on to the far more "dudely," far less pretentious, Hurley. But, thanks to the ever-evolving, deliberate revelations of their backstories, *Lost*'s central characters escape their types and become complex moral human beings we find difficult to judge. The "stupendous stupidity" of *Gilligan's Island* asked nothing from us. When Steven Johnson argues in his recent *Everything Bad Is Good for You: How Today's Popular Culture Is Actually Making Us Smarter* that today's bad TV is a lot smarter than yesterday's version, he might well have made *Gilligan* the poster child for the brainless, implausible TV of several decades past.

Most laughable of all (not meant as a compliment) were the series' preposterous plots. For being a "desert island," *Gilligan's* location was primary destination for a wide variety of strange visitors. An eccentric pilot drops in. A bankrobber makes the island his hideout. A World War II Japanese sailor turns up—twice. An exiled dictator arrives. Two Russian cosmonauts land. A rock group makes the island a hideout from their fans. A mad scientist finds the island a perfect locale for his mad science. A film producer crash lands and wackiness ensues. Other visitors include a surfer, an eccentric painter, a butterfly collector, a game-show contestant, and a big-game hunter. In a 1981 *Gilligan's Island* special that ran 14 years after the series was cancelled (aka, "put out of its misery"), even the Harlem Globetrotters showed up. The voracious need of television to acquire programs somehow transformed Gilligan's island from a land of the lost into a magnet for the farcical and the inane. If the writers of *Lost* decide to import a lepidopterist just to liven things up, fans and critics will proclaim immediately, loudly, and with one voice that their beloved show has "jumped the shark."

Strangely, *Gilligan*, like *Lost*, was full of elements of the fantastic and science fiction. *Gilligan* would offer us episodes in which characters become mind readers, are turned into zombies, switch bodies, and become robots. A robot plummets from the sky and lands on the island. The castaways acquire a rocket pack; find a space capsule; and discover a meteor that causes premature aging. A NASA satellite bound for Mars mistakenly lands on the island and sends back to Houston pictures of the castaways thought to be proof of extraterrestrial life. Every other episode of *Gilligan's* third season makes use of bizarre dream sequences, in one of which Gilligan becomes an on-trial Jekyll and Hyde, Mrs. Howell is Mary Poppins, and Mary Ann plays Eliza Doolittle. *Gilligan* resorted to such motifs not because of a true generic affinity for them but because they made possible the generation of new stories. Finding new material was a special challenge for *Gilligan's* makers, who had to churn out, in keeping with the network demands of the day, over 30 episodes—36, 32, 30—in the show's three seasons.

But for all their shared plot and character elements, *Gilligan's Island* can hardly claim to be a true *Lost* ancestor. *Gilligan* was always lost-at-sea, devoid of any direction, never for a moment aspiring to be anything more than silly rubbish. *Lost* aspires to be suspenseful, mind-blowing, engaging, inventive, memorable. The islands of *Lost* and *Gilligan* are not even in the same archipelago of the imagination.

Jurassic Park—Seeking to reassure Paolo in "Exposé," Nikki insists they not fear the island's Monster because they are not "in Jurassic Park." Michael Crichton's novel now seems almost prehistoric as an ancestor to *Lost*. The "don't mess with Mother Nature" or even sterner "playing God with species creates problems you can't begin to imagine" theme has been used many times, and the special effects that once seemed innovative in Steven Spielberg's cinematic version seem, well, jurassic in comparison to *Lost*'s Smokezilla, much less the level of dinosaur effects showcased in films like Peter Jackson's *King Kong*. Nevertheless, *Jurassic Park* and *Lost* share an island setting in which scientific "breakthroughs" run amok and frighten the island's inhabitants. In *Jurassic Park*, nature defies scientists' expectations, and dinosaurs take matters (and people) into their own claws. With *Lost*'s Season Two inclusion of the DHARMA Initiative and the likelihood that research has indeed gone awry, *Lost* moved closer to *Jurassic Park* in this theme. Spielberg's movie version similarly plays with us through unexpected scares and scenes of growing tension (e.g., a raptor stalks a child in *Jurassic Park*; *Lost*'s Shannon runs toward the unsuspecting Tailies and Ana Lucia's gun). Whereas the temporary visitors to Jurassic Park are able to leave, and new visitors won't likely be invited to this scientific theme park, *Lost*'s castaways aren't that lucky. In fact, they'd probably much rather deal with one consistent reptilian threat than the variety of terrors on their island.

The Langoliers—As a science fiction novella about a bizarre airline flight, later adapted as a 1995 made-for-TV movie, Stephen King's "The Langoliers" naturally makes the short list of *Lost* ancestor texts. Nine passengers, including a British secret agent, a blind, psychic girl, a deranged corporate type, a mystery writer, and, conveniently, an off-duty pilot, all bringing with them substantial extra-baggage, awake on board an American Pride flight from Los Angeles to Boston to discover they are the only people left on a previously full, but now pilotless plane. Thanks to the mystery writer, they figure out they have gone through a time warp that (for some reason) obliterates anyone not asleep. At the Augusta, Maine, airport, now existing in a time-outside-of-time, they encounter the Langoliers, ravenous beings (and laughable CGI effects in the movie) that eat up yesterday in order to make room for tomorrow. Retracing their steps, passing again, this time intentionally, through the time warp, they make it back to LAX, and five of the original nine live happily ever after.

If the characters on *Lost* had been as badly developed as *The Langoliers'* depthless stock figures, if its mysteries had been as cheesily probed and explicated, *Lost* would probably have been cancelled by mid-season rather than becoming a long-running hit. Still, superficial connections do exist. When Nick Hopewell (the secret agent) makes the obvious observation, in conversation with Brian Engle, the pilot, that all the passengers "were going to Boston for different reasons," the far more interesting backstories of the survivors of Ocean 815 come to mind. When Bob Jenkins, the mystery writer, speculates about possible explanations for the disappearance of their fellow passengers, and later Nick Hopewell recalls all the science fiction he has read and wonders if they might now be in the middle of an SF scenario, we can't help but think of all the fan-generated conspiracy theories and speculations inspired by *Lost*. And, at the Bangor Airport, Nick exclaims, in a moment of anger and desperation, a line that might be uttered by any *Lost*away: "I'm starting to feel like Robinson Bloody Crusoe."

Lost Horizon—Not only does the series share "Lost" in the title, but James Hilton's novel and two resulting films (one a musical) have a plane crash in common. Frank Capra brought the novel to the screen in 1937, a much more dramatic and true-to-the-book version than a 1970s musical remake. However, all versions use a plane crash in a mysterious mountain location as the plot device for the survivors to change their lives.

In *Lost Horizon*, a hijacked plane crashes in China; the pilot is killed, and the survivors must figure out where they are and how they are going to survive. Capra's film then tracks the story of the five Westerners who are rescued by the inhabitants of the utopian Shangri-La. Hidden from the rest of the world by high mountains, the inhabitants live in a mystical harmony. The visitors undergo profound changes as they spend time in the Valley of the Blue Moon.

As in *Lost*, the survivors are not alone. Though equally mysterious as the island's Others, the inhabitants of Shangri-La are friendlier. *Lost Horizon*'s characters often parallel those who are *Lost*. The survivors include a self-interested criminal who gradually becomes more "socialized" to the group (i.e., Henry Barnard, Sawyer), a sensitive man who brings humor to the story (i.e., Alexander Lovett, Hurley), and a man interested in the spiritual possibilities of his surroundings (i.e., Chang, Locke).

Lost Horizon's crash survivors learn that Shangri-La can provide them with long life; the valley intends to keep them there, and bad things happen to those who try to leave. Although *Lost*'s survivors do not see benefits of staying on the island (Locke and Rose are the notable exceptions), they learn that leaving is difficult, if not impossible. When the raft departs the island at the end of Season One in search of help, Walt is kidnapped, Sawyer shot, Jin flung overboard, and Michael stranded without his son. In Season Two, Desmond fails to sail away from the island and is washed back to the survivors' beach. The submarine scheduled to take Jack home explodes. Even Michael's and Walt's later departure, with the Others' permission and boat, may be doomed—no one knows if they return home, and their journey is tainted by murder and betrayal. (With Michael's return during Season Four, however, apparently the little boat was more seaworthy than it looked.)

A series of Season Three clues and plenty of fan speculation indicate that time may move differently on the island than in the outside world, a plot thread similar to one in *Lost Horizon*. The x-ray Juliet judges to be of an old woman is really that of a young female island dweller, and healing seems to occur far more rapidly on the island. The reason could be that an island day is far longer in "real time" than an outside-world day. Although the time paradox is not explained in *Lost Horizon*, the problems of leaving the enchanted valley soon become apparent for those long-time residents who try to leave. The 1973 version includes a surprising scene in which a beautiful young woman accompanies her Western lover into the mountains; they plan to leave Shangri-La forever and live in the outside world. Once the woman climbs the mountains protecting the valley, she rapidly ages, looking like a very old woman. Perhaps *Lost*'s island offers the same type of longevity and youthful appearance to its inhabitants, suggesting one reason why people like Ben Linus do not want to leave.

Nash Bridges—Given that *Lost* masterminds Damon Lindelof and Carlton Cuse met while writing for *Nash Bridges* (a show the latter created) and *Lost* directors Tucker Gates, Robert Mandel, and Greg Yaitenes and writer Lynne E. Litt also contributed to it, the set-in-San Francisco police drama, a CBS show which ran for 122 episodes between 1996–2001, must stand as an important, though unlikely, *Lost* ur-text.

With *Miami Vice* star Don Johnson as its eponymous, frequently divorced, yellow-Barracuda-convertible-driving, stylish, yet totally professional cop hero, the head of a police Special Investigation Unit in San Fran, *Nash Bridges* was full of interesting supporting characters, including former stoner comic Cheech Marin as his partner Joe Dominguez (Marin would, of course, later migrate to *Lost*, where he played Hurley's dad in "Tricia Tanaka Is Dead" [3.10]). The cast also included Jeff Perry (now Meredith Grey's father on *Grey's Anatomy*) as techno-wiz and Deadhead Harvey Leek; James Gammon as Nash's somewhat demented father Nick; *Baywatch* alum Yasmine Bleeth as Caitlin Cross, and Daniel Roebuck—*Lost*'s dead-by-dynamite Doctor Arzt—as corrupt cop Rick Bettina.

The roster of guest stars on *Nash Bridges*—a partial list would include Gonzo journalist Hunter S. Thompson, transvestite extraordinaire RuPaul, wrestler Stone Cold Steve Austin, *Sex and the City's* Cynthia Nixon, '70s sex goddess Valerie Perrine, tabloid journalist Geraldo Rivera, controversial baseball great Barry Bonds, Springsteen saxophonist Clarence Clemons, singer Willie Nelson, B-movie queen Shannon Tweed, and *Laverne and Shirley's* (and *League of Their Own* director) Penny Marshall—was truly impressive.

The Prisoner—In the mid-1960s, right in the middle of global upheaval including the Cold War, space race, and various land wars, such as the U.S. involvement in Vietnam, a U.K. television series captured viewers' interest with its unsettling take on reality. In *The Prisoner*, a former government employee (most likely a spy) known only as Number Six is incarcerated and monitored by unknown people in "the Village," a seaside resort from which no one can escape. Is Number Six part of an experiment? Is he a political prisoner? Exactly what's going on? Those were fan questions throughout the series' run—questions similar to those from *Lost* fans not only as Oceanic 815's survivors learn about their bewildering island during the first season, but as more people are heard whispering, glimpsed watching, or caught monitoring the castaways' behavior. Even after four seasons, *Lost*'s mystery continues to deepen about who is behind the island's events, the history surrounding the island's technological development and experiments, and all the possible people who know something but aren't telling. *Lost* boldly goes where *The Prisoner* once dared to tread, making viewers and series' protagonists more paranoid in the process.

The Prisoner's Village resembles the Others' compound, with colorful houses mocking normalcy and providing a home from which its inhabitants cannot escape. On the outside, the Village and the Others' community seem like friendly places with all the amenities needed for a happy life, but they belie a more sinister reality from which the inhabitants feel compelled to escape. Number Six and Jack face repeated interrogation and mind games; Number Six and Karl endure attempted brainwashing. Like Number Six, Jack is a strong man unlikely to break under duress but is severely tested; his vow to escape becomes a primary reason for living.

An important icon for *The Prisoner* was Rover, the large white balloon sent either to pacify or suffocate potential escapees. It could appear anywhere at any time, and because video surveillance covered the Village, Rover could easily be dispatched to avert problems. *Lost*'s smoke monster apparently serves a similar purpose as a "security device," although its method of operation is even creepier than Rover's. Surveillance and punishment are two themes common to both series that, not surprisingly, becoming popular with audiences during times of international stress and mistrust.

Questions of free will also become important elements of both series. Juliet refuses to follow Ben and questions the Others' belief in free will when everyone around her is manipulated into acting against their better judgment. The Prisoner refuses to become a number instead of a man; he may not understand exactly what goes on behind the scenes in the Village, but he rebels against being manipulated into giving his captors information. Both *The Prisoner* and *Lost* explore what makes us human and how "civilization" attempts to break us into easily controllable drones.

Fans of *The Prisoner* demanded answers as they tried to figure out the series' meaning and determine exactly who Number Six was and what he had done. They went so far as to hound Patrick McGoohan, not only the star but a director, writer, and series creator, who had toyed with the ideas leading to *The Prisoner* for years before the series made its way onto television. As a result, McGoohan reportedly went into hiding to avoid fans' fervor. In pre-Internet fandom, *The Prisoner*'s devotees went to extremes to talk with the series' actors and writers, as well as each other. Although only 17 episodes were broadcast, *The Prisoner* achieved cult status and spawned numerous novels, games, and comic books, and a new series has been promised for a few years. *Lost* fans are well known for their similar involvement with the series, although the Internet provides us with outlets for exploring conspiracy theories and sharing information that not even Number Six could have dreamed up 40 years ago.

Solaris—See the entry in Ancestor Texts.

Survivor—Mark Burnett's inventive castaway reality series *Survivor* premiered in the US on CBS in 2000. The original premise: 16 castaways are forced to "outwit, outlast, and outplay" fellow contestants while creating a "new society" on a deserted island as they are competing for a million dollar reward. The series secured a several-season reign at the top of the Nielsen's and has consistently remained in the top ten during new-run episodes.

Separated into two tribes of eight, the contestants spend 39–41 days roughing it in the middle of nowhere, without any modern conveniences or potable water. The castaways forage for their own food (many of the early seasons included a tin of rice for sustenance, but viewer demand for harsher conditions eventually led to full deprivation); locate a water source, build a shelter, start a fire, and compete in bi-weekly challenges for both reward and immunity. Every three days, the losing team has to face the dreaded Tribal Council, where one is ceremoniously voted off the island.

When Lloyd Braun, former head of programming for ABC television, suggested a drama with *Survivor*-like undertones—the show that would eventually become *Lost*—the reception was less than warm. *Survivor*'s appeal to audiences is based on the dramatic component of the challenges and tribal council sessions; group dynamics were simply a sideshow. Marrying *Survivor*'s high concept to drama and suspense required a significant outside force—in the case of *Lost* a big-island mystery that could keep the emotions running high and the audience hooked.

Lost is often linked to *Survivor* in the print media; the first season was often described as "*Survivor* meets *Lord of the Flies* meets *The X-Files.*" Mid-Season One, Fox's *Mad TV* offered a parody of the series, where the *Lost* castaways journey through the dense jungle to discover Jeff Probst, who prompts them to participate in a reward challenge.

To Kill a Mockingbird—In "The Cost of Living" (3.5) Juliet pretends to be putting in a video of *To Kill a Mockingbird* when she instead secretly communicates to Jack her request that he kill Ben during surgery.

To Kill a Mockingbird was Robert Mulligan's award-winning 1962 adaptation of Harper Lee's award-winning 1961 novel about lawyer Atticus Finch's courageous defense of a black man erroneously accused of raping a white woman in Depression-era Alabama. Gregory Peck won an Oscar for his portrayal of Finch. Equally as memorable was child actor Mary Badham's performance as Atticus' young daughter Scout, who narrates both novel and film as an adult.

The Twilight Zone—During the pilot episode of *Lost*, the camera pans to a dark sky teeming with stars, a now-iconic *Lost* image. The shot lingers as the stars twinkle over the castaways. The scene emphasizes the survivors' loneliness and their feeling of being so small in the scope of the universe. According to series' co-creator Damon Lindelof, this scene also welcomes castaways to *The Twilight Zone*.

When *Lost*'s writers and creators were growing up, they loved TV series like Rod Serling's masterpiece. During *Lost*'s first three seasons, fans revisited the *Zone* when they watched *Lost* episodes dealing with everything from parallel universes to time travel to technological problems to sentient machines. Of course, people suffering from their own paranoia and misinterpretation of information create their share of *Twilight Zone* moments, too. Like *Lost*'s island, the *Zone* is a familiar land with weird twists that play with and prey on the imagination.

Like *The Twilight Zone*, *Lost* sets precedents that change the nature of television. Before the end of Season Three, the creative forces behind the series negotiated an ending date for *Lost:* 2010. Although Seasons One through Three involved numerous experiments to determine how best to tell such a complex story while retaining the highest number of viewers, the final "formula" will be 16 consecutive episodes for each season broadcast each year between February and May. *Lost*'s show runners, primarily Lindelof and Cuse, received what they wanted: a finite number of episodes in which to tell a compelling story. ABC received what it wanted, too: an award-winning series that, even with slippage in the ratings, continues to break storytelling ground for three more seasons. Like *The Twilight Zone*, *Lost* will never be duplicated, either in content or in the way the story is told.

Although Serling is often solely credited with *The Twilight Zone*'s development and success, much as J.J. Abrams is often singularly praised for *Lost*, Serling worked with two other writers to craft what many viewers and critics believe is one of the finest science fiction shows ever. Charles Beaumont and Richard Matheson shared writing credits with Serling for the series' episodes. These writers are well known in their own right; in fact,

Stephen King, among other writers, has noted Matheson's influence on his writing. In a six degrees of separation way, Matheson influenced King, who, in turn, influenced Abrams, Lindelof, Cuse, and other *Lost* writers through *The Stand*. The science fiction community is indeed incestuous.

The Twilight Zone provided a different kind of television viewing in the 1950s and 1960s; audiences were accustomed to linear storylines enacted live like a televised play. Science fiction with possibly multiple interpretations offered a new experience, and many viewers were not quite ready. Nevertheless, *The Twilight Zone* built Serling's reputation and begat science fiction knockoffs for generations. *Lost*, too, is a different type of storytelling, one that challenges "standard" television programming, invites imitation, but sometimes is difficult for casual viewers to accept.

As *Lost* has progressed, its plot threads share similarities with many themes that made *The Twilight Zone* a success; like *Zone*, *Lost* at times seems more like science fiction (especially in Season Three), but it never completely enters that realm. During the first season, the drama emphasizes how the castaways survive after the plane crash. Mysteriously, most of the 48 survivors have only minor injuries, when no one should have lived. *The Twilight Zone*'s flights of fancy include "The Odyssey of Flight 33," in which a plane breaks the time barrier and lands in a prehistoric past, and "The Arrival" of a plane whose passengers mysteriously vanished, leaving an empty plane to land.

Even an "outer space" episode suggests a possible interpretation for *Lost*'s castaways' survival. Richard Matheson's "Death Ship" describes the fateful landing of a spaceship near the wreckage of another space vehicle. The crashed spaceship and its dead crew are identical to the newly arrived vessel and its "live" crew, who begin to hallucinate visions of dead friends and relatives. The crew become convinced they are dead, only to "wake up" back in their spaceship, preparing to land on the planet.

Throughout *Lost*'s first four seasons, fans and critics speculated about the fate of Oceanic 815 and its passengers, and the theories sound remarkably similar to those brought to life on *The Twilight Zone*. Season Three's "D.O.C." (3.18) concludes with the startling revelation that Oceanic 815's fuselage had been found in a trench off Bali, all passengers dead, although the castaways on the island seem very much alive. Although it now appears that the crash was faked (by Ben/by Charles Widmore), the possibility of parallel universes, time discrepancies, and other *Zone*-themed explanations don't seem out of the question.

The introduction of the Others into *Lost*'s plot begins an escalation of fear, distrust, and social disintegration, not only for the castaways but the more established Others. Determining who is friend or foe, Us or Them, becomes the motivation for espionage, lies, murder, and betrayal, a theme that reaches its flashpoint during the Season Three finale. The series illustrates just how "lost" people can become when they find it impossible to trust even their supposed friends and how far they might go in trying to protect themselves. *Lost* reflects a current Western culture of fear, similar to the Cold War fears during the time of *The Twilight Zone*.

One of the *Zone*'s most famous episodes, "The Monsters are Due on Maple Street," highlights this fear—a rumored alien invasion seems real when one street after another loses electrical power, and all equipment, including cars, fails to work. One man, however, can start his car, an act that leads to his neighbors' suspicions that he is one of the "aliens." Lights in a few homes flash off and on during the blackout. Certain that the invasion is happening and their street infiltrated by "aliens," neighbors take up arms to fend off these invaders, leading to the accidental shooting and death of an innocent man. The neighborhood plunges into chaos, just as the real aliens, watching from a distance, have predicted. They don't need to invade Middle America; neighbors will soon turn against each other and destroy themselves. By the end of Season Three, *Lost* destroys its own Maple Street.

Other themes, including time travel, space travel, nuclear war, death and the afterlife, and sentient machines, may be tangentially linked to *Lost*. The *Zone*'s first season includes "Mirror Image," a Serling-penned tale in which bus traveler Millicent Barnes discovers that she has a double. Although Millicent is convinced that only one of her selves can survive in this world, the man to whom she tells this story is convinced that she's crazy. His idea abruptly changes, however, when he discovers his own double. The second-season "Back There" sends a modern man, Peter Corrigan, back in history to the day before President Lincoln's assassination. His attempts to change history fail, but one man who heard Corrigan in the 1860s paid attention—back in his own time, Corrigan meets the ancestor of the man who profited from knowing information from the future. In another episode, "The Parallel," astronaut Major Gaines returns to earth, convinced that he is a colonel in a parallel universe. His superiors, colonels them-selves, scoff, until they receive a message from "Colonel Gaines." During Season Three, *Lost* plays with similar themes, especially in scenes involving Desmond, who becomes convinced that he knows—and might be able to change—the future. Time-travel and parallel universe theories have become more popular among fans to explain *Lost*'s convoluted plot twists.

  Lost borrows from the *Zone* in other ways, too. Both series entitle an episode "The Whole Truth," although the plots radically differ. *Lost* references "An Occurrence at Owl Creek Bridge," which becomes a peripheral ancestor text for the series, in "The Long Con" (2.13); *The Twilight Zone* broke tradition by bringing a French film of the short story to U.S. television.

  Lost shares common themes and values with *The Twilight Zone*. The best episodes make viewers think; they scramble audiences' perceptions of the way the universe works; they have a message, although they seldom are heavy handed in delivering it. They bring in elements of the fantastic, but, as characters and viewers discover, the worst monsters come from our imaginations. Human acts resulting from fear, paranoia, and "group think" often provide the greatest terror.

Twin Peaks—The ABC television series *Twin Peaks* (1990–1991) would count as a *Lost* ancestral text even if it hadn't figured prominently in the thinking of both the network executives and show creators who put *Lost* on the air in the Fall of 2004. Virtually every important maker of end-of-the-millennium and early 21st century TV, from Joss Whedon to David Chase to J.J. Abrams, has spoken of a debt to David Lynch and Mark Frost's bizarre tale of Special Agent Dale Cooper's investigation of the murder of prom queen Laura Palmer in the small Northwest town of Twin Peaks. ABC knew full well to expect something out of the ordinary from Lynch (director of *Eraserhead*, *Elephant Man*, and *Blue Velvet*) and Frost (*Hill Street Blues*), though they may not have anticipated a woman who communed with her log, a dancing dwarf, unforgettable dream sequences, crime-solving through Tibetan rock throwing, and a supernatural parasitic being named BOB. Described in one early press story as the "show that will change TV," *Twin Peaks* quickly became a cultural event but flamed out early in its second season, abandoned by a once-huge audience that quickly grew weary of its difficult-to-follow metaphysics and over-the-top quirkiness.

But the thoroughly postmodern (it riffed on/sampled scores of movies, TV shows, and works of literature, from *Double Indemnity* to Arthurian legends) and genre-mixing (was it a soap opera? a sitcom? a police procedural? an FBI drama? a coffee commercial?) *Twin Peaks* did make it possible for television creators to think outside the box. It is hard to imagine ABC allowing J.J. Abrams and Damon Lindelof to morph the basic "plane crashes on an island" idea into the series *Lost* has become without the splendid failure of *Twin Peaks* in its collective past.

Though not quite as PoMo as *Twin Peaks*, *Lost* certainly is genre-bending. As we watch, we are never quite certain which genre-spectacles to don in order to facilitate our close reading of either its present-tense or backstory narratives. An old Sufi tale describes how several men touching different parts of an elephant offer dissimilar reports on the reality before them. Depending on where we encounter the *Lost* elephant, we too might well make very different genre reports.

As Jack operates (in present and past tense) we may think we are watching a medical drama. When Boone sleeps with his stepsister Shannon or Sun and Jin's marriage goes awry, we may think melodrama. As terrifying noises fill the night and a mysterious Monster roams the island, we are afraid *Lost* may turn out to be horror. In the aftermath of Oceanic 815's crash (and in the frighteningly realistic flashbacks to the catastrophic event that broke the plane apart), we might well think we are watching a disaster movie. Flashback after flashback incrementally revealing the backgrounds of all the major characters might mislead us into thinking *Lost* is really an anthology drama. Its many mysteries—Locke's inexplicable ability to walk, the baffling appearance on the island of Jack's father, Walt's psychic ability, the magical power of the numbers that have altered Hurley's life—might make us think *Lost* is some kind of supernatural tale, an exercise in what is sometimes called the fantastic. *Lost*, of course, damn it, never insists on how we should understand it, and in this openness to mystery lies its greatest debt to *Twin Peaks* and its most significant heir, *The X-Files*.

We have detailed elsewhere the many "conspiracy theories" *Lost* has inspired in its avid fans. That too, we should note in closing, is *Twin Peaks*' legacy. One of the first television series to truly energize its fan base (see Henry Jenkins' essay in *Full of Secrets*), *Twin Peaks* inspired obsessive theorizing; its long-delayed answer to its "Who Killed Laura Palmer" central question only fed the flames. In addition to nominating all the usual subjects, fanatics would also suggest that Laura's murderer was (a) an often-used-as-a-transitional-image traffic light and (b) the ceiling fan in Laura Palmer's house. Crazy people enjoy TV, too. But then again, we did learn in *Twin Peaks: Fire Walk with Me*, the series' feature film prequel, that BOB, Laura's actual killer (using her father as his agent), traveled throughout weirdsville via the electrical system, including that ceiling fan at the top of the stairs...

The Wizard of Oz—Even before the title of *Lost*'s three-part Season Four finale—"There's No Place Like Home," clearly a reference to Dorothy's signature line in Victor Fleming's classic 1939 film—*The Wizard of Oz* had already come to the island. Anyone who's seen the movie version remembers Dorothy's Uncle

Henry. He isn't the smartest man, leaving the handling of Miz Gulch to his wife, but he's polite and sincere. Nevertheless, he undoubtedly is the head of the family. Henry Gale of Kansas might be considered a good figurehead for his small family. Although as the man of the household he oversees the farm and its workers, audiences understand that he really isn't the one in charge.

Lost may have appropriated the character name of Henry Gale as an original wink to yet another ancestor text. "Fake" Henry Gale says he arrived on the island in a bright smiley-faced balloon, but he merely takes the name of the balloonist he buries ("One of Them," 2.14). Gale's driver's license lists an address of 815 Walnut Ridge Road in Wayzata, Minnesota. Wayzata is featured in the TV series *90210*, while Minnesota was the home state of Judy Garland, the movie's Dorothy.

Ben Linus may borrow the name Henry Gale, but he is more akin to another *Oz* character, the Wizard himself. Ben's Season Three backstory, appropriately named "The Man Behind the Curtain" (3.20), recalls a pivotal scene in *The Wizard of Oz* when Toto tugs back the curtain hiding the man manipulating controls to project the Wizard's powerful image. "Pay no attention to the man behind the curtain," the Wizard proclaims, but the secret is out: The Great and Mighty Wizard of Oz is merely an average man who puffs himself up in order to frighten followers and maintain control of Oz (itself a wink to Australia, departure point for Flight 815).

Perhaps the "man behind the curtain" is the real Ben Linus. For years he keeps his followers in line with threats and a few magic tricks, but he is just as much stuck in Oz as they. Since the sky turned purple and then the submarine blew up, no one seems able to leave the island (until the Season Three finale reveals that at least Jack and Kate do make it back to LA). Michael and Walt, who earlier received permission (and coordinates) to head for home, may never be able to return to the island, á là the "wizard" flying away from Oz but being unable to visit, even if he so wished. Although Walt again seems to "teleport" his essence as a vision to a castaway, this time Locke ("Through the Looking Glass," 3.22-23) sees the vision; much like the Wizard's disembodied head, Walt only appears as a holographic image to dispense his wisdom. One man with some of the answers, Ben, technically may know how to leave the island but so far hasn't been motivated to take that one-way trip; he warns Jack that he doesn't know what he's doing by communicating with a boat waiting off shore; "rescue" from the island seems to be Jack's undoing. Although he tries to return to his "Oz," Jack's travels across the Pacific seem futile.

A late Season Two fan comparison between *Lost* and the movie noted parallels between *Oz* and *Lost* characters: Ben (the Wizard), Dorothy (Kate), Scarecrow (Jack), Tinman (Sawyer), and Cowardly Lion (Hurley). Kate, the spunky Dorothy, runs away from home in the Midwest (Kate's Iowa instead of Dorothy's Kansas). Scarecrow Jack seeks knowledge and develops a close friendship with "Dorothy." Sawyer needs a heart, or at least to show it more often, and Hurley's lovely locks are reminiscent of the Lion's curly mane. Like the Lion, Hurley shows surprising courage as the story progresses. Although this analogy works within the framework of late Season Two episodes, further plot development in Season Three renders it less tenable.

Although Ben controls the lives of those he keeps captive (early in Season Three), he doesn't provide the group a "quest" that may help them gain what they most desire. He does, however, promise Jack a way home if Ben's tumor is successfully removed ("The Glass Ballerina," 3.2) but then is unable to fulfill his part of the bargain ("The Man from Tallahassee," 3.13). Locke receives a "quest" that, if he succeeds, permits him to join the Others and "come home" to the island rather than leave. Like the Wizard demanding proof of the Wicked Witch of the West's death (her broomstick), Ben requires Locke to bring the dead body of his father ("The Brig," 3.20). Locke successfully shoulders this burden, which rids him of the father he hates and initiates him into the Others' society.

The original L. Frank Baum *Oz* adventure was published in turn-of-the-20th-century America, just when the rise of technology began to encroach upon rural society. On the island, the hatches and Others' community have higher levels of technology than the castaways' "rural" community on the beach. The struggle to gain technology, and then manage and maintain it, is as much a part of the island's history as of Baum's America. Like the diminishing rural communities, by the end of Season Three the beach community is not as "natural" as it originally was; contact with the Others and ever-increasing presence of technology essentially changes the way the castaways live.

The X-Files—One of *Lost's* key characters, Hurley, does share a last name with Agent Monica Reyes (Annabeth Gish) from *The X-Files'* final season (2001–2002), and Robert Patrick (Agent John Doggett on the series [2000–2002]) and Terry O'Quinn (who appeared in a second season episode ["Aubrey," 2.2] and in *The X-Files* movie [1998]) do show up on *Lost*—as Hibbs, the man who sets up Sawyer to kill his namesake in Australia in "Outlaws" (1.16), and Locke, respectively. The Fox Television series *The*

X-Files (1993–2002) shared fewer story elements *with Lost* than *Gilligan's Island* or even *Lord of the Flies*, and yet it stands as a key ancestor text in many respects.

Created by Chris Carter, *The X-Files* followed the investigations of two FBI special agents: the "I want to believe," open-to-all-things-occult, convinced "the truth is out there" Fox Mulder (David Duchovny) and the medical doctor and skeptic Dana Scully (Gillian Anderson), assigned to investigate the agency's most "out there" cases. (The series had its own ancestor texts, of course: the Watergate hearings, television programs like *The Night Stalker* (ABC, 1972–1975) and *Twin Peaks*, books like John Mack's *Abduction: Human Encounters with Aliens* [1994].) The show became first a cult hit and then a mainstream success that played a pivotal role in the establishment of Fox as a bona fide network.

Its fan base was rabid, producing some of the most brilliant, comprehensive, and ingenious websites to date and penning tons of fanfiction that not only consummated (at last!) the PST (Prolonged Sexual Tension) of Mulder/Scully but slashed all sort of other characters as well, including Mulder and Director Walter Skinner. But Fox was not kind to its fans, often shutting down websites for copyright infringement when they were contributing mightily to the series' growing popularity. In a later century, the creators of *Lost* would stroke the very fans Fox would counterproductively alienate.

Though *Lost* has no FBI agents and offers no police procedural, it does replicate several *Filish* traits: its pairing of believer and doubter (on *Lost*, Locke and Jack, respectively); its casting of relative unknowns in its key roles, Matthew Fox as Jack and Evangeline Lilly as Kate, replicates the Duchovny/Anderson pairing (both the male leads were somewhat better known; both the women were complete unknowns), but perhaps the greatest similarity between the two series lies in their similar openness to the mystery.

The X-Files was a show so resistant to closure—to satisfactory resolution of the myriad questions each individual story, and its over-arching "mythology" episodes, introduced—that it even self-referentially joked about it. "Whatever 'out there' truth Mulder and Scully discovered in the hour—whatever evidence they accumulated, by means of his intuitions or her careful science, of the existence of the paranormal or the supernatural or of vast conspiracies—dissipated or evaporated before the closing credits" (Lavery 243). In *Lost's* *Black Rock*, Dark Territory, Others, polar bears, the Monster, the hatch, we find echoes of *The X-Files'* reliance on its own recurring mysteries: the alien bounty hunter, the black oil, the Cigarette-Smoking Man, the Syndicate, the Well-Manicured Man, the bees, the alien rebels, supersoldiers.... By the end of its run, however, many, if not most, *X-Files* regulars had grown tired of its mysteries-without-end. Marketing, on TV and in print, constantly promised that our questions would be answered, but they never were and even more were raised.

Writing recently about *The X-Files'* unhappy end in *The Chicago Tribune*, Joshua Klein would, not surprisingly, think of *Lost*: "TV watchers may currently sense a similar situation in the mysterious *Lost*, the finale of which angered viewers by failing to answer any of the many questions raised during its first season." Klein asked the man himself, *X-Files* creator Chris Carter, what he thinks of *Lost*.

I'm a big fan of J.J. Abrams. I think he's really creative, and I'm a big fan of what he does. But I know there are pits to fall into, and you've got to avoid them every step of the way. It takes a lot of thought and gut instinct. I can tell you that with mythology shows, if you stumble, you fall.

Lost's makers are well aware of the dilemma and demonstrate in podcasts and interviews their clear desire to avoid taking a fall.

CHAPTER TWO

THE LOST PLAYLIST

Not everyone on the island lives in harmony, and few are bona fide musicians, but a surprising number of castaways and Others enjoy music and at least attempt to sing or play an instrument. Whether in a flashback or -forward, or somewhen between, music captures a time and place and enhances our enjoyment of a scene. Few opportunities for music making occur in Season Four, a time of great transition: the arrival of the freighter folk, "war," time travel, rescue for some, death or transformation for others. As well, with musician Charlie Pace's death, many opportunities for musical interludes died with him. Composer Michael Giacchino's original "danger" score receives more onscreen time this season, and the few times that golden oldies are used make audiences even more aware of a character's emotion or mindset.

Throughout four seasons, music quite literally provides a soundtrack for the *Lost* islanders' lives, uniting viewers and characters through mutually remembered songs and artists and reminding us that music is a common note in our lives. It sets the scene in many ways: through characters who sing or play instruments on the island and in their backstories, in the background popular music from roughly the past sixty years, by references to bands (real or imagined), and with an original score. Music helps characters find themselves; it's the ultimate "comfort food" for the soul. In this chapter we look at the many ways that a selection's lyrics, theme, time period, or pace creates a mood and enhances audiences' understanding of a scene. Michael Giacchino's award-winning compositions subtly underscore the danger, pathos, and joy of island living; by carefully selecting instruments and tones— and knowing just when music should enter and leave a scene, he creates a unique soundtrack for this rare television series.

THE MUSICAL CASTAWAYS

As the lone identified professional musician/songwriter/singer on the island, Charlie Pace sings snippets of songs in several episodes in Seasons One through Three. They range from the high-pitched chorus of "You All Everybody" (sung twice in the pilot episode, including a scene cut from broadcast but appearing on the Season One DVD extended episodes, or when parodied during "Fire + Water" as "You All Every Butty"—an advertisement for diapers) to the Kinks' "He's Evil" ("The 23rd Psalm," 2.10). More memorably (and better in tune), he plays bass and sings with DriveShaft ("Homecoming," 1.15; "Fire + Water," 2.12; "Greatest Hits," 3.21). During backstories' quieter moments or between island crises, he plays guitar or composes songs. For three seasons, Charlie's life really was all about the music. We don't know if music plays a part in his rather active afterlife, but "ghost" Charlie's heaven probably includes at least a few jam sessions. As the Righteous Brothers reminded us, "if there's rock 'n' roll in heaven, you know they have a helluva band."[8]

A surprising number of other characters manage a few bars here and there. Before Claire agrees to give up her soon-to-be-born child for adoption, she asks the prospective parents to promise to sing "Catch a Falling Star" to the baby ("Raised by Another," 1.10). She quickly and self-consciously sings a few lines to make sure they know the song. For Claire, motherhood involves little things like bedtime lullabies; if she won't be there to sing to her baby, she wants him/her at least to have that comfort from someone else. (Sadly, however, Aaron's "mom" Kate and some-time-surrogate dad Jack don't seem like the lullaby types. Jack, at least, prefers reading bedtime stories to Aaron ["Something Nice Back Home," 4.10]). Such a sweet song as "Catch a Falling Star" provides an ironic twist to Claire's wishes once she crash-lands on the island. Perry Como's lighthearted recording lends an eerie note to "Maternity Leave" (2.15) as Ethan Rom plans to give Claire's baby to "a good family"—the Others.

Baby Aaron brings out Hurley's musical talents, too. When Charlie runs out of songs for the crying newborn, he asks Hurley to help out. The big man bursts into a rousing rendition of James Brown's "I Feel Good"—which only makes Aaron cry more loudly ("The Greater Good," 1.21). The music becomes not only part of the characters' "dialogue," but the way they sing and their song choice let audiences know more about them. Hurley is *Lost*'s "feel-good" character, and the song that comes immediately to his mind reflects his propensity to find the lighter side of island life.

Almost any occasion can spark a song. Desmond drunkenly sings "The Celtic Song" for his favorite football (soccer) team after downing a bottle of Mariah Vineyards' finest ("Catch-22," 3.17). He mostly mumbles the chorus, as sung by Glasgow's Celtic fans: "For it's a grand old team to play for / For it's a grand old team to see /

And if you know the history / It's enough to make your heart go / 9 in a row."[9] Desmond only makes it roughly through the first three lines before Brother Campbell "fires" him as a monk.

Buoyed by the possibility of escape from the island, Sawyer sings Bob Marley's "Redemption Song" ("Exodus," 1.24) as he sets sail on the raft near the end of Season One. The song may have been an embedded spoiler for what is to come, as the first line is "Old Pirates, yes, they rob"—perhaps alluding to Walt's kidnapping from the "Pirate-d" Others. Sawyer again sings (albeit badly) during "Stranger in a Strange Land" (3.9) Irving Berlin's "Show Me the Way to Go Home"—it seems sailing gets Sawyer in the mood for serenading. That's not the only thing: He also knows the value of music to set the mood. When he suggests Kate share a little "afternoon delight" ("Catch-22," 3.17), he not only cites the title of a 1976 Starlight Vocal Band hit but promises a mix tape to get her in the mood after she declines his invitation. Kate is suitably impressed, although surprised, when Sawyer later hands her a cassette of Phil Collins' greatest hits ("borrowed" from Bernard).

Even the most serious characters surprisingly relax by playing the piano. On the eve of Jack and Sarah's wedding, the couple massacre "Heart and Soul" on the piano; Jack is the more accomplished musician, but he lets Sarah peck a few notes ("The Hunting Party," 2.11). Jack's cold feet before marriage should have signaled a greater concern about the doomed relationship. The couple's marriage will echo the disharmony in their pre-wedding duet; although Jack seems to love Sarah "heart and soul," he questions his ability to be a good husband. Later he tries to take full responsibility for their breakup, although Sarah willingly accepts her share, too.

When Jack plays piano solo in his "home" at the Others' encampment ("Left Behind," 3.15), the scene again echoes Jack's feelings: He is hopeful at the possibility of going home, but he is also alone and lonely. When Kate sees Jack playing the piano in such a "normal" setting, she suddenly realizes just how much she doesn't know about him. Music reveals a very different side to Jack, and as with other characters, subtly indicates his deepest feelings.

In a scene mirroring Jack's solo during his stay at New Otherton, Ben also de-stresses in a similar way ("The Shape of Things to Come," 4.9) by playing Rachmaninov's "Prelude in C# Minor." The camera in his scene mimics Kate's quiet entry into the same house, but instead of Kate watching Jack, the camera allows the audience voyeuristically to watch Ben in what seems to be a rare unguarded moment. He, like Jack, becomes absorbed in the solace of making music, a revealing insight into the common interest of two increasingly desperate leaders. Of course, Ben's tendency to plan for any contingency comes in handy when Locke and Sawyer interrupt his reverie with a phone message: Code 14J. Ben immediately reverts to command mode—his first act is to grab a gun conveniently stored inside the piano bench.

Although the characters have fewer reasons and less time to sing or play during Season Four, audiences still can see how, on a fundamental level, music uncovers emotions usually kept beneath the surface.

CHOOSING THE RIGHT SONG FOR THE SCENE

Paying attention to the lyrics, as well as the artist, time period, musical genre, and emotional timbre of a song is crucial to getting the most out of *Lost*'s storyline and real-world soundtrack. Not only does song selection often expose hidden parts of a character's personality, but it also can foreshadow what will happen:

- Until the batteries finally die, Hurley spends relaxation time on the beach listening to music through his headset ("House of the Rising Sun," 1.16).

- The memorable "Delicate," by Damien Rice, plays over scenes of the castaways' beach camp and abruptly stops right before Sun removes her coverings to stand in her bikini, marking her freedom ("...in Translation," 1.23). Here, lyrics also may foreshadow what we soon come to learn about Sun's extramarital affair, as the content of the song deals with a secret love affair.

- Willie Nelson's "Are You Sure" ("...In Translation," 1.23) must echo the feelings of the uncertain castaways beginning to realize rescue isn't coming any time soon: "The lonely faces that you see / Are you sure that this is where you want to be? / These are your friends / But are they real friends?"[10] At this point the alliances among castaways are still tentative, and true friendships have yet to be forged from sharing continued dangers.

- During a flashback in which we learn more about Shannon, Dave Matthew's "Stay (Wasting Time)" plays in the background, another foreshadowing perhaps—as Shannon is killed at the end of the episode ("Abandoned" 2.6).

- When the newly opened hatch provides a turntable and plenty of vinyl, Hurley and Charlie happily try to revert to their pre-crash selves by listening to music ("The Hunting Party," 2.11). Music becomes a shared interest that further binds the two friends, but Sayid finds their choices "depressing."

- Staind's "Outside" plays in a bar as Ana Lucia hunts down the man who caused her to lose her child, Jason McCormick. The bitter lyrics mirror Ana Lucia's frame of mind, "And I taste / What I could never have / It's from You"[11] ("Collision," 2.16).

- Desmond's return to Penny in "Flashes Before Your Eyes" (3.8) features Sarah McLachlan's "Building a Mystery,"[12] a song that refers to a "beautiful, strange man" (Desmond).

- Nikki dances to "Rump Shaker" in "Exposé" (3.14) right before her death scene in the mystery drama of the same name.

- Even after the hatch implodes, Hurley still finds recorded music. Three Dog Night's "Shambala" brings back memories of his childhood; it blasts from the 8-track while Hurley and Charlie joyride in the DHARMA Initiative's van ("Tricia Tanaka Is Dead," 3.10). Hurley's music lightens the mood and gives viewers—as well as castaways—a respite from drama.

- Charlie occupies a sidewalk singing Oasis' "Wonderwall" in "Flashes Before Your Eyes" (3.8) (and in "Greatest Hits," 3.21). The lyrics, "maybe you're gonna be the one that saves me," reflect Charlie's need to save his friends and family, always a strong motivator in his life. They also specifically foreshadow his impending death, which Desmond tells him is necessary in order for Claire and Aaron to be rescued from the island.

- Bonobo's "If You Stayed Over" ("The Economist," 4.3) appropriately summarizes Sayid's desire for a normal life with a woman he loves—a future denied to him on or off the island. As he makes love with Elsa, the lyrics taunt him with possibilities: "If I breathe in the future / Breathe out the past, yeah / Savor this moment / As long as it lasts."[13]

The way that music is edited within a scene also powerfully supports the visuals and dialogue of even an "ordinary" scene, such as Kate's visit to Sawyer's New Otherton home in "Eggtown" (4.4). Making himself at home, Hurley starts watching *Xanadu* on TV, but Sawyer, who prefers to read, asks him to turn down the volume. Their interplay is interrupted when Kate knocks at their door. Just as Olivia Newton-John entices her love to "open your eyes and see what we have is real,"[14] Sawyer opens the door and takes off his glasses; he truly sees Kate as the woman he wants and, soon after, invites her to stay with him in the Others' abandoned town. Sawyer pictures a sheltered life there; he and Kate can share a little house and enjoy a few comforts while remaining secluded from the rest of the world. For Sawyer, this scenario would be ideal, his version of Xanadu as a mystical, perfect place where predestined love can overcome obstacles of time and space (and the clichéd long arm of the law). Kate, on the other hand, doesn't believe that life can be so simple, especially for (emotionally stunted and morally challenged) con artists like she and Sawyer. "Xanadu," as a theme song and a romantic ideal, converge in this scene and provide insights into Sawyer's more romantic, less pragmatic side.

Sometimes a song seems to have been chosen simply to throw the audience off. Perhaps the best example plays at the close of Season Three, when a bedraggled Jack drives to a funeral listening to "Scentless Apprentice," a song released in 1994 by Nirvana. Although we first expect this scene to be a flashback, Jack (in the series' first flashforward episode) is listening to the song on April 5, 2007—three years after the crash (and thirteen years after the death of Nirvana frontrunner, Kurt Cobain). Musical misdirection also can surprise us with revelations about characters' lives. Sayid enjoys a night at the opera with his new lover, Elsa ("The Economist," 4.3), a woman he meets while on a business trip to Berlin. The veneer of cultural sophistication and elegance indicated by an opera contrasts with the gritty reality that the two not-so-coincidental "lovers" are paid assassins who soon try to kill each other.

CHANNELING THE DEAD

Ever notice how many songs featured on *Lost* are by now-dead artists? The list is long, including Glenn Miller, Patsy Cline, Bob Marley, Otis Redding, Perry Como, Skeeter Davis, Cass Elliot, Kurt Cobain, and Buddy Holly. Although some lived to see old age, most of these artists died unexpectedly while relatively young. Some, such as Miller, Cline, and Holly, died in plane crashes. Of course, songs by living bands and artists also provide a soundtrack for the castaways' *Lost* lives, but somber music often sets the mood, not so much because of the lyrics or melody but for the images it evokes of artists once popular but now gone.

After Sayid finally fixes the radio for Hurley ("The Long Con," 2.13), they test it on a quiet starlit night on the beach. Sayid finally tunes the radio so that it pulls in a song—Glenn Miller's "Moonlight Serenade." Appropriately, Sayid and Hurley are serenaded in the moonlight, but sci-fi-friendly Hurley feels compelled to comment that maybe the signal is coming from another time. Given Desmond's later penchant for playing with timelines, Hurley may have been right. *Lost* has a way of bringing back the dead, or at least making their presence heavily felt by the castaways.

Buddy Holly's "Everyday" recreates the 1950s as young Emily prepares for her date with an unseen "older man" against her mother's wishes ("Cabin Fever," 4.11). Irony, a frequent element in pairing music with scene, permeates Emily's happiness (and a light-hearted love tune) with the next scenes of the teenager being hit by a car and prematurely giving birth to baby John. The lyrics "Every day it's a-gettin' closer / Goin' faster than a roller coaster / Love like yours will surely come my way"[15] also ironically foreshadow the mother's (and, much later, the son's) difficulty in finding true love. As loyal *Lost* fans know from previous flashback episodes, Emily's "love" is con man Anthony Cooper, who uses Emily not just for sex but to meet adult John in order to "steal" his kidney. Mentally unstable adult Emily sets up her son in exchange for cash.

John doesn't fare much better on his own. Although as a newborn he overcomes illness as a result of being born several months prematurely (and as an adult regains mobility after being paralyzed in a fall), he can't seem to overcome commitment issues in order to love. When he gives his heart completely—to his birth parents, for example—he ends up bitter and disappointed. When girlfriend Helen truly loves him, John manages to squander what may be his one chance at happiness ("Walkabout," 1.3; "Lockdown," 2.17; "The Man from Tallahassee," 3.13). Within this context, Buddy Holly's cheerful vocals promising love just around the corner seem as naïve as the teenager trying to look sexy for her big date but having no idea how sinister he may be.

Patsy Cline's artistry provides the perfect soundtrack to Kate's pre-island life, although other characters, such as Christian Shephard, also appropriate Cline's country sound for sad life stories. Surprisingly, only two of her more famous songs are used in flashbacks: "Walkin' After Midnight" ("Left Behind," 3.15; "Two for the Road," 2.20; "What Kate Did," 2.9) and "Leavin' On Your Mind" ("Tabula Rasa," 1.3). The lyrics of the much-used "Walkin' After Midnight" seem appropriate for Kate and Christian in these episodes; both search for the missing ones they love. Even Cassidy, who talks with Kate while the song plays in the background, has lost Sawyer, the man she loves who abandoned her.

Cline's haunting voice describes loneliness and longing: "I'm out walking after midnight out in the moonlight / Just hoping maybe you're somewhere walking after midnight searching for me." The lyrics and lazy tempo capture the feeling of being lost and alone. The title "Leavin' on Your Mind" aptly fits Kate, discovered trying to slip away from the ranch where she's been hiding out. As her former employer Ray Mullen drives her toward town, they discuss the universality of Patsy Cline music—a last fond moment between the two before Kate realizes that Ray plans to turn her in for the reward money.

Even after Kate has been living on the island for three months, Cline's music continues to haunt her. "She's Got You"[16] foreshadows Kate's split from Sawyer, who remains in New Otherton with Locke's followers when Kate returns to the beach and Jack. In the song, a woman looks at the mementos of her now-ended love affair; all that has changed in her life is that someone else now has her lover, but her feelings for him haven't changed over time. Kate listens to this song while she waits for Sawyer ("Eggtown," 4.4) in his house, but she suspects that their respite in the Others' "paradise" will be short lived. The lyrics indicate a future Kate separated from Sawyer but still somewhat in love with the man she can't have: "I got your memory / Or has it got me? / I really don't know / but I know it won't let me be." A later episode ("Something Nice Back Home," 4.10) reveals Kate's future with Jack, and, true to Cline's "prediction," Kate jeopardizes what could be a normal married life to fulfill a promise to Sawyer. Cline's music always provides an appropriate musical metaphor for Kate's emotional rollercoaster of a love life.

Whereas Cline's melancholy love songs provide both text and subtext for Kate's romantic entanglements, Cass Elliot's music offers ironic counterpoint to characters' embittered lives. Elliot's hits are better known for upbeat lyrics and a bouncy beat; her classic pop hits "Make Your Own Kind of Music" and "Getting Better Every Day" emphasize just how far from perfect, or even normal, Desmond's and Michael's lives are.

Cass Elliot's cover of "Make Your Own Kind of Music" offers emotional irony in Desmond's scenes ("Man of Science, Man of Faith," 2.1; "Flashes Before Your Eyes," 3.8). Stuck in the hatch for what he thinks quite possibly may be the rest of his life, Desmond plays the bouncy 1970s pop tune as part of his morning routine—wake up, exercise, eat breakfast ("Man of Science, Man of Faith," 2.1). He has little control over his life, a mockery of the song's theme of self-determination. Even when he sees "flashes" of the future, shortly after the hatch implodes, he wavers between grasping at hope that he can change the future and despairing that fate thwarts his actions.

When Desmond hears "Make Your Own Kind of Music" from a jukebox in a London pub, he thinks he knows the future: a fight will soon erupt. The song ends, but the brawl doesn't occur. Desmond concludes that the premonition was wrong. During a second night in the bar, however, he rejoices when his vision comes true after the same song plays on the jukebox. He was only a night too early with his prediction, and for a fleeting moment, he believes he just might be able to change the future and permanently regain his life with true love Penny. Before he can celebrate this possibility, Desmond inadvertently gets in the way of an angry patron, takes a punch to the head, and wakes up back on the island ("Flashes Before Your Eyes," 3.8). Every time he takes Mama Cass' musical advice to "sing your own special song/even if nobody else sings along," a possible reunion with Penny slips away again. He plans to sacrifice Charlie as part of a vision that implies that doing so would result in Penny's arrival on the island, for example, but then saves him at the last second. The future is changed, and Naomi, not Penny, crash-lands. Such a lighthearted song as "Make Your Own Kind of Music" provides a strong emotional counterpoint to Desmond's life-or-death choices and his fear of tempting fate.

"It's Getting Better" ("Meet Kevin Johnson," 4.8) again provides an ironic accompaniment to a character's life, this time Michael Dawson (soon to be known by the freighter folk as Kevin Johnson). As the episode opens, Michael prepares to commit suicide. While Elliot cheerfully sings about life getting better every day, Michael accelerates his car toward a metal dumpster. Although he and Walt are living in New York, just as he planned if he ever left the island, Walt refuses to talk to him, and Michael can't live with both the loss of his son and his guilt over what he did to get them home. Heaping even more irony on the scene, the island has another surprise for Michael—he can't kill himself. "The island won't let you," a bemused Tom Friendly tells him when he recruits the former castaway to work for Ben.

Perhaps, to Michael, this last chance at redemption—by protecting his island-bound friends from certain death at the hands of Charles Widmore's attack force—means that his life may be getting better. His "better" half, Kevin Johnson, is a handyman and general flunky on the *Christiane* by day and Ben's "man on the boat" by night. Michael plans to save his friends but dies doing so (a self-prophesy fulfilled in "There's No Place Like Home," 4.13). The only way Michael can fathom to "better" his life is an afterlife of peace that he can't find anywhere on earth.

Michael's "ghosts" continue to plague him on the freighter. He plans to blow it up, only to hear Cass Elliot's refrain eerily playing once again and Libby, one of the women he killed, beseeching him not to detonate the bomb. Although the device is a fake, a "test" from Ben, the song choice paired with Michael's depressing reality makes his life seem even further removed from any possibility of happiness. The upbeat music also recalls Cass Elliot's sad and untimely death after giving the world a series of life-affirming hits. Even "happy" music unearths some serious truths on *Lost*.

MAKING THE BAND

Elvis' explosion into rock 'n' roll, as well as the British Invasion of the 1960s, brought immediate attention to the phenomenon of rock bands. Making the band became a dream for would-be stars who wanted the celebrity and perks afforded to the Beatles or Rolling Stones. During the intervening decades, the popularity of certain groups has signaled cultural changes, and young fans' idolatry of band members can influence everything from fashion to slang to sociopolitical point of view. The rise of a group's or an artist's popularity often accompanies shifts in popular consciousness and trends in popular culture. (Look at the close association between the Beatles' visits with Mahareshi Mahesh Yogi in the late 1960s and increased Western interest in meditation and Eastern-flavored music; the Bee Gees' *Saturday Night Fever* soundtrack, with its many #1 hits, and the rise of disco in the mid-1970s; the *British/American/Australian*, etc. *Idol*'s current television craze and the public's "control" over new artists' careers; or dozens of examples from other musical genres and other decades.) Being a hit rocker carries a lot of cultural weight.

Even today, with as much emphasis on individual artists as bands, fascination with rockers' lives continues. For more than forty years, confessional stories of and by roadies and groupies have fueled popular interest in what it must be like to record and tour; celebrity tabloids and entertainment news chronicle every up and down in musicians' lives. Bands and their music are adopted as prophets or proponents of cultures or countercultures; their fortunes wax and wane with the sales of their songs. The desire to be one of the few who attain such stardom motivates many young musicians to form bands and attempt to turn professional. It's no wonder that *Lost* explores how musicians find and lose themselves in celebrity as much as in the music.

"*Lost*" music is appropriate for *Lost*'s analysis of the association between fame and music: three bands mentioned within the first three seasons are now defunct. In "Homecoming" (1.15), Francis Price Heatherington, father of Charlie's then-girlfriend Lucy, describes his long-gone band, Protestant Reformation. He admits that the name is a groaner and explains that he gave up the band when he "grew up" as a husband and father. Frank and Charlie share an interest in music as well as some insights into what it's like to be with the band. The message is clear to Charlie: To be man enough to provide for Lucy, he needs a regular job. Being a musician is fine when he's single, but at some point he'll need to settle down…and just settle, like everyone else.

Charlie's own band, DriveShaft, attempts a comeback that fizzles when his brother Liam refuses to go on tour. The band has one hit, two albums, and a few European tours before its perhaps not-so-tragic demise; a belated "Greatest Hits" collection becomes popular after Charlie's reported death. Although DriveShaft provides Charlie with a wider audience and greater opportunity as a songwriter, it simultaneously restrains his unique—if not as commercially viable—artistic voice.

The third band, Geronimo Jackson, is the only one with (possibly) real-world origins. Its greatest claim to fame is being mentioned on *Lost*; Geronimo Jackson memorabilia pop up in flashbacks and on the island. They too represent a bygone era in music and American history, fading quietly into obscurity.

Why is there so much interest in these "lost" bands? Music offers one more way that people become "lost." But what happens to no longer famous musicians? Do they become lost in the past, or do they move on to other jobs in the industry, working as agents or producers? Do they, like Frank Heatherington, successfully leave behind that part of their lives? Or do they still think about what might have been?

Protestant Reformation, DriveShaft, and Geronimo Jackson may be gone, but they're not forgotten. Former fans, like Kate's friend Beth ("Pilot," 1.1), remember the music long after it's no longer on the Hot 100. Locke likes DriveShaft and knows enough about the band to give Charlie a critique: The first, self-titled CD was better than the second, *Oil Change* ("The Moth," 1.7). When Eddie wears his dad's old Geronimo Jackson T-shirt around the commune, Locke and other adults recall the band's music. It might not have been much to Eddie's taste, but the "older generation" sitting around the picnic table remembers the band ("Further Instructions," 3.2).

Lost's focus on has-beens fits the series' motif, but they also represent the majority of musicians who struggle to be on top, even briefly, but are more likely (and lucky) to scrape out a living doing what they love. *Lost* bands make audiences think about why fame seems so important and what people will do to keep or regain it. A closer look at Geronimo Jackson and DriveShaft provides greater insight into "making the band" and the popularity of these groups with *Lost* fans.

GERONIMO JACKSON

A lesser *Lost* mystery, but one causing fan speculation for almost two seasons, is whether Geronimo Jackson ever was a real band. On the Season Two DVD, writers Edward Kitsis and Adam Horowitz mention that the band existed briefly in the San Francisco area in the late 1960s. Kitsis explains that Geronimo Jackson released one album, tried to make that perfect second album but couldn't, and disappeared after a Woodstock appearance in 1971. According to the writers, like so many young musicians in the 1960s, Kentuckian Keith Strutter eventually migrated to San Francisco, where he founded the band.[17] Later, official podcasts claimed similar information.[18] Some fans even supported that statement by writing online about their memories of seeing the folk rock group at Woodstock. However, these memories are often questioned by other fans—the only online documentation of the group is fan speculation (e.g., one fan site mimicked a real Geronimo Jackson site for a few weeks before taking it down in 2005), and no paper trail leads back to the group. Most *Lost* fans think that the band is yet another inside joke for the series' creators.

Even *Lost*'s characters provide contradictory "evidence" about the band's popularity, although it undoubtedly was a real group in their fictitious world. Charlie, who claims to be an expert on all music, has never heard of Geronimo Jackson ("The Hunting Party," 2.11), but the members of Locke's commune, closer to Locke's age than Charlie's, have ("Further Instructions," 3.2). When newcomer Eddie sports a band T-shirt, commune leader Mike asks him if he liked the band. Although Eddie isn't a fan, his father was, and Eddie wears his vintage shirt.

Some fans speculate that Mike's interest comes from being a member of the mysterious band. Yet another theory posits that Geronimo Jackson was the DeGroots' band.[19] Although not now a possibility, a "future theory" influenced by Desmond's early Season Three "flashes" stated that Charlie is one of the castaways able to travel back and forth to the island from the future; he becomes the founder of Geronimo Jackson.[20]

Whether Geronimo Jackson is indeed a clue to *Lost*'s overarching mystery still invites speculation, although only one new clue arrived during Season Four. A Geronimo Jackson poster flashes on screen as young John Locke opens his school locker ("Cabin Fever," 4.11). Appearances in multiple episodes and even a puzzle, however, suggest some revelations involving Geronimo Jackson may still be possible. The band makes three appearances: "The Hunting Party" (2.11; Hurley discovers the album), "The Whole Truth" (2.16; Locke flips through albums, including *Magna Carta*), and "Further Instructions" (3.2). Geronimo Jackson's yellow-and-orange logo even turns up in *Lost* Puzzle #1, The Hatch, which promised insights into the series' mysteries.

The band gained even more notoriety in mid-2006; lyrics and references popped up frequently in The *Lost* Experience. DJ

Dan's podcasts proclaimed that the band's founder, Keith Strutter, also had been a member of the band Karma Imperative,[21] a name strangely similar to the DHARMA Initiative. Rachel Blake's blogs also quoted lyrics, and The *Lost* Experience incorporated information by and about the band throughout the game. If, as the producers originally promised, information from The *Lost* Experience eventually becomes more important to the episodes' canon, Geronimo Jackson has a potentially important (yet-to-be-revealed) role in *Lost*'s mythology. This type of band seems a likely favorite of the idealistic workers in the DHARMA Initiative, and with future revelations about the DI promised in Season Five, Geronimo Jackson may yet return to the island's soundtrack.

DRIVESHAFT

DriveShaft is not a real band, although series' fans continue to treat it like one, even after Charlie Pace's death. *Lost*'s most famous band likely has been derived from Oasis; both Mancunian bands share a musical style as well as two frequently feuding brothers, one named Liam, fronting the band. Charlie plays Oasis' "Wonderwall" twice during Season Three: when Desmond recognizes him from the island as he plays for money near a subway station ("Flashes Before Your Eyes," 3.8), and a similar scene without Desmond, when a sudden rain shower breaks up the crowd and Charlie's path intersects that of a young woman being mugged in a nearby alley ("Greatest Hits," 3.21).

As noted earlier in this chapter, "Wonderwall" lyrics seem to haunt Charlie's final days, and saving others is a recurrent theme in Charlie's backstories: Jack's rescue from a cave-in ("The Moth," 1.7); his mother telling him to save the family with his music and his island vision/dream of saving Aaron ("Fire + Water," 2.12); the previously mentioned confrontation with Nadia's London mugger ("Greatest Hits," 3.21); and that fateful handwritten message before he drowns ("Through the Looking Glass," 3.23). Even after his death, a surprisingly solid "ghost" Charlie tries to look after his surrogate family, especially Hurley and Aaron. He frequently chats with Hurley, who, after initially freaking out over the encounters ("The Beginning of the End," 4.1), shares his friend's messages with Jack ("Something Nice Back Home," 4.10). Until all his friends are "saved" from their island troubles, Charlie seems determined to stick around. "Wonderwall" remains a metaphor for Charlie's life as a musician and a possible savior.

DriveShaft isn't an Oasis clone, however. The first season *Lost* DVD includes a commentary about the making of DriveShaft ("Backstage with DriveShaft," Disk 7). Inspiration for the band's lyrics comes from many places: inane dialogue from a talk show (leading to "You All Everybody" as a song title), the series' creators' feelings about music from their generation, and Dominic (Charlie) Monaghan's interest in music and ability to identify with rockers.[22]

In *Lost* canon, the band's name is derived from a family heirloom, a DS ring passed from a relative, Dexter Stratton, to Megan Pace, to her older son Liam, who then hands over the ring to his brother when he believes Charlie is more likely to become a stalwart family man someday. Ironically, Charlie becomes the misfit who dies before fathering a child (Liam gains sobriety after the birth of daughter Megan). Before his one-way mission to the Looking Glass, Charlie passes on his treasured DS ring to surrogate son Aaron ("Greatest Hits," 3.21). In a scene fraught with symbolism, Claire fails to find the ring in Aaron's crib as she and her son prepare to leave the beach; the ring, enlarged by close-up, remains behind in the empty crib while Claire walks away with the baby. With all the frenzied activity surrounding the arrival of the freighter folk, Charlie's DS ring may be long lost. In a late Season Four interview, Emilie (Claire) de Ravin admitted that she, too, wondered what happened to that ring[23] and if this thread someday will be woven into the story.

Although in flashbacks the band often seems more of a burden than a blessing to both Liam and Charlie, who don't handle their fame or fortune well, "Greatest Hits" (3.21) provides one positive glimpse of DriveShaft on the road. The beat-up vehicle carrying the band to Clitheroe has a flat tire, and Charlie and Liam become soaked in a deluge while trying to fix it. At that low point—tired, wet, dirty, and frustrated with the van, Liam, and the upcoming gig[24]—Charlie hears "You All Everybody" on the radio for the first time. The instant joy from hearing themselves on the radio keeps the band together and becomes one of Charlie's top five memories. The simple pleasure of early success far outweighs pleasure from DriveShaft's later fame.

How Charlie deals with being a has-been rocker while still a young man, instead of the middle aged rocker initially envisioned in the role, offers audiences another way of looking at the redemptive quality of music versus the "soulless" music business. Charlie's identity, especially in the first two seasons, is so caught up in DriveShaft that he has little self outside the band.

He seems to veer between two extremes: the drive for commercial hits and the need to honor his musical muse. When he works on songs from the heart, such as the few bars of "Saved" sung during "Fire + Water" (2.12)—"Funny now, you finally see me standing here / Funny now, I'm crying in the rain / All alone, I try to be invincible / Together now we can be saved"—music seems likely to redeem him. When he writes music just for commercial gain, the result is more likely to be a "You All Every Butty" diaper commercial ("Fire + Water," 2.12) or "Monster Ate the Pilot" ("Born to Run," 1.22). As his lyrics for "Saved" indicate, Charlie needs to work with or on behalf of a group in order to be saved; isolating himself from others, whether on the island or from the "common folk" by acting like a rock god, usually causes him problems.

His escape from life's hardships—even torture—is writing music. Monaghan explained the way that Charlie deals with a brutal interrogation in "Greatest Hits" (3.21): "Instead of dwelling on the…bad side of being tortured, he goes into his head and he starts to write a song."[25] He explains to one of his captors that all he needs to finish is the bridge. (Perhaps symbolically his life is nearly complete as he approaches the "bridge" leading from life into death, or the afterlife, as Catholic Charlie may believe.) A few scenes later, his final act of crossing himself before he drowns alludes not only to his religious upbringing but spiritually crossing a bridge to the afterlife.

Charlie's knowledge of music comes in handy when he has the opportunity to help his friends escape the island—and learn about their potential rescuers. Who else among the castaways would know the Beach Boys' "Good Vibrations" chorus well enough to confidently key it as a computer code? The Other who guards the station recalls the code only as a long series of numbers, but Charlie translates the notes—programmed by a fellow musician years ago—into keystrokes to stop the Others' jamming signal ("Through the Looking Glass," 3.23). In this episode, his love of music and desire to save others merge, transforming "sorry excuse" Charlie into a sacrificial savior. As the *Connecticut Post*'s Amanda Cuder noted in the first of a series of music-related *Lost* blogs, "Charlie's death was particularly sad, as he was one of the show's most effective and sympathetic characters. Initially depicted as self-involved and morally weak, he eventually proved sensitive, brave and even heroic. The music associated with him reflects his many layers."[26]

DRIVESHAFT'S AND CHARLIE'S REAL-WORLD POPULARITY

Perhaps based on Monaghan's popularity (as well as his and fellow former hobbit Elijah Wood's high-profile deejaying and highly publicized interest in undiscovered avant garde bands), DriveShaft received a lot of attention early on from *Lost* and *Lord of the Rings* fans. In 2004, after one line of "You All Everybody" in the pilot episode and the song's later guest appearance on another J.J. Abrams' series, *Alias*,[27] fangirls clamored for more. Rumors buzzed that DriveShaft might release an album.

Fans soon created fake DriveShaft websites and began to develop their own merchandise. "You All Everybody" and "Saved" can be downloaded from the DriveShaft MySpace site. This site remains active and, by the end of Season Four, listed more than 3300 friends and almost 60,000 site views. One of the best fan sites, the realistic Second Tour of Finland—The Unofficial DriveShaft Site, provides notes from Liam Pace; lyrics for several CDs; biographies of band members Charlie and Liam Pace, Adam "Sinjin" St. John, and Patrick Gleason; a swag shop; and fanvid tributes that feature clips of Monaghan himself as often as clips of Charlie. On September 22, 2007 (three years after the crash of imaginary Oceanic 815), a memorial event raised funds for the real Make Poverty History campaign. At that time, the site officially closed, although it continues to be available for fans who want to light a virtual candle and post a tribute to Charlie. In May 2008, a year after Charlie's death scene, more than 2,300 candles had been lit. (Only 700 candles burned soon after "Greatest Hits" and "Through the Looking Glass" were broadcast; fans added hundreds of tributes in 2008.)

A *Lost* "tribute" band called You.All.Everybody shares four songs on their MySpace website (http://www.myspace.com/youall-everybodyband), two added in the year after Charlie's death. "Nerve aka Charley's [sic] Song" is a direct tribute to Charlie Pace, but other songs "Polar Bear," "The Numbers," and "Speared aka For Goodwin" humorously describe other aspects of island living (or dying).

Other fan sites, such as Remember Charlie Pace, provide a biography complete with photos from *Lost* backstories, DriveShaft's discography, and the now-requisite memorial page.[28] YouTube, the bastion of many humorous or dramatic *Lost* fanvids and clip tributes, added more than 30 Charlie (or Charlie/Claire) videos 2007–2008, such as the eight-minute "In Memory of Charlie Pace" and "Please Remember—Charlie & Claire."[29]

Of course, fan interest led to DriveShaft merchandise, which continued to be sold after the Season Three finale. When the band's CD cover briefly appeared on screen in the Hurley back-story "Everybody Hates Hugo" (2.4), unofficial merchandise, including T-shirts, as well as officially licensed products, showed up online. The attention-grabbing red-and-black DriveShaft logo on the CD mirrors the band's tempestuous offstage life. The briefly shown logo and Charlie's DS ring provided the patterns for other merchandise. Creation Entertainment sold official red-and-black DriveShaft coffee mugs and a "bloody rock god" Charlie T-shirt; the fan club once gave logo bumper stickers to new members. The "prize" accompanying McFarlane Toys' Charlie action figure is a life-sized DS ring. Like many aspects of *Lost*, fictitious DriveShaft developed a real-world presence, not only in the series' marketing campaigns but in fandom. A fan site like Second Tour of Finland looks just as authentic as any other unofficial fan site for real bands; fans wear DriveShaft T-shirts and download songs just as they would for any other band.

Perhaps with all the attention given to DriveShaft, and with many of Charlie's or Monaghan's fans angry over the character's demise, it's not strange that the post-death popularity of Charlie Pace mimics that of real dead-before-their-time rockers. Morbid fascination with famous people (especially hard-living rock stars) who die suddenly or horrifically often increases an artist's posthumous popularity. *Lost* briefly touches on this phenomenon when Naomi tells Charlie about a huge memorial service for him and the resurgence of DriveShaft in the wake of his reported death and the discovery of Oceanic 815's fuselage ("Greatest Hits," 3.21).

Although Lindelof and Cuse affirm that Charlie is truly dead, even if he occasionally pops up in flashforwards, hardcore Charlie fans choose to cling to the hope that, with all *Lost*'s time-traveling and lively after-death possibilities, Charlie somehow survives. In September 2007 Monaghan fueled speculation at London Film and Comic Con by giving out "I Was Here Moments Ago" stickers; such a sticker is shown on Charlie's guitar in a "Greatest Hits" (3.23) flashback but not in a similar street music scene in "Flashes Before Your Eyes" (3.8). Fans wondered if Desmond somehow altered time, preferably to keep Charlie alive. Although the actor later said that his character was definitely dead (but doing well in heaven) and might return in flashbacks or flashforwards,[30] active fanfiction writers keep Charlie alive through long, complex, and well-written virtual episodes and time-travel stories[31] that provide Charlie with fame as a current rock star.

THE GENIUS OF MICHAEL GIACCHINO

In a May 2008 review of Michael Giacchino's music for *Speed Racer* [a film starring Matthew (Jack) Fox], *iF Magazine* reports how well the composer has "scored" with such well-publicized films as *The Incredibles, Ratatouille, Mission Impossible 3* (written and directed by *Lost* creator J.J. Abrams), and *Cloverfield* (produced by Abrams). Even in the *Speed Racer* review, *Lost* was prominently mentioned. Soundtrack Editor Daniel Schweiger reminded *Lost* fans that they should be grateful that "Giacchino is still bringing all of his big-screen inventiveness to the engaging, jungle-driven rhythms of the ABC show. And with two discs on hand here [in the long-awaited *Lost* Season Three soundtrack], this new *Lost* compilation is a feast of melodic mystery that continues to unravel with engaging results."[32]

Now that their association seems firmly cemented, it seems strange to remember that when J.J. Abrams first approached Michael Giacchino about writing a score for *Alias*, the composer was surprised and didn't know what to expect. After working with Abrams on that series, however, Giacchino didn't need to receive a formal invitation to work with *Lost*; he naturally became a part of this series from its inception. His original soundtrack (aided by other songwriters, including J.J. Abrams) incorporates unusual sounds to highlight the island's creepiness; even plane wreckage serves as percussion at times. The recurring original themes enhance each scene's emotional impact.

Giacchino is no stranger to film, television, or video games; he has a great deal of experience with storytelling through music. For a composer, he has an interesting academic background in film as well as music. Giacchino studied at Juilliard but also earned a film degree from New York's School of Arts. He has won a BMI award, an Annie, and an Emmy—for *Lost*—as well as being nominated for a Grammy. Nevertheless, his creative process for *Lost* differs from his many other projects.

To retain an element of surprise and to stay in the moment (so that audiences also have a sense of anticipation as they watch a scene), the composer scores one scene at a time and doesn't skip to the end of a script to see how the episode ends. In this way he creates "uncomfortable" music, "something completely opposite what you would have [expected] in an action or jungle setting."[33] Like *Lost*'s story, the soundtrack offers something different and unexpected. Giacchino insists that the series' original music should make audiences understand what it means to be spiritually lost; he "wanted something *not* typical for what you would get about a show about characters stranded on an island."[34] Reviewers and fans agree that Giacchino succeeded in his musical mission.

Giacchino, like many other creative talents behind *Lost*, is well known among the series' fans. Whereas the composers behind most other television shows, past or present, are seldom recognized in public, Giacchino has a higher profile. During a panel at the first official *Lost* fan convention, presented by Creation Entertainment in June 2005, Giacchino joined writers and producers Javier Grillo-Marxuach, Damon Lindelof, and Bryan Burk to talk with fans about the behind-the-scenes' aspects of the series. Since then, Giacchino has been interviewed on official *Lost* podcasts, and fans visit his website (www.michaelgiacchino.com) for the latest news about *Lost* and his many other projects.

SOUNDTRACKS FOR SEASONS ONE, TWO, AND THREE

Lost is highly unusual in today's television production: It incorporates an original orchestrated score into each week's episodes. One of Giacchino's initial fears about composing for the series was that he wouldn't be able to work with a live orchestra, a process generally deemed too expensive and time consuming for the fast pace and tight budgets of most series. Nevertheless, Giacchino got his wish and incorporates unusual combinations of instruments into his orchestra, which records the *Lost* soundtrack in Los Angeles' Eastwood Scoring Stage.

The resulting soundtracks were released in March (Season One) and October (Season Two) 2006 and May 2008 (Season Three, with two disks). Although some cuts are the same on each season's CD (e.g., the Main Title or "*Lost* opening theme"), each soundtrack's selections highlight character themes and major plot points of that season's episodes. The first CD's twenty-seven tracks have titles like "Oceanic 815" and "I've Got a Plane to Catch" to illustrate key scenes from the first season. Season Two's musical highlights in twenty-six tracks include the hauntingly beautiful "Rose and Bernard" as well as the harsh, suspenseful "Peace through Superior Firepower." Season Two's CD offers more musical variety, but both soundtracks capture the series' extremes in emotion and evoke memories of specific episodes. Season Three's soundtrack, although released almost a year after episodes were first broadcast, has two disks and boasts perhaps the best original music to date.

The CDs have received good reviews from critics and fans, which might seem unusual for a television soundtrack featuring no famous covers or hummable tunes. The brilliance of *Lost*'s soundtrack, and a likely reason why it won Giacchino an Emmy after Season One, is that it captures the changing mood of the island and its inhabitants. The music foreshadows the danger of the Monster or the hatch, but it also poignantly conveys the castaways' mercurial emotions in response to their plight. *iF Magazine*'s soundtrack editor glowed that the first season soundtrack "dazzles with its hodge-podge of cool styles, alternating from bold melodies to exotic percussion and castaway poignancy. It's almost enough to make you wish they'd never get rescued so that Giacchino could continue to spin out such tantalizing, complex stuff."[35]

THE SIGNIFICANCE OF AN EFFECTIVE SOUNDTRACK

Giacchino creates themes for characters and then interweaves those themes with the on-screen action, in effect creating an "opera as far as these intersecting character lines and themes."[36] One of the composer's favorite characters is Hurley, whose life blended of comedy and tragedy allows Giacchino to create some lighter moments in the score. Hurley has three themes, including one introduced during "Numbers" (1.18), Hurley's first backstory episode. When Hurley first hears the lottery numbers, odd, quizzical sounds begin. These few weird notes recur during several scenes. Whenever Hurley believes the eerie numbers might be creating havoc, the theme again begins. The upbeat, syncopated "I've Got a Plane to Catch" underscores Hurley's lighter moments, such as dashing through the Sydney airport to catch Flight 815. Reviewer Nick Joy called it the "most bizarre cue" on the CD, "a jaunty 'Flying Down to Rio' Calypso-type affair,"[37] probably because such a lighthearted theme is unexpected within the darker context of the series. The second season collection showcases a theme for quieter moments, such as when Hurley distributes food from the hatch. "Hurley's Handouts" features a guitar gently strumming an upbeat tune; a violin next plays a wistful counterpoint to the main melody. No matter which other instruments playing other characters' themes become part of the song, Hurley's continues in the background; his theme's presence in the song, just like Hurley's in the scene, holds everything together.

Although every character may not have as many distinct themes, each has at least one unique musical signature. Appropriately, scenes emphasizing Charlie often feature piano or guitar, his two instruments. "All's Forgiven...Except Charlie" begins with piano chords, but the guitar becomes more prominent; this track ends with ominous strings and shift in key. Rose and Bernard receive their own self-titled theme in their backstory "S.O.S." (2.19), the episode in which Bernard comes to understand that he and Rose can't leave the island because she is unafflicted by a terminal disease as long as she stays. The musical accompaniment to this emotional scene reflects the couple's abiding love. The song is a bit sweet, a bit sad. As the melody deepens, more instruments are added: The opening piano sequence gives way to a cello solo before violins take up the same theme, this time with a cello counterpoint. Unlike many *Lost* themes, this song lacks an abrupt, scary, or surprising conclusion. Instead, the peaceful ending is a testament to Bernard's and Rose's enduring relationship.

Giacchino's selection of instruments to create this variety is unusual. Not only are parts of the fuselage used to create unusual percussion,[38] but traditional instruments are used in unexpected ways. The score relies on four trombones, a string section (including harp), percussion, and piano. To create what bass player Karl Vincent calls "auditory hallucinations,"[39] Giacchino might use odd note combinations to create a more sinister effect. "You don't often get beautiful harp lifts on *Lost*," Giacchino explains, "but you do get the lower five notes."[40] Striking one lower-register note ominously in a scene literally harps on the danger quotient. Strings used in more traditionally uplifting themes illustrate hope and exhilaration; Giacchino's score contrasts the "danger" scenes with the beautiful "Parting Words" as Jin, Michael, Walt, and Sawyer depart on the raft at the end of Season One. As the makeshift craft gains speed and the island-bound castaways run along the shore to say farewell, the score soars, increasing in number of instruments and volume. Danger is never far away, however; the final notes—the single-note "bong" of a harsh harp—reminds viewers of the series' darker undercurrent. For all the castaways' hopes and good wishes, the little raft sails into treacherous waters.

More typical of *Lost*, scary scenes involving the likelihood of death or the introduction of a new danger require Giacchino to make the audience just as nervous as the castaways. Season One's "Toxic Avenger" harshly introduces percussion instruments that aren't easily distinguished, which matches the anxiety factor. The unusual use of percussion—lots of sticks, clangs from unidentifiable sources—creates a running pace and thrumming beat in Season Two's "Peace through Superior Firepower." The single harp note, heard in similar scenes, warns of new danger.

Deciding when not to include music, thus making music more important when it is used, sometimes helps to build the appropriate mood. Silence, or the occasional sound effect, can increase a scene's emotional punch. Three life-or-death scenes involving Charlie clearly illustrate Giacchino's judicious use of musical themes. When Kate and Jack discover Charlie hanging from a tree ("Whatever the Case May Be," 1.12), they desperately cut him down and try to revive him. The score provides an ominous death knell—a single note tolling Charlie's apparent demise. While Jack performs CPR, the music stops; the only sounds are Jack's and Kate's frantic pleas. The absence of music appropriately illustrates the absence of life signs. When Charlie gasps for air and unexpectedly comes back to life, a more traditional score begins and adds to the emotional impact of the castaways' reunion.

A similar pattern builds tension in "Greatest Hits" (3.21) and "Through the Looking Glass" (3.22–3.23). Strings underscore the emotion in Charlie's decision to undertake a suicide dive to open a jammed communication link. The music switches to thrumming "danger sounds" as he swims toward the moon pool inside the Looking Glass station. The music ends with his entry into the (surprise! not flooded) station, and Charlie's gasps become the primary sound. The audience also can breathe again as the scene's tension briefly ebbs.

During the season finale, "Other" Mikhail shows Charlie a grenade—pin pulled—just outside a porthole. When the grenade explodes, the chamber—possibly the whole station—will be flooded. To stop Desmond from entering the communication room to talk with Penny, and thus be in harm's way, Charlie seals it off the only possible way: from the inside. Once he accepts the inevitability of his death, his piano theme from previous episodes rises for several bars; a single violin enters, and the poignant music "remind[s] the audience that the person they're losing is someone they were...quite fond of."[41] Desmond and Charlie have no dialogue, but a warning message written on Charlie's hand becomes his final words. The music, emphasized by lack of dialogue, elevates the emotional scene.

With such game-changing plot shifts and emotionally wrenching scenes in Season Three's final two episodes ("Greatest Hits" and "Through the Looking Glass"), perhaps it's not surprising that music from these episodes makes up the second disk of the two-disk soundtrack. Whereas musical highlights from "Greatest Hits" plays for almost eighteen minutes, the soundtrack from "Through the Looking Glass" is fifty-eight minutes long! The length alone is testament to the significance of Giacchino's score to the storytelling complexity and overall emotional impact of *Lost*.

The recurrence of musical themes and the careful matching of music with action make *Lost*'s soundtrack crucial to a scene's dramatic or comedic elements. The visual context, however, is lost on a CD, and although musical cues undoubtedly alert fans to the scenes which a track originally enhanced, many listeners may have to rely on the CD's playlist to figure out which music accompanies which scene. If anything is criticized about the CDs, usually it is the choice of titles, which sometimes are groaningly bad puns.

The first season CD includes "Booneral" (played during Boone's funeral) and "Shannonigans." "McGale's Navy" is played during the second season finale, when Others' leader Henry Gale gives a rickety motorboat to Michael; older fans may recall the TV series *McHale's Navy*, a wartime comedy based on a tropical island and often featuring a makeshift navy. "I Crashed Your Plane, Brotha" echoes Desmond's accent and his horrified confession during a pivotal scene. "Bon Voyage, Traitor" mirrors fans' thoughts toward Michael as he abandons his friends and heads for home with son Walt. Of the sixty-seven tracks on two disks from Season Three, several continue the trend of humorous or ironic titles. "Leggo My Eko" and "Eko of the Past" indicate how Eko dies but also play on words, whether from the popular Eggo commercial or a clichéd phrase. "Looking Glass Half Fool" indicates the rising water in the Looking Glass station as well as Charlie's perhaps foolish bravery in sealing himself inside. "Naomi Phone Home" plays on the classic *E.T.* line but helps listeners remember Naomi checking her phone to see when she could receive or send a signal to her friends on the freighter. The song titles indicate what happens in the highlighted scene, but they sometimes are a bit too cute for critics.

The not-yet-released soundtrack for Season Four offers new riffs on old "danger" themes to introduce the freighter folk. Jacob's cabin, a truly creepy, ever-shifting domain, benefits from the inclusion of anxiety-producing music quietly leading in to a "boo!" moment—such as when an eye looks back through Jacob's window or the cabin "appears" in front of Hurley, no matter where he turns. The menacing music increases audience anticipation of what will happen. The music sometimes shrieks, providing a *Psycho*-reminiscent slash as a powerful exclamation point to an unnerving scene. Emotions are heightened when the music—as well as the visuals—startles listeners.

As equally moving as the uplifting raft theme from Season One's finale is the soaring, life-affirming theme at several emotional points in Season Four's finale, including the Oceanic 6's reunion with their families. At the conclusion of the first hour, the music unites several separate story lines on the island. Over scenes of captured Kate and Sayid following Richard Alpert through the jungle, Sawyer and Jack heading out to rescue Hurley at the Orchid station, and Hurley, Locke, and Ben at the Orchid, the music defiantly crescendos to an emotional peak. Typical of other *Lost* themes, the beautiful melody soon is undercut with discordant notes. Danger music again replaces the free-flying melody, and the audience is left hanging until the next part of the finale (broadcast two weeks later in the U.S.). Giacchino's Season Four score provides brief, life-affirming interludes that make the danger seem worth surviving (and the next CD worth anticipating).

Whatever the tracks are called or how much fans and critics like/dislike the titles, Giacchino's musical prowess is undisputed. His ability to create music that shifts emotional gears within a scene creates a memorable, unique soundtrack for this on-the-edge series. Audiences "feel" as well as hear the music; it supports but never overshadows what happens visually. *Lost*'s soundtrack captures the essence of what it means to be lost within oneself or from the world; it aurally illustrates what it means to be human.

LISTENING RECOMMENDATIONS: ARTISTS AND SONGS YOU SHOULD KNOW

Song, Album/CD Year	Artist	Music & Lyrics	What You Should Know	Why You Should Listen
"Walkin' After Midnight" Released first as a single, the song gained prominence on the *Patsy Cline* debut album. 1957	Patsy Cline	Alan Block & Don Hecht	The country song originally faced criticism as being "too pop." Cline won a talent competition on *The Arthur Godfrey Show* by singing this song. It clearly stood out from other "country" songs.	The song—and Cline's rendition—have been called haunting, elegant, lonely—perfect terms to set the scene for *Lost* loves. Cline's music may be categorized as "country," but this song differs from the cowboy country of the 1950s or even the pop genre it seemed to cross into. Like *Lost*'s characters, the song and artist are memorable because they are unique.

Song, Album/CD Year	Artist	Music & Lyrics	What You Should Know	Why You Should Listen
"She Has You" Released as a single. 1962	Patsy Cline	Hank Cochran	This song became so popular outside country music that Cline was invited to perform it on *American Bandstand*.	This song was a #1 country hit, surpassing "Walkin' After Midnight," which only made it to #2. On the U.S. Hot 100 chart, however, "Walkin'" was #12 and "She Has You" a close #14. Both songs attest to Cline's ability to sell a good, if sad, love song.
"Make Your Own Kind of Music" *Bubllegum Lemonade*, *Something for Mama*, *The song is also featured on Mama's Big Ones: The Best of Mama Cass*. 1969	Cass Elliot	Barry Mann & Cynthia Weil	Although "Make Your Own Kind of Music" debuted in October 1969, it achieved hit status in the early 1970s. It was one of Cass Elliot's big hits as a solo artist after her Mamas and Papas days. The song also was covered by leading	The song became an anthem for young pop singers in the early 1970s and embraced the optimism often at odds with Vietnam- and Watergate-era turmoil. Perhaps Desmond needed this reminder of unwavering optimism during his own turbulent times in the hatch.

continued on next page

Song, Album/CD Year	Artist	Music & Lyrics	What You Should Know	Why You Should Listen
"Make Your Own Kind of Music"			artists in the early 1970s (including teen idol Bobby Sherman and the Carpenters).	
"It's Getting Better" *Bubblegum, Lemonade, Something for Mama* 1969	Cass Elliot	Barry Mann & Cynthia Weil	This first track set the tone for an upbeat album.	This tune, although not as popular as other cuts from the album, epitomized youthful optimism and "sunny" music associated with Cass Elliot.
"Wonderwall" *(What's the Story) Morning Glory?* 1995	Oasis		A "greatest hits" compilation, *Stop the Clocks*, released in 2006, featured "Wonderwall." "Wonderwall" was perceived as a tribute to the Beatles and an attempt to rekindle the British Invasion of the 1960s.	Probably this is the closest you'll come to hearing a "DriveShaft" hit (or CD, for that matter), although the Pace brothers' band never matched Oasis' smoothness, longevity, variety, or success.

Song, Album/CD Year	Artist	Music & Lyrics	What You Should Know	Why You Should Listen
"Scentless Apprentice" *In Utero* 1994	Nirvana	Kurt Cobain, Dave Grohl, and Krist Noveselik	The song is based on the German novel *Perfume* about a boy born without body odor that later becomes a serial killer.	Jack certainly seems to identify with the song's angst-filled lyrics. His Season Four flashforwards emphasize his guilt over the fate of his former island friends and his inability to live a lie, turning him into a pill-popping addict.
"Good Vibrations" First released as a single, "Good Vibrations" also is on the *Pet Sounds* album. The song was re-released on the Beach Boys' *Rarities* album and as a 40th anniversary special single. 1966	Beach Boys	Brian Wilson (music), Brian Wilson & Mike Love (lyrics)	"Good Vibrations" is listed as one of the Rock and Roll Hall of Fame's 500 Songs That Shaped Rock and Roll. Charlie Pace or the Looking Glass programmer would appreciate that fact.	"Good Vibrations" set a new standard in the recording industry: Brian Wilson layered the tracks after recording each separately, creating the rich sound. Long before computers mixed tracks for composers, Wilson created a masterpiece "by hand." The song features instruments, such as cello, unusual on a pop rock song. It would be a standout that a musician/programmer might want to immortalize in his daily work.

Song, Album/CD Year	Artist	Music & Lyrics	What You Should Know	Why You Should Listen
"Downtown" First released as a single, "Downtown" became the title cut of Clark's 1964 album. It has been re-recorded and covered several times in the following three decades. 1964	Petula Clark	Tony Hatch	"Downtown" was the first song by a British female artist to make Billboard's Hot 100. It won a Grammy in the U.S. and was a bestseller in both English and French. Although *Lost*'s Juliet favors the original version, Clark re-recorded the song three times in different styles (including disco).	The lyrics about forgetting worries or cares are pertinent to Juliet's situation: "When you're alone and life is making you lonely," "You can forget all your troubles, forget all your cares." Juliet's previous urban life would allow her to find solace surrounded by traffic, people, and busy places. When she lacks that solace now, she may still go "Downtown" in her memories.

"MUST-HEAR" TRACKS FROM THE LOST SOUNDTRACKS, SEASONS ONE AND TWO

Season	Trk#	Title	What You Need to Know	Why You Should Listen
1	1	"Main Title"	*Lost*'s weekly theme is really the anti-TV theme: short (only 16 seconds), definitely not hummable, weird—in short, perfect for the series.	The echoing sounds indicate just the unexpected or strange may follow; it ideally sets the mood for the series. Just as *Lost* is different from previous TV shows, so its main title differs from any other series' opening.
1	4	"Credit Where Credit Is Due"	A recurring theme, first heard as "Credit Where Credit Is Due," often provides background music for emotional scenes in Season One. A three-note phrase moves "up" the scale, creating a more hopeful mood; strings carry the tune and build emotion during a scene.	(Usually shorter) variations of this track's primary melody can be heard in "Booneral" (Track 21) or Season Two's "Final Countdown" (Track 3), among others.

Season	Trk#	Title	What You Need to Know	Why You Should Listen
1	9	"Crocodile Locke"	Locke's eerie theme includes more percussion in this cut than when his theme is repeated in other episodes. Its distinctive "melody" creates a dark, mysterious, brooding mood.	Locke's theme sometimes accompanies other "mysterious" scenes involving danger, the hatch, or the Others. The end of Season Two's "Final Countdown," for example, briefly features his theme.
1	10	"Win One for the Reaper"	*Lost*'s "death" theme often is played in the series' quiet, somber moments, not always involving a death but evoking strong emotions.	One of *Lost*'s most frequently repeated themes, a variation is played in the middle of Boone's death-scene song, "Life and Death" (Season One, Track 20) and Charlie's near-death scene ("Charlie Hangs Around," Track 12). The song has a traditional, final ending, atypical for the surprising endings to many tracks. Like life, this track comes to a conclusion before the notes fade into memory.

Season	Trk#	Title	What You Need to Know	Why You Should Listen
1	24	"I've Got a Plane to Catch"	The bouncy, lighter tune, one of Hurley's three themes, is a striking contrast from other tracks. It is probably the most "visual" song; Hurley's stops and starts on the way to catching his flight are captured with the music's pace, shift in instrumentation, or occasional lingering pauses.	Many atypical instrument combinations, even for *Lost*'s soundtrack, are featured; for example, a harmonica blends with strings. The mixture of unusual instruments and the bouncy, bubbly pace reflect Hurley's personality.
1	26	"Parting Words"	One of the most beautiful orchestrations on this or any soundtrack, "Parting Words" conveys the castaways' many emotions as the raft sets sail at the end of Season One.	The long cut (more than 5 minutes) builds momentum in the same way that the raft gains speed once it's launched. The epic, soaring melody is undercut in the last bars with an ominous note, a "surprise" ending typical of many Lost tracks.

Season	Trk#	Title	What You Need to Know	Why You Should Listen
2	3	"The Final Countdown"	Several tracks provide "danger music" appropriate for the spookier aspects of island life. "The Final Countdown" excels with bursts of sound to help viewers recall Rousseau, the Others, and, in general, the unfamiliar and feared.	The "danger" music, with sharp, quick notes, sudden changes in tempo or accent, and harsh tones, also features short sections of other, more familiar themes, including Locke's mysterious theme.
2	6	"Hurley's Handouts"	In particular, the strumming guitar sets a quiet, relaxed pace appropriate for Hurley's distribution of the hatch's goodies. As Hurley approaches different castaways, new instruments carry the melody and then fade, allowing the next instrument to gain prominence.	An interesting blend of instruments, from harp and cello to piano to guitar, create a laid-back mood for a quiet, campfire scene. A variation of "Credit Where Credit Is Due" appropriately makes a brief appearance in this song.

Season	Trk#	Title	What You Need to Know	Why You Should Listen
2	19	"Rose and Bernard"	This theme is different from any other characters' and hasn't been repeated (at least by the end of Season Three).	Beautiful and melodic, featuring instruments frequently used on *Lost* (harp, piano, full strings), Rose and Bernard's theme manages to be different from any other track and is a loving tribute to this couple's relationship.
2	26	"End Title"	Fans who haven't yet heard the ending (over the credits) music should hear this track to appreciate the way the mystery "closes."	The driving, almost mechanical end title still sounds suspenseful but is more precise and "calculated" than the opening track.

CHAPTER THREE

BETWEEN THE LINES: LOST AND POPULAR CULTURE

Just as *Lost* returned from hiatus in April 2008, *MadTV* featured a *Lost* parody starring former cast member Dominic (Charlie) Monaghan.[42] As the actor rides with *MadTV* regular Bobby Lee to a fan convention, the pair become lost. They encounter another series regular, Crista Flanagan, who acts strangely just before Monaghan shoots her with a speargun. Flanagan, however, comes back from the dead to warn Lee that no one can be trusted, but Monaghan and his trusty speargun kill her once again (not long before he, too, is suddenly speared by another cast member, Nicole Parker). The black smoke monster envelopes Parker and drags her, screaming, out of the scene. Lee awakens in 2010, just like a *Lost* flashforward so popular in Season Four, but instead of finding his (surprise!) wife awaiting him in the shower, (even bigger surprise!) Monaghan awaits him, a la Bobby Ewing in *Dallas'* shark-jumping shower scene. In addition to being surreal humor, the skit skewers *Lost* just as deftly as those deadly spears hit their marks.

Monaghan and Lee's ride is reminiscent of Hurley and Charlie's joyride in the DHARMA Initiative van ("Tricia Tanaka Is Dead," 3.10). When Lee takes a wrong turn, all the irony and four years' of bad puns of the series' title make the actors' predicament humorous. "It's not like we're *Lost*," Lee smirks a second before a rifle-wielding woman stops their vehicle. *Lost*'s complex plot is ripe for parody; the skit's (and *Lost*'s) characters aren't who they initially seem to be, and strange coincidences are commonplace. Monaghan, for example, finds the ancestral family speargun in the jungle and uses it to kill Flanagan just as she warns Lee how much danger he's in. Of course, Monaghan's reassurance that he actually saved Lee instead of killing someone about to divulge a deep, dark secret leads to a familiar *Lost* plot device: a flashback. Even Monaghan's death scene recalls a late Season Three episode in which an arrow runs him through ("Catch-22," 3.17).

Lost provides *MadTV* with plenty of material. An earlier episode featured guest Jeff Probst (*Survivor*) finding the castaways. As *MadTV* writer Brian D. Bradley explains, the series prides itself on humor based on popular culture icons and would be remiss if it didn't parody *Lost*. "The more something takes risks, the more you think it's funny," adds Bradley, and *Lost* is definitely known as a risk-taking series.[43]

Pop icon *Lost* truly has become part of the national culture consciousness. *Saturday Night Live* (which Matthew Fox hosted in December 2006) also parodied the show, and even other networks' characters talk about *Lost*. On NBC, the mystery of Oceanic 815's crash is part of the top secret information reluctant spy *Chuck* uncovers.[44] When the white-collar employees of *The Office* are forced to meet dock workers for what management hopes will be greater understanding, the office gang refers to their counterparts as "the Others." In *Lost*'s four seasons it has been referenced in "real life" on dramas and comedies (e.g., *Notes from the Underbelly, American Dad, Family Guy, The Simpsons*).[45] Writers assume that anyone watching TV has at least heard of *Lost* or, more likely, is a regular viewer.

Why is popular culture so important? The Popular Culture Association, a scholarly organization devoted to its study, defines popular culture as "the life and culture of real people,"[46] including all the things that interest them: material culture, comics, music, movies, television, fashion, games, books, magazines—in short, what we like to do and how we like to do it. Most simply, popular culture identifies us with and binds us to others with similar interests and behaviors. It provides the code by which members of the group "in the know" understand each other. It gives us a way to interpret and make meaning of our lives.

No nation is more obsessed with popular culture than the U.S., and because American TV series and movies (along with other products) are exported globally, what's "common knowledge" in the U.S. rapidly is becoming known everywhere else. *Lost*'s writers understand that and make the series "real" by showing us that Hurley, for example, likes comic books just as much as we might, or that Locke, just like some of us, reads *The Brothers Karamazov* but also keeps up with rock music. Ben may share Locke's fondness for *VALIS* and play classical music on the piano, but he also keeps a copy of Olivia Newton John's *Xanadu* around the house. Understanding a reference to a book, movie, TV character, or scene adds depth to our understanding of *Lost* and the background of key characters, and so far, international audiences seem to understand the many references to popular culture sprinkled throughout episodes.

Like the majority of *Lost* viewers, the series' characters grew up with television. Younger castaways don't remember a (pre-crash) time when television, movies, music, videogames, and computers weren't part of their everyday experience. They are likely to identify with pop culture icons. Hurley invokes *Star Wars* when he reveals he was something of a warrior back home ("Confidence Man," 1.8), and Charlie wanted to be a rock god whom others idolize. Pop culture icons, whether real people or fictitious characters, have become the heroes that people like Hurley and Charlie not only revere but want to become.

So when Hurley says that Jack creates a "Jedi moment" by talking Shannon through an asthma attack ("Confidence Man," 1.8), we understand Hurley's level of respect or even reverence for what Jack has done. Like Obi-Wan Kenobi with his ability to make others think and then do what he wants (e.g., "These are not the droids you are looking for"), Jack seems capable of great focus and mental persuasion; he can do what ordinary people can't.

Star Wars and comic books must have played a big role in Hurley's childhood. He reads a comic book on ill-fated flight 815 ("Exodus," 1.24), and when Desmond first indicates that he knows the future, Hurley's response is to ask whether Desmond is going to "Hulk out" ("Further Instructions," 3.2). The Incredible Hulk of comic books, TV, and film changes into a superhero (or monster, depending on one's point of view) when he becomes angry; this transformation of an average guy into the Hulk comes about after a lab explosion, perhaps similar to the hatch's implosion. For Hurley, the similarity between the two explosions makes him wonder about Desmond's new "superpower."

A discussion of immense importance concerns whether the Flash or Superman is the better/faster/smarter superhero. Hurley (expounding upon the Flash's superiority) is matched by Charlie (arguing for Superman) in a passionate exchange as they hike through the jungle ("Catch-22," 3.17). Such a debate, moments before Charlie narrowly escapes death-by-arrow, seems "normal" and underscores the abnormality of the rest of their island life.

Science fiction and fantasy are important touchstones for many young people. On the island, young men far more often than women use popular culture references to infuse their language with meaning. *Star Wars* is mentioned more than any other movie, and Season Four is full of references to the film series. Just before his death, Karl tells Alex that "It's quiet…too quiet," a line used several times in *Star Wars*. Just to make sure that all viewers pick up the reference, the enhanced episode, complete with pop culture references and explanations of the plot to date, explains the *Star Wars* connection ("Meet Kevin Johnson," 4.8). When audiences see Jack briefly contented with his life as Kate's live-in lover and Aaron's surrogate dad, the camera focuses on a miniature Millennium Falcon on the kitchen floor. Jack smiles as he picks up his son's toy ("Something Nice Back Home," 4.10).

Television, as the medium with which the male characters in their 20s and 30s grew up, provides the source of most other references. Boone explains the concept of "red shirts" to Locke when they traipse through the jungle in search of Claire and Charlie ("All the Best Cowboys Have Daddy Issues," 1.11). He details Captain Kirk's typical process of leading crew on dangerous missions, which usually involve a crewman wearing a red shirt being dissolved in phaser fire or suffering some other gruesome death (a series cliché at the heart of a running joke in 1999's *Galaxy Quest*). Whereas fans of classic *Star Trek* usually revere Kirk as a fine commander, Locke isn't impressed. "Sounds like a piss-poor captain," he tells Boone, who, ironically, is carrying a red shirt and soon dies while under Locke's leadership. Fans similarly refer to extras cast as unnamed survivors or Others as "red shirts," because these characters are most likely to die. Blogs and message boards frequently list fan comments about who is or should be a red shirt, depending on how annoyed bloggers have become with a particular character. TV terms used by later TV series and becoming popular vernacular in discussing TV shows is a perfect example of the power of popular culture.

Boone also refers to his mother as the "Martha Stewart of matrimony" ("All the Best Cowboys Have Daddy Issues," 1.11). Locke seems to understand this reference much better; Martha Stewart as the ideal hostess, homemaker, designer, etc., indicates just what a detail-oriented perfectionist she must be and explains a lot about Boone's and Shannon's family dynamic.

Charlie refers to British literature, such as author Jane Austen ("Homecoming," 1.15) or William Golding's *Lord of the Flies* ("What Kate Did," 2.9), a novel also mentioned by Sawyer ("…In Translation," 1.17). He, too, has been influenced by U.S. imports; he angrily laments that he's not part of the *A-Team* when he's left out yet again ("Everybody Hates Hugo," 2.4) and compares Hurley, in his search for Rousseau, with crazed "Colonel bloody Kurtz" from *Apocalypse Now* (and *Heart of Darkness*, "Numbers," 1.18). (Sawyer also refers to Colonel Kurtz in Season Four.) Nevertheless, most of Charlie's popular culture-based comments provide insight into his pre-crash life in the U.K.: the way that afternoon tea, shared between Charlie and Claire, makes those with a British background more civilized ("Raised by Another," 1.10), banoffee pie as a favorite dessert ("Confidence Man," 1.8), documentaries about polar bears, which Charlie loved to watch "on the Beeb" (BBC) while high ("Further Instructions," 3.2).

New British character Charlotte Staples Lewis introduces another prominent British author whose references pepper Season Four episodes. Being familiar with the name C.S. Lewis immediately helps audiences understand a bit more about Charlotte's well-educated background and British society in general.

Clive Staples (C.S.) Lewis perhaps is best known for his *Narnia* series of fantasy/quasi-religious novels, but his closest link to *Lost* may be *The Great Divorce*. Readers familiar with Lewis' works may recall this story of the dead who must decide whether to abandon their attachment to their earthly lives (including their self-deceptions) or to find salvation. Just as in *Lost*, one soul/person can't inhabit both heaven and hell; at some point a character must decide whether to repent and find salvation or to remain unfulfilled and sinful in hell.

Just about everyone makes a popular reference at some point, as the list in Table 3 illustrates.

POPULAR CULTURE REFERENCES, SEASONS ONE THROUGH FOUR

PC Reference	Origin	Said By	Said To	Episode
Johnny Fever	WKRP in Cincinnati deejay	Hurley	Jack, about feverish marshal	"Tabula Rasa" (1.3)
Captain America	Comic book hero	Shannon	Boone	"Walkabout" (1.4)

PC Reference	Origin	Said By	Said To	Episode
Jethro	*The Beverly Hillbillies* backward young hill-billy	Hurley	Sawyer	"Walkabout" (1.4)
White Rabbit, Alice in Wonderland	Lewis Carroll's *Alice in Wonderland*	Locke	Jack	"White Rabbit" (1.4)
Adam and Eve	Biblical first couple	Locke	Jack	"House of the Rising Sun" (1.6)
Eve	Biblical first woman	Kate	Jack, about herself	"House of the Rising Sun" (1.6)
Jedi reference: "I'm known as a warrior at home."	Star Wars	Hurley	Himself	"Confidence Man" (1.8)
"Jedi moment"	Star Wars	Hurley	Jack, after he talks Shannon through an asthma attack	"Confidence Man" (1.8)
Red Shirts	Star Trek	Boone	Locke, as Boone explains who gets killed on away missions	"All the Best Cowboys Have Daddy Issues" (1.11)

PC Reference	Origin	Said By	Said To	Episode
"Martha Stewart of matrimony"	Well-known homemaking expert	Boone	Locke, about Boone's mother	"All the Best Cowboys Have Daddy Issues" (1.11)
Jane Austen	Popular British romance novelist, knowledge-able about proper Victorian manners	Charlie	Group of young women in a bar	"Homecoming" (1.15)
Queen Mary	Luxury cruise ship	Michael	Jack, about the raft	"...In Translation" (1.17)
"Colonel bloody Kurtz"	Officer who goes insane in *Apocalypse Now* (and Joseph Conrad's *Heart of Darkness*)	Charlie	Hurley, when he looks for Rousseau	"Numbers" (1.18)
"steam rollered Harry Potter"	J.K. Rowling's *Harry Potter* books and films	Hurley	Sawyer, about his new glasses	"Deus Ex Machina" (1.19)
Huggy Bear	*Starsky and Hutch*	Johnny	Hurley	"Everybody Hates Hugo" (2.4)

PC Reference	Origin	Said By	Said To	Episode
A-Team	*The A-Team*	Charlie	Locke	"Everybody Hates Hugo" (2.4)
Lord of the Flies	William Golding's *The Lord of the Flies*	Charlie	Kate	"What Kate Did" (2.9)
Hulk	Comic book hero, the Incredible Hulk	Hurley	Desmond	"Further Instructions" (3.3)
Beeb	BBC	Charlie	Locke, about television documentaries	"Further Instructions" (3.3)
Eye for an eye	Biblical justice	Alex	Jack	"Flashes Before Your Eyes" (3.8)
"I'm sorry. You were right. Those pants don't make you look fat."	What women want to hear—all men need to be able to say	Jin	Sawyer	"Tricia Tanaka Is Dead" (3.10)
(Slap) "Snap out of it!"	Cher's line to Nicholas Cage in *Moonstruck*	Hurley	Charlie	"Tricia Tanaka Is Dead" (3.10)

PC Reference	Origin	Said By	Said To	Episode
"Victory or death!"	Many U.S. historic references: motto of 32nd Army Armored Regiment; code word for 1776 attack on Trenton, NJ; battle cry at the Alamo, etc.	Charlie	Hurley	"Tricia Tanaka Is Dead" (3.10)
Nadia Comaneci	Famous Olympic gymnast	Mikhail	Sayid, about a cat	"Enter 77" (3.11)
Phil Collins	Pop music star, very popular in the 1980s	Sawyer, giving her a mix tape	Sawyer, giving her a mix tape	"Catch-22" (3.17)
"Afternoon Delight"	Hit song by Starland Vocal Band, but more importantly, a euphemism for sex	Sawyer	Kate	"Catch-22" (3.17)
The Flash	Comic book character	Hurley	Charlie	"Catch-22" (3.17)
Superman	Comic book character	Charlie	Hurley (as they debate who is faster/ better: Flash or Superman)	"Catch-22" (3.17)

PC Reference	Origin	Said By	Said To	Episode
AWOL	Absent Without Leave, a military term	Sawyer		"Catch-22" (3.17)
"Bridge on the River Kwai" theme	Song prominently used in World War II movie	Charlie and Jin whistle it as they march along the beach, a scene made ironically humorous because a Brit and an Asian (although Korean instead of Japanese) are friends, instead of the enemies portrayed in the movie, and because both Jin and Charlie know the same song		"Catch-22" (3.17)
Catch-22	Joseph Heller's novel, which Naomi carries; more importantly, a popular reference to a no-win situation, like the one in which Desmond finds himself	Episode Title		"Catch-22" (3.17)

PC Reference	Origin	Said By	Said To	Episode
The Man Behind the Curtain	Episode title; a Wizard of Oz reference applied to Ben Linus, the island's apparent "Wizard" or "man behind the curtain"			"The Man Behind the Curtain" (3.20)
Rambo	Fierce jungle fighter played in the movies by Sylvester Stallone	Bernard says he's not Rambo	Rose	"Through the Looking Glass" (3.22)

The Hurley-Sawyer Connection

Not surprisingly, the character with whom most of us identify, "everyperson" Hurley, is one of two characters referring to popular culture most often. He recalls popular TV characters (probably seen on reruns while he was growing up), including Jethro from *The Beverly Hillbillies* and Johnny Fever from *WKRP in Cincinnati.* In backstories, Hurley's pal Johnny mentions Huggy Bear (*Starsky and Hutch*) and Pony Boy (*The Outsiders*) ("Everybody Hates Hugo," 2.4). Hurley's movie preferences run to science fiction (*Star Wars*) and fantasy *(Harry Potter).* It's not surprising that Sawyer's dark, taped glasses remind Hurley of a "steam roll-ered Harry Potter" ("Deus Ex Machina," 1.19).

From what we know from Hurley's backstories, he was a slim boy who became traumatized by his father's abandonment ("Tricia Tanaka Is Dead," 3.10); perhaps his feelings of rejection caused him to retreat to food and fantasy as a way to escape a troubled home life. Adult millionaire Hurley also feels rejected and cursed—his beloved grandfather dies suddenly ("Numbers," 1.18); his father reappears when Hurley becomes a millionaire; his mother eagerly, and to Hurley's disgust, rather passionately, welcomes her estranged husband home; his best friend Johnny abandons him and steals the one woman Hurley feels he has a chance to date ("Tricia Tanaka Is Dead," 3.10). On the island, Hurley is belittled by Sawyer and alternately befriended and manipulated by Charlie (whose death further reduces Hurley's number of close pals). His one chance at true love seems to be a budding relationship with Libby, who dies before Hurley can even finish their first date ("Two for the Road," 2.20). As one of the Oceanic 6, Hurley finds brief happiness back home, even traveling to Korea to visit Sun and her new daughter ("Ji Yeon," 4.7). Soon, however, Hurley once again retreats to a fantasy life (sometimes complete with imaginary friend Dave [2.18], or dead-but-still-here buddy Charlie ["The Beginning of the End," 4.1; "Something Nice Back Home," 4.10]); real life is too much to face some days.

It's also not surprising that Hurley, out of all the castaways, actively seeks ways to break the monotony of island life and make people forget for a few minutes the dangers surrounding them. Hurley wants to be liked and goes out of his way to create a happy fantasy of a normal life (just like on a TV sitcom or in a superhero comic book with a happy ending), even if the illusion is temporary. He distributes goodies from the hatch so that everyone can indulge their culinary vices, from coffee to chocolate to peanut butter ("Everyone Hates Hugo," 2.4). He builds a golf course ("Solitary," 1.9). He finds a VW van in the jungle and invites a depressed, marked-for-death Charlie to ride along ("Tricia Tanaka Is Dead," 3.10). He cons Sawyer into doing nice things for the castaways, including sponsoring a barbecue ("Left Behind," 3.15). He travels halfway around the world to meet baby Ji Yeon and remind lonely new-mother Sun that she's not alone ("Ji Yeon," 4.7). He introduces Sayid, who has no one to meet him at the plane, to his family, and the Oceanic 6 are invited to Hurley's birthday bash ("There's No Place Like Home," 4.13).

What might be surprising is that, for all their differences in background, life experiences, and outlook on life, Hurley and Sawyer have something in common: a love of popular culture. Both men probably share feelings of abandonment and betrayal from childhood through adulthood, but they've developed different ways of coping. Sawyer prefers to stay outside society and maintain an "outlaw" façade so that he seems tougher and meaner than anyone else. He shows moments of softness,

however, and at times defends the quieter moments of his childhood. When he mentions "Little House" to Kate, she scoffs at
his familiarity with the family TV series. Sawyer defensively
explains that he had mononucleosis as a child, which required
him to stay in bed at home. The family TV picked up only one
channel, so *Little House on the Prairie* became his companion
during the afternoons ("Tricia Tanaka Is Dead," 3.10). Justifying
his obvious enjoyment of this childhood memory reveals a hidden
softer side to the killer con man. Sawyer's concept of frontier
justice, as well as his need to protect (at least some) women and
children, may stem from his early identification with TV characters. After Charlie's death, Sawyer looks after Claire, risking
his life to rescue her from the attack on New Otherton ("The
Shape of Things to Come," 4.9) and taking care of baby Aaron
after Claire's surprising trek into the jungle with her dead father
("Something Nice Back Home," 4.10).

Sawyer's self-education and at least some of his socialization
seem based on popular culture. In prison and on the island, he
often reads books. Because he started his career as a con man
at 17, Sawyer must have made up for what he felt he lacked by
reading as much as possible. On the island, he voraciously reads
everything—from children's (*Watership Down*) and teen literature
(*Are You There, God? It's Me, Margaret*) to women's magazines
(*Cosmopolitan*) to "shocking amounts of pornography" ("Flashes
Before Your Eyes," 3.8).

Our knowledge of this literature helps us get the joke. When
Sawyer explains that he's reading *Watership Down* because it's a
nice little book about bunnies, we know better; this is a decep-
tively dark tale. Sawyer's complaint about *Are You There, God?
It's Me, Margaret* is that it doesn't have enough sex. Of course,

the title alone indicates that this might not be a steamy novel, but understanding the subject matter gives us a better sense of Sawyer's sense of humor, best illustrated when Sawyer uses what he's learned from women's magazine, *Cosmo*. Notorious for being a magazine written by women for women, *Cosmopolitan*'s infamous love/sex quizzes and how-to's for getting a man obviously create a lasting impression. Sawyer's poor track record for long-term relationships makes his "expert" advice to Jin even more humorous. He teaches his friend all the English that he'll ever need to speak to Sun: "I'm sorry. You were right. Those pants don't make you look fat" ("Tricia Tanaka Is Dead," 3.10).

More than any other character, Sawyer peppers his conversation with nicknames and frequently sarcastic references to movies and television. (A fun feature of the Season Two DVD set is a rapid-fire montage of Sawyerisms, mostly nicknames.) He may not have a college education, but he keeps up with what's going on in the world, which to him is more readily accessed through popular media. Knowledge of pop culture is one way for Sawyer to feel "equal" with the richer, better educated people he loves to con.

His word choices, however, sometimes reflect his lack of understanding. He scathingly calls Sayid "Al-Jazeera" ("Tabula Rasa," 1.3)—Charlie derisively tells him that's a news agency, not a person. Calling Hurley "Barbar" is meant to refer to his large size; Hurley corrects Sawyer by reminding him the elephant's name is Babar ("One of Them," 2.14). In the face of criticism, Sawyer shuts up, but he quickly comes back with more. Other nicknames for Hurley include Stay-Puff ("Raised by Another," 1.10), Pillsbury ("The 23rd Psalm," 2.10), Jabba ("Fire + Water," 2.12), Hoss ("Fire + Water," 2.12), Rerun ("One of Them," 2.14), Mongo ("Lockdown," 2.17), Avalanche ("Enter 77," 3.11), and

Jumbotron ("Tricia Tanaka Is Dead," 3.10). Re-naming others happens so often that Sawyer becomes annoyed when he loses a ping pong bet and is forbidden to call anyone by a nickname for a week ("Enter 77," 3.11).

During the first three seasons of *Lost*, Sawyer primarily uses his word choice to feel superior to those he considers weaker. On the island, his most likely targets are Hurley and Charlie, each vulnerable in his own way. Because Hurley is self-conscious about his girth, Sawyer usually chooses nicknames referring to large, soft, or round characters: a huge wrestler (Avalanche), large, stupid cowboy (Mongo), cartoon gorilla (Grape Ape), soft doughboy (Pillsbury), or round, soft (and, in *Ghostbusters*, huge and out of control) Stay-Puff Marshmallow Man. Charlie may believe he stands tall in the music industry, but his height is much less than Sawyer's or that of most men on the island. Sawyer's nicknames for him cut him down to size: Munchkin (a short person in *The Wizard of Oz*, as well as a name given to diminutive children), Jiminy Cricket (a tiny singing Disney cartoon character), Chucky (not only a childish variation of Charles, but a demonic blond toy brought to life in the *Child's Play* series). Although Sawyer most often uses these nicknames in front of Hurley, Charlie is frequently discussed in these terms when he's not around or just as he arrives on scene—he's being talked about, rather than talked with.

Although Sawyer's relationship with Sayid changes substantially during the castaways' first 100 days on the island (roughly the first three seasons), to Sawyer, Sayid probably will always be first an Iraqi and then a man or even a friend. Nicknames for Sayid always refer to his nationality or Middle-Eastern culture (e.g., Al-Jazeera, falafel). Even when he refers to Sayid with what Sawyer would probably term respect for his special interrogational "talent," Sayid is called "our resident Iraqi" ("One of Us," 3.16). To Sawyer, Iraqi = Torturer, a comparison Sayid sometimes resents but more recently finds useful as a weapon against the Others.

During their trek to New Otherton, leader Locke's destination when the island is threatened, Sawyer disagrees with Locke about the need to keep Ben alive. He mocks Locke's explanation of his vision of a more mature Walt by referring to "Taller Ghost Walt" and sneeringly nicknames Locke "Johnny" ("Confirmed Dead," 4.2). As with Charlie, Sawyer tries to put Locke in his place by giving the older man a childlike form of his name.

Sawyer's choice of nicknames indicates the way he identifies the people around him: Hurley = Fat, Charlie = Small or Boyish, Sayid = Iraqi, Locke = Naïve or Ineffectual. The labels aren't always negative, however. His choices for Jack might be sarcastic, but they indicate his acknowledgment of Jack's skills: famed poker player Amarillo Slim or frontier miracle worker Dr. Quinn.

With the increasing danger and impending annihilation of the island and its inhabitants during *Lost*'s Season Four, Sawyer has fewer chances for lighthearted nicknames or scathing comments. The few he bestows on Hurley show a shift in their relationship. With Charlie gone and Hurley mourning his loss, Sawyer appoints himself as Hurley's protector; perhaps he understands how difficult it is to be vulnerable and admires Hurley's determination to go with Locke, look after Claire and Aaron, and follow Charlie's last message that the Freighter Folk aren't who they say they are and thus might be dangerous. Although Season Four's dark side provides fewer opportunities for the insertion of popular culture references, Sawyer does manage to get in a few.

Like Hurley, Sawyer often refers to television or movies in his choice of nicknames or references. Although Sawyer's repertoire is much greater than Hurley's, the most common references are to science fiction (sometimes horror) and fantasy movies and television series: *Ghostbusters, Indiana Jones and the Temple of Doom, Star Wars, The Wizard of Oz, Child's Play, Pinocchio, The Green Hornet, Star Trek, Fantasy Island*. The sheer number of references (see the following table) indicates just how much time Sawyer has spent reading, watching TV or movies, and listening to the news.

SAWYERISMS

PC Reference	Origin	Said To	Episode
Al-Jazeera	Iraqi media outlet	Sayid, to refer to his being Iraqi (Charlie corrects Sawyer's usage)	"Tabula Rasa" (1.3)
Playboys	Playboy magazine	Jack	"Tabula Rasa" (1.3)
Pork Pie	Food reference; also a round hat	Hurley	"Walkabout" (1.4)
Mr. Miyagi	The Karate Kid series of films	Kate, about Jin	"White Rabbit" (1.5)
Omar	Sarcastic appropriation of Middle Eastern name	Sayid	"House of the Rising Sun" (1.6)
Dr. Quinn	*Dr. Quinn, Medicine Woman*, about a frontier doctor	Jack	"Solitary" (1.9)
Stay-Puff	Brand of marshmallows; Stay-Puff Marshmallow Man attack in *Ghostbusters*	Hurley	"Raised by Another" (1.10)
Tattoo	*Fantasy Island*	Walt	"All the Best Cowboys Have Daddy Issues" (1.11)

PC Reference	Origin	Said To	Episode
"VH1 Has-Beens"	Music network known for retro-spective specials about "has-been" bands and performers	Walt, about Charlie	"All the Best Cowboys Have Daddy Issues" (1.11)
Dr. Do-Right	Combination of medical refer-ence and Dudley Do-Right cartoon about a straitlaced Mountie	Sayid, about Jack	"All the Best Cowboys Have Daddy Issues" (1.11)
Hoss	Gun reference to the Western *Bonanza*	Jack	"Homecoming" (1.15)
Mohammed	Reference to Sayid's Middle Eastern origins and being Muslim	Sayid	"Outlaws" (1.16)
Bruce	Bruce Lee, martial arts expert	Jin	"…In Translation" (1.17)
"Lord of the Flies time"	William Golding's *The Lord of the Flies*	Jin, who is accused of theft	"…In Translation" (1.17)
Betty	Asian spy's Americanized name	Sun, when he accuses her of being a "double agent" between her husband and the castaways	"…In Translation" (1.17)

PC Reference	Origin	Said To	Episode
Captain Falafel	Combination of military reference (Sayid was in the Iraqi Republican Guard) and food	Sayid	"...In Translation" (1.17)
Short Round	*Indiana Jones and the Temple of Doom*	Walt	"Numbers" (1.18)
Kato	*The Green Hornet*	Michael, about Jin	"Do No Harm" (1.20)
Chucky	Variant nickname of Charles; also a demonic toy in the *Child's Play* series	Charlie	"The Greater Good" (1.21)
Baby Huey	Oversized cartoon baby	Charlie, about Aaron	"The Greater Good" (1.21)
Chewy and Han	*Star Wars*	Jin and Michael	"Exodus" (1.23)
Kazoo	Alien on *The Flintstones*	Walt	"Exodus" (1.23)
Hoss	*Bonanza*	Michael, when he tries to fire a wet gun	"Adrift" (2.2)
Bluebeard	Famous pirate	Michael, about the Other who kidnapped Walt	"Adrift" (2.2)
Shaft	Shaft	Ana Lucia, about Mr. Eko	"Orientation" (2.3)

PC Reference	Origin	Said To	Episode
Howdy Doody	Children's TV series	Ana Lucia	"Orientation" (2.3)
Rambina	Feminine variation of Rambo, *Rambo* action movie series	Michael, about Ana Lucia	"Everybody Hates Hugo" (2.4)
"Beam us up"	*Star Trek*	Michael	"Everybody Hates Hugo" (2.4)
Hot Lips	*M*A*S*H* sexy but stuck-up nurse	Ana Lucia	"Everybody Hates Hugo" (2.4)
Mr. Ed	*Mr. Ed*	Mr. Eko	"…And Found" (2.5)
Chewy	*Star Wars*	Jin	"…And Found" (2.5)
Ponce de Leon	Famous explorer	Ana Lucia	"Abandoned" (2.6)
Chewy	*Star Wars*	Jin	"Abandoned" (2.6)
Pillsbury	TV pitchman doughboy	Hurley	"The 23rd Psalm" (2.10)
Mr. Clean	Bald TV pitchman	Locke	"The Hunting Party" (2.11)
Mount Vesuvius	Tall volcanic mountain	Locke, about their path through the jungle	"The Hunting Party" (2.11)
Daniel Boone	Historic frontiersman	Locke	"The Hunting Party" (2.11)

PC Reference	Origin	Said To	Episode
Zeke	"Hillbilly" name	Tom (aka Mr. Friendly)	"The Hunting Party" (2.11)
Jabba	*Star Wars*	Hurley	"Fire + Water" (2.12)
Jethro	*The Beverly Hillbillies*	Hurley	"Fire + Water" (2.12)
Hoss	*Bonanza*	Hurley	"Fire + Water" (2.12)
Sheena	*Sheena, Queen of the Jungle* comic book and movie	Kate	"The Long Con" (2.13)
Dewey decimal system	Book-classification system for libraries	Locke, as he arranges books in the hatch	"The Long Con" (2.13)
Tokyo Rose	Famous spy	Locke, about Sun	"The Long Con" (2.13)
Cowboys and Indians	Children's game	Locke	"The Long Con" (2.13)
Hoss	*Bonanza*	Locke	"The Long Con" (2.13)
Donkey Kong	Videogame	Jack, as Sawyer input the Numbers	"The Long Con" (2.13)
Rerun	*What's Happening?*	Hurley	"One of Them" (2.14)
Barbar	Mistakenly saying that instead of Babar, the elephant in a children's story	Hurley	"One of Them" (2.14)

PC Reference	Origin	Said To	Episode
Thelma	*Thelma and Louise*	Kate	"Maternity Leave" (2.15)
Amarillo Slim	Famous poker player	Jack	"Lockdown" (2.17)
Cool Hand	*Cool Hand Luke*	Jack	"Lockdown" (2.17)
Mongo	*Blazing Saddles*	Hurley	"Lockdown" (2.17)
Mutton-chops	Large sideburns	Hurley	"Lockdown" (2.17)
Deep Dish	Style of pie, usually pizza, sometimes fruit	Hurley	"Dave" (2.18)
"I'm walking here!"	Dustin Hoffman's famous line from *Midnight Cowboy*	Christian Shephard	"Two for the Road" (2.20)
Grape Ape	Large cartoon character from a 1970s TV series	Hurley	"Three Minutes" (2.22)
Pippi Long-stocking	Young female heroine of books and movies	Kate	"Three Minutes" (2.22)
Red Beret	Iraqi Republican Guard uniform (also not a Green Beret, the U.S. elite unit)	Sayid	"Three Minutes" (2.22)
Dirty Dozen	Military unit on a special mission, as in the film *The Dirty Dozen*	About castaways headed into the jungle to find Walt	"Three Minutes" (2.22)

PC Reference	Origin	Said To	Episode
Chachi	*Happy Days, Joanie Loves Chachi*	Karl	"A Tale of Two Cities" (3.1)
Shortcake	Food tasting like strawberries	Kate	"The Glass Ballerina" (3.2)
Chinatown	Jack Nicholson's character, who wore a bandage across his nose, in *Chinatown*	Pickett	"Every Man for Himself" (3.4)
Costanza	*Seinfeld*	Mr. Friendly	"Every Man for Himself" (3.4)
George	*Of Mice and Men*	Ben	"Every Man for Himself" (3.4)
Sheena	*Sheena, Queen of the Jungle*	Alex	"Not in Portland" (3.7)
Underdog	*Underdog* animated TV series, also "dog" reference to digging	Alex	"Not in Portland" (3.7)
Lollipop	Sweet, child-like reference	Alex	"Not in Portland" (3.7)
Wookiee	*Star Wars*, referring to a scene in *Empire Strikes Back*	Aldo	"Not in Portland" (3.7)

PC Reference	Origin	Said To	Episode
Cheech	*Cheech & Chong*; also interesting because episode co-author Carlton Cuse once created *Nash Bridges*, which starred Cheech Marin (who also plays Hurley's father)	Karl	"Not in Portland" (3.7)
Captain Bunny Killer	Creating an "official" title for a character	Kate, about Ben	"Stranger in a Strange Land" (3.9)
Magellan	Explorer, in reference to Kate deciding which direction their boat should turn	Kate	"Stranger in a Strange Land" (3.9)
Bobby, Brady Bunch	*Brady Bunch*'s middle son	Karl	"Stranger in a Strange Land" (3.9)
Sally Slingshot	Made-up alliterative name	Karl, about Alex	"Stranger in a Strange Land" (3.9)
Are we there yet?	Typical child's reaction to a long trip	Kate	"Tricia Tanaka Is Dead" (3.10)
Little House	*Little House on the Prairie*	Kate	"Tricia Tanaka Is Dead" (3.10)

PC Reference	Origin	Said To	Episode
Snuffy	Snuffleupagus, of *Sesame Street*, sometimes called Snuffy, is large and cuddly	Hurley, who hugs Sawyer	"Tricia Tanaka Is Dead" (3.10)
Oliver Twist	*Oliver Twist*, referring to Charlie's British origins, possibly his height, and his ability to steal from Sawyer	Charlie, accused of taking Sawyer's stuff	"Tricia Tanaka Is Dead" (3.10)
Munchkin	*Wizard of Oz*, referring to Charlie's short stature	Desmond, about Charlie	"Tricia Tanaka Is Dead" (3.10)
Jin-bo	Variation of Jimbo, a Southern nickname	Jin	"Tricia Tanaka Is Dead" (3.10)
Hooked on phonics	A method of teaching reading and language skills	Jin	"Tricia Tanaka Is Dead" (3.10)
Skeletor	Comic book and TV character from *Masters of the Universe*	Hurley, about Roger (dead Other)	"Tricia Tanaka Is Dead" (3.10)
International House of Pancakes	U.S. restaurant chain	Jin, about Hurley	"Tricia Tanaka Is Dead" (3.10)
Jumbotron	Large video screen for stadiums; also sounds like a made-up name for a transformer	Hurley	"Tricia Tanaka Is Dead" (3.10)

PC Reference	Origin	Said To	Episode
Jiminy Cricket	Animated character in *Pinocchio*	Hurley, about Charlie	"Tricia Tanaka Is Dead" (3.10)
Zorro	Legendary literary, TV, and movie character, an early Californian Hispanic "Robin Hood"	Paolo	"Enter 77" (3.11)
Crouching Tiger, Hidden Dragon	*Crouching Tiger, Hidden Dragon*	Sun, Jin	"Enter 77" (3.11)
Grimace	Large McDonald's mascot	Hurley	"Enter 77" (3.11)
Scotty	Desmond's Scottish origins, plus TV's most famous excited Scotsman, "Beam Me Up" Scotty from *Star Trek*	Desmond	"The Beginning of the End" (4.1)
Colonel Kurtz	Scary *Apocalypse Now* leader	Locke	"Confirmed Dead" (4.2)
Chicken Little	Children's book character who warned of the sky falling	Hurley	"The Shape of Things to Come" (4.9)
Yoda	Jedi mentor and sage in *Star Wars* saga	Ben	"Something Nice Back Home" (4.10)

PC Reference	Origin	Said To	Episode
Yahoo	People that Gulliver meets on his travels, also slang for an unsophisticated person (e.g., yokel, hick)	Frank	"There's No Place Like Home" (4.13)
Shaggy	Character in *Scooby-Doo*	Frank	"There's No Place Like Home" (4.13)
Genghis	Genghis Khan, renowned ruthless leader	Miles	"There's No Place Like Home" (4.13)
Sundance	Outlaw buddy of Butch Cassidy, doomed partner in crime in *Butch Cassidy and the Sundance Kid*	Jack	"There's No Place Like Home" (4.13)
Kenny Rogers	Country singer, whose beard, to Sawyer, might seem similar to Frank's scragglier salt-and-pepper facial hair	Frank	"There's No Place Like Home" (4.13)

Hurley, like Kate and Sawyer, knows what it feels like to be an outsider, although Hugo probably understands much more than Kate ever could how Sawyer may have relied on imaginary heroes to help him through a rough childhood. Sawyer and Hurley likely have been socialized primarily through popular culture, moreso than by family or friends. Perhaps that's why Hurley, the most likely target for Sawyer's witticisms and criticisms, is the best person to socialize Sawyer for island life. Whereas the Others couldn't change him with torture and deprivation, Hurley knows how to motivate Sawyer. He understands better than Sawyer realizes that they both may not fit in with the "popular kids" but can't survive on their own.

Two prime examples of Hurley's influence over Sawyer occur in Season Three. When Hurley finds a broken-down van in the jungle, he coerces Sawyer to help get it running by offering him beer from the back of the van. Although Sawyer grouses about its quality, he nevertheless sticks around to bond with Jin and join Hurley and Charlie on a joyride ("Tricia Tanaka Is Dead," 3.10). A few days later, Hurley cons Sawyer into thinking that the castaways' little society will banish him if he doesn't "play nicely." Hurley also realizes that Sawyer may need to step in as the group's leader, if Jack, Sayid, and Locke fail to return to camp (which they later do). By forcing Sawyer to realize that he can't live well on his own (evident after a disastrous attempt at fishing), Hurley supervises while Sawyer "plays politician": praising baby Aaron, hunting boar, and making a special barbecue sauce for the community barbecue ("Left Behind," 3.15).

The Hurley-Sawyer connection grows even stronger in Season Four. When Hurley seems to have a tough time keeping up with the group meeting up with Jack at the fuselage, Sawyer lags behind to make sure his companion is all right. He even offers to listen if Hurley wants to talk about Charlie ("Confirmed Dead," 4.2). Whereas Hurley could cry with Claire as they mutually mourned Charlie, Sawyer never befriended the musician, and Hurley seems reluctant to share that part of himself with Sawyer—perhaps because the former con man usually attacks when he finds a vulnerable spot. Sawyer's concern continues when Hurley is separated from the group, only to rejoin the rest of the castaways with Locke in tow.

In New Otherton, Sawyer and Hurley become domestic. They play horseshoes ("The Other Woman," 4.6) and Risk ("The Shape of Things to Come," 4.9), and only Kate's timely arrival prevents Sawyer from watching *Xanadu* with Hurley ("Eggtown," 4.4).

Hurley, however, still has the same type of control over Sawyer that he had in Season Three. When Sawyer likely would've killed Ben on the trek back to the Others' compound ("Confirmed Dead," 4.2), Hurley quickly shakes his head, a subtle "no" that speaks louder than Locke's many reasoning words why Ben's life should be spared. Ben recognizes that Hurley, like Locke, is "special" and may be useful in future dealings with the elusive Jacob. When Ben commands that Locke and Hurley accompany him to Jacob's cabin, Hurley agrees—perhaps out of curiosity or a sense of duty. Only he can "call off" guard dog Sawyer, who fails to understand why Hurley would go anywhere with Ben. Retaining his threatening stance, Sawyer vows to kill Ben if "so much as one hair on [Hurley's] curly head is hurt" ("Something Nice Back Home," 4.10). Sawyer even convinces Jack to hike to the guarded and heavily fortified Orchid station because that's where Hurley was headed with Locke and Ben ("There's No Place Like Home," 4.13). After more than 100 days on the island, Sawyer is clearly loyal to Hurley.

Loyalty and love for others culminates in Sawyer sacrificing his spot on the helicopter headed for the freighter and, presumably, rescue. When the damaged helicopter needs to lighten its load to conserve fuel, Hurley looks distinctly worried, but Sawyer comes up with a better solution. After whispering to Kate and sealing the deal with a prolonged kiss, Sawyer leaps from the helicopter ("There's No Place Like Home," 4.13). The Sawyer who crashed on the island three months previously more likely would've pushed Hurley out the door; after his "socialization" on the island, largely through Hurley's friendship, Sawyer reveals a nobler personality.

Of all the unlikely friendships to develop on the island, the strengthening Sawyer-Hurley relationship is one of the strangest. The important bond of popular culture and its significance in their lives brings together such unlikely duos as Hurley and Charlie or Hurley and Sawyer.

THE POWER OF POPULAR CULTURE

Popular culture is more than a retreat or an escape, although it sometimes serves that purpose for die-hard fans who find television, film, or literary characters more understanding or desirable than the real people around them. Popular culture helps us draw comparisons of our very personal, unique experiences with common public experiences and knowledge. We know exactly the shade of meaning provided by a common cultural reference.

Season Four's episode title to Juliet's backstory, "The Other Woman" (4.6), takes on a double meaning, one cultural, one purely *Lost*-related. Juliet is (or was) one of the Others, and this backstory clearly indicates her place within and history with this group. She also is "the other woman" via her affair with the adulterous Goodwin, whose wife is introduced in this episode. Juliet's duplicitous nature takes on another dimension when viewers see that she often has led a double life: as the other woman in a love triangle, as a secret saboteur within Ben's "family," as Ben's spy on Jack and his friends. Juliet's continuing ability to convincingly live a double life makes her seem even more dangerous and less trustworthy. Throughout her adult life but especially on the island, Juliet lives comfortably as "other" from accepted social norms.

Connotations are often important in understanding the deeper meanings behind cultural labels. We all understand "has-been," but when Sawyer describes Charlie as a star of VH1 Has-Beens, we interpret this insult as more scathing than just a reference to defunct DriveShaft. VH1 is a middle-of-the-road music network increasingly heavy with retrospectives and lists (e.g., one-hit wonders). That Charlie's life can be reduced to a sound bite on VH1 is truly an insult to a man who thinks he was a significant rock star. It makes his slide into oblivion more embarrassing. Most people face some setbacks or failures in their careers; Sawyer knows that Charlie's can be broadcast internationally and replayed hundreds of times.

Sawyer's ability to create a nickname that sounds plausible, even if it refers to no specific TV or movie character, shows just how much popular culture is an integral part of his vocabulary. He creates a "titled" nickname for other characters who have (even temporary) authority over him. Sayid becomes "Captain Falafel" ("…In Translation," 1.17), a combination military title and Middle Eastern food that Sawyer turns into an ethnic slur; Sawyer labels Ben "Captain Bunny Killer" ("Every Man for Himself," 3.4).

These pop culture references and a preference for inserting them in everyday conversations mark Hurley and Sawyer as Americans; the TV series and movies on which "Sawyerisms" are based are clearly stamped Made in the U.S. With the exception of Charlie's comments, influenced not only by British traditions and television but U.S. imports, and the occasional offhand references by Claire (e.g., her love of peanut butter, unusual for an Australian) and Kate (e.g., Patsy Cline is popular everywhere, not just in the U.S.), the culture being referenced is mainstream Hollywood. Count the number of references to U.S. television programs broadcast between the mid-1960s and 1990s, when Hurley, Boone, and Sawyer, in particular, would've been watching U.S. TV in first-run or syndicated rerun episodes (see the table on p. 167). During the first three seasons of *Lost*, Sawyer alone mentions *Dr. Quinn, Medicine Woman*; *Bonanza*; *Fantasy Island*; *The Flintstones*; *M*A*S*H*; *Mr. Ed*; *Star Trek*; *The Beverly Hillbillies*; *Happy Days*; *Seinfeld*; *Underdog*; *The Brady Bunch*; and *Little House on the Prairie*, among others. That's quite a range!

Better educated characters, including Jack, and older characters such as Locke don't use popular culture references themselves. Locke prefers nature-based metaphors or stories, such as his comparison of the moth's journey to Charlie's ("The Moth," 1.7); what's most important to Locke is the island (nature). He also discusses literature with the ease of someone who's read classic books. Jack understands what Sawyer means when the con man calls him Amarillo Slim ("Lockdown," 2.17) or Dr. Quinn ("Solitary," 1.9), but he doesn't use the same vocabulary. Popular culture (especially film and TV) seems to be the province of the younger, less highly educated, male, and multimedia-friendly castaways—the "common men" among the group, which is appropriate, because popular culture is "of the people."

Even the Others use popular culture to bridge the gap between themselves and the castaways. Ben knows that baseball is an important metaphor for life, especially to Jack. Christian Shephard repeatedly said that the unlikely would happen "when the Red Sox win the Series" ("Exodus," 1.24), a phrase akin to "when hell freezes over." Ben wants to impress upon Jack the fact that the Others access current technology and can truly send him home; to convince him, he shows Jack the latest televised World Series game, the night when the Red Sox finally win ("The Glass Ballerina," 3.3). Believing what he sees on TV is normal even for cynical people like Jack, who then changes his opinion of the Others' capabilities. Television becomes a bargaining chip; when he's cooperative, they roll a television near his cell. Watching taped programs—or secret messages—on TV becomes one way for the Others, especially Juliet, to communicate with Jack.

LOST AS REFLECTOR AND CREATOR OF POPULAR CULTURE

But what about the rest of the world in which popular culture isn't so heavily reliant on television or film? During Season Four, a few non-U.S. cultural references have come into play, but with few exceptions, mostly U.S.-based cultural references have become part of *Lost*'s dialogue.

In a flashback sequence ("Ji Yeon," 4.7), Jin buys a huge plush panda to present to a business client shortly after the birth of his grandson; the baby gift, carefully tied with a blue ribbon, helps seal future deals between the businessman and Jin's employer, Mr. Paik. Even this symbol of friendship between two parties is understood outside Chinese culture. Especially since the early 1970s, when Ling-Ling and Hsing-Hsing were given as a goodwill gift from China to the U.S., Americans have linked China to the image of giant pandas. The idea of blue as a "boy" color is common in many countries, too, and Jin's careful selection of the proper bow doesn't seem specific either to Korean or Chinese culture.

Similarly, our brief glance at the funeral of Sayid's wife, Nadia, provides minimal insight into Iraqi funereal traditions. Sayid is one of several male pallbearers carrying a simple casket bedecked with flowers, but this sight seems as appropriate to Nadia's and Sayid's Westernized lives as to their Middle Eastern upbringing ("The Shape of Things to Come," 4.9).

"Other" Mikhail Bakunin shares the name of a father of anarchism and Russian revolutionary, a reference perhaps lost on many U.S. viewers, but this nod to Russian history doesn't occur often. Hermann Minkowski may be the Lithuanian-born father of spacetime theory, but *Lost's* namesake George Minkowski, the hapless victim of yo-yoing between the past and present, is definitely American. (U.S. audiences are more likely to recognize famous names in French or British politics, science, or philosophy, such as Rousseau, Locke, or Burke.) *Lost* is, of course, a U.S. TV series made primarily for those at home, although with the series' huge international following, it may seem surprising that a series boasting international characters with widely divergent views on religion and politics offers few "insider" references from other cultures.

The reasoning behind this decision may be twofold. From a pragmatic perspective, *Lost is* popular culture, promoting the U.S. just like any other product exported internationally, no different from Levi's, Coca Cola, or McDonald's. *Lost* exports knowledge of U.S. products, past and current, as well as the American way of life. From a story perspective, the castaways would be even more "lost" without their understanding of U.S. popular culture. Almost everyone on the island(s) seems to understand Sawyer-speak; few references need to be explained. With the exception of Karl, who's never seen *The Brady Bunch* and doesn't know why Sawyer calls him "Bobby" ("Stranger in a Strange Land," 3.9), no one seems "lost" in their understanding of U.S. popular culture—a political statement itself. Everyone in the world has been exposed to U.S. television and movies, at least as much as and usually more than critically acclaimed literature from the past thousand years.

Lost doesn't limit its references to only the best-known television series or movies. Only *Lost*'s literary references truly span the globe (see Chapter 1 for a complete rundown of ancestor texts). Many characters seem to have read and reference the same books: Locke and Henry/Ben analyze Dostoevsky's *The Brothers Karamazov*; Ben and Sawyer discuss *Of Mice and Men*; Desmond adores the works of Charles Dickens but also reads Irish author Flann O'Brien's *The Third Policeman*; Locke remembers *Gilgamesh* when filling out a crossword; the Others seem to read everything from Stephen King's *Carrie* to Stephen Hawking's *A Brief History of Time*; Jack reads *Alice in Wonderland* to toddler Aaron, just as his father read the book to him as a favorite bedtime story.

More than most entertainment series, *Lost* brings previously obscure works to the public's attention; it makes some usually-overlooked books popular, simply because *Lost* fans go out of their way to find (and often buy) any possible source of clues to the series' mysteries. Fans who may never have heard of, much less read, "An Occurrence at Owl Creek Bridge" expand their literary knowledge once the story is shown on *Lost*. Dickens is a well-known author, but *Our Mutual Friend* is hardly as commonly read as *Oliver Twist* (which Sawyer calls Charlie, "Tricia Tanaka Is Dead," 3.10) or *A Christmas Carol*. H.G. Wells' lesser-known *The Shape of Things to Come* (4.9) serves as an episode title as well as a clue to the castaways' post-island future. In the same episode, Ben uses "Dean Moriarty" as his alias during a trip to Tunisia; although "Moriarty" is commonly associated with Sherlock Holmes, Dean Moriarty is a principal character in Beat novelist Jack Kerouac's *On the Road*. *Lost* not only references pop culture but makes less well-known works more popular among the series' fans—and with an audience in the multimillions internationally, previously little known artists or works gain quite a bit of notoriety. (The same process occurs, if more subtly, with music. See Chapter 2 for a discussion of artists and songs used in episodes.)

Television audiences around the world not only are "bonding" over the widely syndicated and highly successful *Lost*, but they also are learning even more about Western popular culture by investigating the meanings behind *Lost*'s many references. *Lost* is socializing fans to the pervasive, now international culture promulgated by television and film, but it also pays a great deal of attention to the literary tradition; it's helping to bring everyone up to speed on cultural touchstones that the series' creators (and thus their characters) believe are important.

Although *Lost* remains trend setting, and many critics and fans believe Season Four's episodes are the best ever—or at least as good as those in groundbreaking Season One, toward the end of Season Three, series creator and frequent writer Damon Lindelof stated that *Lost* is moving back into "cult TV" status instead of remaining a mainstream hit.[47] The writers' strike, which caused all U.S. series, including *Lost*, to be shut down for months until a settlement could be reached, ironically may have returned *Lost* to mainstream hit status. The first eight episodes of Season Four were broadcast in January and February 2008, a time when other primetime series had run out of new episodes. Not only having something new to watch, but having highly anticipated new *Lost* episodes, gave the series a powerful boost. Tighter writing, faster revelations, and even deaths of key characters also helped keep ratings high, as well as keep cast and audience confident that the series is moving in the right direction toward its 2010 conclusion.

The series' instant first-season success couldn't be sustained indefinitely; *Lost* has made an amazing comeback after a largely disappointing third season. Popular culture changes rapidly, and audiences eagerly anticipate the next big trend. In 2005 it was serials and more science fiction, based in large part on *Lost*'s success, which almost every producer wanted to copy. The trend in 2007 was to move away from complex serials and back toward shorter story arcs and easy-to-understand plotlines. Although 2007–2008 saw the arrival of more quirky fantasies (e.g., ABC's *Pushing Daisies* or *Eli Stone*), devilish supernatural comedies (e.g., *Reaper*) or vampiric romances (e.g., *Moonlight*), nothing in this shortened TV season captured audience's attention as much as *Lost* did during its first season. Even if *Lost* is no longer the shiny new series people "have" to see, it continues to grab the attention of clue-seeking, mystery-loving, detail-obsessed fans and critics. Whether *Lost* eventually ends its planned six-season run as a mainstream phenomenon or "merely" a cult favorite, it has changed the landscape of popular culture.

CHAPTER FOUR

WAKING THE DEAD

The cliché says "You can't keep a good man down." On *Lost*, that's very true, but not only for good men—or women. Even the questionably good, downright bad, as yet unknown, or simply mysterious have the chance for a cosmic "do-over." One of the best "buried" treasures, and one that resurfaces far more often than might be expected, is the "dead" who have quite an active afterlife on *Lost*. Despite Lindelof's and Cuse's repeated denial that *Lost*'s island setting is some kind of purgatory or even their multicultural, multireligion approach to life after death, the fact remains that an increasing number of the physically dead somehow return to thicken the plot.

In fact, by Season Four, fans are so accustomed to seeing the dead return to the series, either in flashbacks or current time, that when John Locke (or Jeremy Bentham) was revealed to be the man in the coffin, they didn't worry too much about the loss of a favorite character. Ben's instruction to Jack to bring Locke's body along with them on a return to the island seems to portend greater things (including reanimation?) yet to come for one of the island's greatest defenders. Even characters who might not seem as important in the overall story, such as Ben's gunned-down daughter Alex, may return in Seasons Five or Six. Tania Raymonde confided to *TV Guide* that she'd been asked if she'd be willing to come back to the series and would be open to returning. The possibility of turning up again, possibly as one of the undead, "would be *so* cool."[48] As the cast began filming Season Five episodes in August 2008, one of the hottest news items was the return of Ana Lucia, presumably in a Hurley-centric episode, but whether she becomes one of the waking dead or enacts a flashback was carefully kept secret.[49]

As M. Night Shyamalan taught us in *The Sixth Sense*, we "see dead people." The dead are always with us—and in full view of at least some characters—throughout *Lost*'s first four seasons, with some characters making multiple guest appearances. In fact, all we know of Jack's father, Christian Shephard, comes from flashbacks and his often-mute visits to the island. Only in a webisode shortly before Season Three began does Christian voice a line on the island; he instructs Vincent to awaken Jack, who has just survived a plane crash, because "he has work to do."[50] Once Christian makes himself at home in Jacob's cabin, he apparently becomes much more talkative. The dead seem to know much more than their living friends or relatives; because they seem more at peace after death than they ever were while alive, the living castaways and audience want to know just how they came by that peace. The living are lost; the dead seem to have found everything they needed but lacked in life.

The interest in life after death generally increases during times of global stress. Although traditional religions or even unconventional spiritual practices help many seekers during difficult times (e.g., Rose's Christian faith, Locke's belief in "the island"), the supernatural becomes more intriguing for many people who want confirmation that there is life after death or hope that an afterlife is peaceful. *Lost* offers no answers but presents many possibilities, which can be interpreted scientifically or metaphysically, depending upon the viewer's life experiences and belief system. In the *Lost*verse, three types of "metaphysical human entities" regularly show up to offer advice or give direction to the castaways of Oceanic 6: supernatural spirits (i.e., Jacob), apparitions (e.g., Christian, Charlie, Libby), and dream-visions. The table below lists some of *Lost*'s strange encounters with characters known or presumed to be dead. (Jacob and Dave, for example, aren't included in this table because we don't know if they are once-living people or a completely different type of manifestation.)

THE LIVING DEAD

Season/ Episode	Character	Sighting	By	Type of Encounter	Message from Beyond
"Walkabout" (1.4)	Christian Shephard	On the island	Jack	Vision/ Hallucination	None— seen but not heard
"White Rabbit" (1.4)	Christian Shepard	On the island	Jack	Vision/ Hallucination	None— seen but not heard
"?" (2.21)	Ana Lucia	On the island	Mr. Eko	Vision/ Hallucination	Presence makes Eko aware of her death
"?" (2.21)	Yemi	On the island	Mr. Eko	Dream	"Help John"

Season/ Episode	Character	Sighting	By	Type of Encounter	Message from Beyond
"The Cost of Living" (3.5)	Yemi	On the island (in Eko's tent)	Mr. Eko	Dream	Warning of danger
"The Cost of Living" (3.5)	Yemi	On the island (close to his plane's crash site)	Mr. Eko	Vision/ Possible encounter with Smoke Monster	Eko forced to justify his actions
"Further Instructions" (3.3)	Boone Carlyle (showing Locke still-living castaways' future)	On the island (in Locke's sweat lodge)	Locke	Vision/ Hallucination	Clean up your mess, among others
"The Beginning of the End" (4.1)	Charlie Pace	In a convenience store (California)	Hurley	Apparition	None— seen but not heard
"The Beginning of the End" (4.1)	Charlie Pace	In a police interrogation room (California)	Hurley	Apparition	"They need you," written on Charlie's hand
"The Beginning of the End" (4.1)	Charlie Pace	At Santa Rosa mental institution (California)	Hurley and another mental patient	Apparition	"They need you," among others

Season/ Episode	Character	Sighting	By	Type of Encounter	Message from Beyond
"Meet Kevin Johnson" (4.8)	Libby	In a New York City hospital	Michael	Possible hallucination	None—seen but not heard
"Meet Kevin Johnson" (4.8)	Libby	On the freighter	Michael	Apparition	"Don't, Michael"
"Something Nice Back Home" (4.10)	Christian Shephard	In the jungle	Claire	Apparition	None—seen but not heard, as he happily holds Aaron and then leads Claire into the jungle
"Cabin Fever" (4.11)	Horace Goodspeed	On the island	Locke	Dream	Directions for finding a map to Jacob's cabin
"Cabin Fever" (4.11)	Christian Shephard and (possibly dead) Claire	In Jacob's cabin	Locke	Apparition	Claiming to speak for Jacob, Christian reveals the message: "Move the island"

Season/ Episode	Character	Sighting	By	Type of Encounter	Message from Beyond
"There's No Place Like Home" (4.13)	(possibly dead) Claire	In Aaron's bedroom in Kate's house, Los Angeles	Kate	Dream	Hovering near her child, Claire warns Kate not to let "him" take Aaron back to the island

Although the "undead" have the mysterious island and death in common, their experiences in life and their purpose in the story vary. In this chapter, we'll look at some interesting and different roles the dead play in this series.

JACOB

On *Lost,* many people die but still live on in the story and return as messengers to the living, but one of the most enigmatic characters, Jacob, brings not general advice, warnings, or even comfort—only instructions. Viewers don't know exactly who or what Jacob is, but undoubtedly he will play an important part in the story during the next two seasons. Is his the eye peering back at Hurley through the cabin window ("The Beginning of the End," 4.1)? Is Jacob the one in the rocking chair—or is the glimpse really of Christian Shephard, who seems very familiar with Jacob's cabin and later tells Locke that he speaks on Jacob's behalf ("Cabin Fever," 4.11)? Does Jacob exist in nebulous form waiting for his body to return to the island? Is he the spirit of the island who periodically chooses a true believer to assist him? Whatever/whoever Jacob is, his orders are followed to the letter, and he seems a daunting taskmaster. Who else could command "move the island" and have master game-player Ben and faithful Locke rush to the Orchid station to make the seemingly impossible come true ("Cabin Fever;" 4.11, "There's No Place Like Home," 4.12)? If the island indeed can move in space and time, is Jacob truly timeless, or is he, like his island followers, lost between geographic or interdimensional worlds?

Although Jacob hasn't revealed himself to the audience, we do know who sees Jacob, or who claims to have seen Jacob, and these people have links among themselves. Locke, even before he rivaled Ben Linus for control of the Others, received messages from the elusive Jacob and was called to Jacob's cabin, where he heard Jacob say, "Help me" ("The Man Behind the Curtain," 3.20). Although Locke didn't know what to make of this message, more importantly, he heard it. That message was enough to convince Ben that his days as the Others' leader were coming to a close. In the Season Four finale, the long-time leader turns over the reins of power to Locke. Ben knows that only he can move the island, and so he sacrifices his leadership role so that he may save the island ("Cabin Fever," 4.11). We don't yet know what happens to John Locke after this momentous shift in power, but, by the end of the Season Four finale, Locke (aka Jeremy Bentham) is dead, and Ben says that Jack needs to take Locke's body back with them to the island.

Perhaps this power shift and travel to safety in another place and time hint at what Jacob is or how Jacob "lives" on the island without a body. Some fans speculate that John Locke may, in fact, be Jacob. In any case, Locke has at least heard Jacob on several occasions. In "Cabin Fever" (4.11), when Christian Shephard and Claire claim to be Jacob's representatives, Locke receives further instructions from his unseen but fully believed "boss." If Locke's body, along with the physically living former castaways, must return to the island in order to save it, John may not be able to escape Jacob's commands, even after death. Whether Jacob and Locke are one and the same, or two very different entities, the link between them likely continues beyond death.

Those who have seen or heard Jacob have prior supernatural experiences. Locke receives visions while on the island. In a vision that eventually leads to Boone's death, Locke sees his mother and an airplane, a message which guides him to the downed plane containing the remains of Mr. Eko's brother, Yemi ("Deus Ex Machina," 1.17). During a vision quest in a sweat lodge, Locke learns from now-dead Boone what he should do to help save his friends from the Others ("Further Instructions," 3.3).

Hurley, who some characters, including himself, consider to be crazy, frequently sees people who aren't visible to others. These encounters occur throughout his adult life: before the crash, during his stay on the island, and after his rescue, prompting his return to a mental institution. In Season Four, while lost from his friends on a trek across the island, Hurley stumbles across Jacob's cabin and becomes scared when a face peers back at him through the window ("The Beginning of the End," 4.1). Ben and Locke later coerce Hurley to accompany them on the search for Jacob's cabin, because Hurley may be the only one who knows how to get there ("The Shape of Things to Come," 4.9). Although Locke, not Hurley, once again finds the cabin (when Locke has another prophetic dream leading to a map to the cabin—"Cabin Fever," 4.11), Hurley's ability to receive messages from the dead may yet lead him back to Jacob. It will be interesting to see if Jacob has a further claim over Hurley in Seasons Five and Six.

With so many surprising and mysterious twists on the island, plus Cuse and Lindelof's stated premise that every event can have a supernatural as well as scientific explanation, having a character like Jacob as mastermind behind the island and its chief protector isn't all that surprising.

APPARITIONS

Apparitions primarily are messengers to the living. During Seasons Three and Four, Boone Carlyle, Charlie Pace, and Libby all appear to still-living characters, and we must determine whether these encounters are real or imaginary. Although these characters lived, however briefly, in "real time" in the story and return later to haunt their friends, one character—who may turn out to be an important key to these buried treasures—has "lived" only in flashbacks. When the pilot episode introduces *Lost* via a horrendous plane crash on a mysterious island, Christian Shephard already is dead, his corpse part of Oceanic 815's cargo that lands on the island.

CHRISTIAN SHEPHARD

"Those who are dead aren't dead / They just live inside my head"[51] may be a popular *Coldplay* lyric, but Jack (as well as Hurley) could sing this song with equal conviction. In an early Season One episode ("Walkabout," 1.4), Jack first sees an apparition of his father. He doesn't speak; he simply appears, looks at his son, and then wanders into the jungle. After another sighting ("White Rabbit," 1.5), Jack follows his father, eventually finding water in the caves, something the newly appointed island leader needed to do. Jack is initially afraid to follow his vision, because he fears he may be going crazy. Locke counsels him that it doesn't matter whether Jack's vision is real, as long as he believes in it (a philosophy foreshadowing Locke's upcoming visions and dreams that guide him throughout much of the series). That advice seems to be a recurring theme concerning the living dead in the *Lost*verse.

Throughout the next three seasons, Christian Shephard gained a more prominent role in the series, especially in flashbacks. Through flashback episodes, we learn more about his and Jack's troubled relationship, as well as his fathering an out-of-wedlock child, Claire. Whenever Christian Shephard appears in flashbacks as a living man, he seems emotionally isolated from his children. Jack feels he can never live up to his father's expectations but also judges his father's actions harshly when Christian increasingly turns to alcohol to relieve stress (e.g., "All the Best Cowboys Have Daddy Issues," 1.11; "Do No Harm," 1.20; "Man of Science, Man of Faith," 2.1). Claire only meets her father when he visits Sydney after her mother's car crash; when Christian suggests that Claire pull the plug on her comatose mother, she tells him she doesn't want to have anything to do with him ("Par Avion," 3.12). After death, however, the returned Christian Shephard acts more fatherly, for better or worse. The mere sight of him prompts Jack to feel guilt over what he has or hasn't done; when Claire sees her father on the island, he is joyfully cradling grandson Aaron. Christian talks most to John Locke, however, explaining Jacob's message to him and claiming to speak on Jacob's behalf.

Dear old dad may not need words to convey messages to his children. His larger than life presence ensures that, dead or alive, he can unnerve his son. In Season Four, for example, he appears in present time to Jack at the hospital where father and son once worked together ("Something Nice Back Home," 4.10). He doesn't say anything, but his presence rattles Jack. It probably doesn't help that this encounter begins with a nagging beep-beep-beep of a fire alarm, which Jack investigates. When he finds the apparently malfunctioning smoke detector in a dark, quiet hospital lounge, he sees his father comfortably sitting on a couch, watching as Jack turns off the alarm. Jack probably wishes he could so easily turn off the alarm bells going off in his life—and his father's presence reminds him that no matter how long he may choose to ignore the warning signs, or sounds, sooner or later he'll have to deal with recurring island issues.

Christian Shephard also makes a sudden, surprise visit to Claire and, for the first time, sees his grandson Aaron ("Cabin Fever," 4.11). Awakened one night during her trek back to the beach, Claire sees her father kneeling by the campfire. Perhaps her last word as a living being is "Dad?", which may be a fitting introduction to a new (after)life. Fans speculate that Claire is now one of the living dead, although Cuse and Lindelof promise that she will become an important future part of the story. Claire serves as a messenger to the living when, via a dream, she tells Kate not to let "him" take Aaron back to the island ("There's No Place Like Home," 4.13). In this way Claire, like Charlie, mysteriously looks after the baby even though she isn't physically part of his present life.

Miles later tells Sawyer that he watched Claire follow her father into the jungle, but whether both are dead (as many fans suspect) or whether Claire simply can see her dead father hasn't yet been confirmed. Her changed demeanor in Jacob's cabin and simply the act of leaving her baby behind—when she has been so protective of him to this point—indicate that the "new" Claire is vastly different from the character we've come to know.

BOONE CARLYLE

Another one of the early dead characters coming back to life is Boone Carlyle. He appears to Locke during a vision quest

("Further Instructions," 3.3), and he seems to know what's going on with other characters on the island. During that vision quest, Boone shows Locke that Kate and Sawyer will flirt and for a time be together. The dream/vision also features Desmond as a pilot surrounded by beautiful flight attendants; perhaps it is no surprise that Desmond flies off to become reunited with true love Penny ("There's No Place Like Home," 4.13). Boone also tells Locke that Claire, Charlie, and Aaron will be "OK—for now," but his tone and word choice foreshadow troubled times for the little family. The information Boone provides helps Locke decide what to do next. Boone, like Christian Shephard and Claire, seems to be working on behalf of the island to ensure the reality it wants/knows to come true will turn out as planned.

Locke's vision helps him deal with his guilt over Boone's death. Although he comes to accept that Boone needed to be "sacrificed" for the island, he probably also feels guilt over the young man's death. When Boone becomes Locke's spirit guide in the dream/vision, Locke trades roles with his former mentee, who followed Locke's commands even to his death. When Boone appears as his guide, Locke gets a chance to apologize for his actions, as well as to honor the young man by following his counsel.

Charlie Pace

Another active dead character is Charlie Pace. In the Season Four opener ("The Beginning of the End," 4.1), Charlie fans were relieved to see their favorite character reappear in the present. When his pleas for understanding and his multiple appearances don't seem to get the message across to Hurley that he's returned from the dead, Charlie slaps his friend, a very physical metaphysical wake-up call. During these initial encounters, he consistently reminds Hurley that "they need you." Seeing Charlie convinces Hurley that he is indeed crazy, and he willingly returns to the Santa Rosa Mental Health Facility.

Charlie must visit his friend there regularly, because Hurley later tells Jack that Charlie has left a message for him ("Something Nice Back Home," 4.10). In fact, Charlie tells Hurley to write down the message—Jack shouldn't raise Aaron—so that he won't forget it. At that time, Jack is playing "daddy" to Aaron and living with Aaron's new "mommy," Kate. Charlie, who in life loved Aaron and looked after the baby, would certainly seem to have a vested interest in the child's welfare. After all, he sacrificed his life in order to pave the way for his "family's" rescue.

Seeing Charlie as one of the living dead not only helps Hurley come to grips with his friend's death, but it allows Charlie fans closure. By giving him a further role in the story, as well as showing him as a sexier, more confident man in the afterlife, the writers help fans get on with the story, just as Charlie gets on with his new (after)life.

Hurley also visits with Mr. Eko and tells Sayid he regularly sees dead people ("There's No Place Like Home," 4.13). In fact, his chess game with Eko is in progress when Sayid arrives. Chess, like backgammon, is an important game on *Lost*. Not only is it a game of strategy, but black-and-white symbolism has been important since the early episodes. For Hurley to be playing chess with the dead suggests his greater role in the story. If *Lost* represents the "game" of life, black-and-white symbols, such as backgammon or chess pieces, indicate the importance of opposites but, more importantly, that life can't be reduced to absolutes. Everyman Hurley may be the best character to come to understand that such apparent oppositions (e.g., black/white, life/death) may not be as opposite as we would like to think. Hurley's journey to this understanding may be "crazy," but it may turn out to be our journey as well. By identifying with lovable, average Hurley, audiences may see just how strange or extraordinary "reality" can be.

LIBBY

In addition to Charlie and Boone, Libby also makes several appearances as one of the living dead in Season Four. She has unfinished business with Michael, who accidentally shot and killed her in Season Two ("Two for the Road," 2.20). When Michael is grievously injured in an aborted suicide attempt, Libby appears to him in the hospital ("Meet Kevin Johnson," 4.8). She also visits Michael when he is moments away from detonating a bomb on the freighter and tells him not to do so. When he disregards Libby's plea, he discovers that the bomb isn't real but merely a test from Ben Linus. Michael apparently needs to learn to listen to the dead. He becomes grateful for Christian Shephard's message shortly before a real bomb explodes on the freighter, killing him. Christian tells Michael that his work is finished and, in essence, gives him permission to move on to death. He had told his former friends from the island he expected to die on the freighter as part of his penance for killing Ana Lucia and Libby, as well as leaving the island behind. Although Michael didn't seem to be a highly spiritual character, his ability to receive "supernatural" messages may not require belief in an afterlife. The dead who need to talk with him about his actions may have been sent by the island, and who better to get his attention, especially at first, than a woman he killed?

DEATH BECOMES THEM

A not-so-great film's title noted that *Death Becomes Her*, a theme taken to heart on *Lost*, where the dead gain new gravitas once freed of their earthly challenges. Perhaps Jacob, or the island, changes characters after they die, once their earthly troubles are behind them. Christian Shephard seems more decisive and confident in his role as messenger and an "insider" to Jacob's plan; as Claire lounges in the cabin, she too seems less concerned with her duties as Aaron's mother and acts as if she understands a grander plan, one in which she accepts that Aaron is exactly where he should be ("Cabin Fever," 4.11). Only in Kate's dream ("There's No Place Like Home," 4.13) does Claire seem agitated, adamantly telling Kate to keep Aaron away from "him"—whether Jacob, Locke, Ben, or another character is unclear.

Charlie, although not associated with Jacob directly (at least through information gleaned from Season Four), also seems more confident and even tempered during his visits with Hurley. He relays messages to his friend as well as helps him understand the circumstances surrounding his drowning; he may not understand exactly how he can visit as a corporeal being, but he confidently explains that he's dead but also here in Hurley's present ("The Beginning of the End," 4.1).

Life after death imbues these characters with greater authority and self assurance, not only about what they need to do but who they are. Whether their roles and images are produced by another entity or whether they really are the living dead has not yet been revealed, but the sheer number of characters whose personalities generally are improved by death indicates that whatever afterlife awaits helps characters find themselves so that they can help their friends and family. Through death, these characters may have found themselves, making them more likely to want to help the still-lost living.

Surprisingly, because conventional ghost wisdom indicates otherwise, the dead aren't bound to the place where they died, or even to the island. Christian died in a Sydney alley but first appears on the island and later in Los Angeles; Charlie died in the Looking Glass station but visits Hurley in California; Libby died in the hatch but travels to a New York hospital and a South Pacific freighter to visit Michael. Even Claire turns up in Kate's dream in Los Angeles. Although each appearance might be logically explained as a character's hallucination due to stress, medication, or mental illness, the number of otherworldly visitations suggests many other possible interpretations.

Other dead characters do appear in dreams or waking visions, but of the Oceanic castaways, Libby, Boone, and Charlie may make future appearances in the continuing *Lost* saga. When Jack tells the reporters in Honolulu about what happened to Oceanic 815's passengers, he specifically mentions Libby, Boone, and Charlie ("There's No Place Like Home," 4.12). The actors playing these characters have expressed interest in continuing their roles in future episodes. *Lost* doesn't separate the living from the dead, but makes life a continuum, from life to death to afterlife. Whether these characters are figments of imaginations, messengers sent from the other side, or hallucinations induced by island experiments, what is important is that we believe in the messages they provide.

MESSAGES FROM BEYOND

Many supernatural messages come from an unknown source of knowledge and most often are passed along to the living by the dead who had some connection with the recipient. To date, only two messengers prove exceptions: Christian Shephard and Dave. Jack's father doesn't have an as-yet-revealed prior connection to Michael, and although Dave may have been a real person in the mental institution with Hurley, he may have been an "imaginary friend" or even a "spirit" who, for some reason, latched onto the troubled man. Most often, the dead provide the living with reminders of what they know they need to do but may not want to.

Jack may not always want to figure out what his father intends him to do, but Christian Shephard's mere presence makes Jack feel guilty or question his latest actions. By following in his dead father's footsteps, Jack is reminded that he can't forget the island and must follow his instincts about what to do next. In many ways, the dead "nag" the living, and Christian and Charlie seem most adept in this role. In addition to nagging his friend to do things he should, Charlie uses Hurley as a go-between to get to Jack, possibly because Jack only seems to see, but not hear, the dead. Hurley gives voice to Charlie's messages in a way that Jack can't ignore.

Libby and Boone are more traditional "spirit guides," as are some visions of Yemi. Charlie, and possibly Mr. Eko, act as companions to Hurley. If these "ghosts" are real, they may simply enjoy spending time with Hurley, rather than just providing information and disappearing. Perhaps Hurley is reluctant to let go of his relationship with friend Charlie, or maybe he feels guilty over his lack of understanding Charlie's goodbye hug. Perhaps the dead also want to maintain contact with the living, and Hurley, more than most people, can easily see and interact with them.

PROPHETIC DREAMS AND VISIONS

Many characters who return after death also received "supernatural" messages in life. In a dream, Yemi alerts Eko to danger in his tent and saves his life ("The Cost of Living," 3.5). Ana Lucia appears to Eko on the beach hours before he learns of her death, and Yemi directs his brother and Locke to a new hatch ("?" 2.21). This hatch provides Locke with more information about the Others and leads Eko to a new mission. Although Locke begins to question the spiritual nature of the island at this point, he must prove to himself that the island does indeed have the type of power he originally attributed to it. Locke's crisis of faith, initially instigated by interpreting a vision, is later resolved by more dream-vision guidance that he believes comes from the island. Mr. Eko, however, isn't as fortunate in the outcome of his "visions." What he thinks is a waking vision of dead Yemi ("The Cost of Living," 3.5) turns out to be a manifestation of the Smoke Monster, which evaluates and later kills him.

It likely isn't a coincidence that Charlie's dream/vision includes Hurley, who seem linked in life and death. Catholic Charlie's dreams involve the most important people in his life—Claire, his mother, Hurley—telling him to save his surrogate son Aaron; these characters appear in the dream wearing Biblical dress ("Fire + Water," 2.12), which would be an important way of getting Charlie's attention by playing into his belief system.

These types of links between characters further integrate the dead with the living or illustrate ways in which the living dead interacted with each other in life:

- **Locke and Hurley**. Jacob forges this link. Although Locke hears Jacob and later receives messages via dreams that lead him to Jacob's cabin and to do Jacob's will, Hurley sees the cabin and seems to gain information about it through waking visions, in which the cabin is in whatever direction Hurley tries to run ("The Beginning of the End," 4.1).

Hurley may not want this information, and he certainly doesn't seek it out as Locke does, but both characters are linked by their messages from the island and involving those beyond the grave.

- **Claire and Hurley.** Jack asks Hurley to look after Claire in the aftermath of the crash ("Pilot," 1.1), thus beginning their platonic friendship. They were Charlie's closest friends on the island, and Charlie expressed love for both. Hurley tells Claire about Charlie's death and comforts her ("Confirmed Dead," 4.2), as well as later provides messages to Jack about Aaron's upbringing ("Something Nice Back Home," 4.10).

- **Libby and Hurley.** They were planning their first date when Libby was killed ("Two for the Road," 2.20), but they may have met earlier. In a flashback, Libby sits across the room from Hurley at the Santa Rosa Mental Facility ("Dave," 2.18). Although she hasn't yet appeared to Hurley, it wouldn't be surprising if someday he sees her as well.

- **Charlie and Locke.** Charlie was mentored by Locke ("The Moth," 1.7), but when Locke believed Charlie had returned to heroin, the disappointed former mentor beat him ("Fire + Water," 2.12). At that point, Charlie wanted little to do with Locke but nevertheless assisted him with a vision quest in the shell of the church that he and Mr. Eko were building ("Further Instructions," 3.3).

- **Charlie and Mr. Eko.** In addition to their individual problems and reconciliations with the Catholic Church, they started building a church ("S.O.S." 2.19) and prayed together over Yemi's remains, which they found in the shell of the drug runners' plane ("The 23rd Psalm," 2.10).

The characters who have the greatest potential as messengers from the other side seem to be linked with those most likely to receive and accept messages from beyond. The big exception is Christian Shephard, who seems to have a separate purpose and whose link to the Others is peripheral through Jack and Claire.

Just who has visions in service of Jacob or the island is questionable, because many characters see things they can't believe are real. Some "messages" or "visits" don't seem to carry much weight beyond being strange encounters. Charlie, Hurley, Locke, Eko, and Jack have had more meaningful dream-visions or supernatural visits, but even skeptical Kate has seen a black horse from her past ("What Kate Did," 2.9), and Sayid and Sawyer, among others, can attest that the island "whispers" (e.g., "Solitary," 1.9; "Outlaws," 1.16).

When Ben wistfully confides to Locke that he "used to have dreams" ("Cabin Fever," 4.11), he indicates that those chosen by Jacob to help the island may be "given" insightful dreams, such as the one from which Locke has just awakened. In that dream, Horace Goodspeed—forever chopping down a tree to make a getaway cabin—tells Locke that the location of Jacob's cabin can be found in a map in the dead man's pocket. Locke remembers the pit where the bodies of the DHARMA Initiates, killed in the Purge, are decomposing, and he finds Horace's body—and the map—there. Perhaps, as many fans have speculated over the years, the island does indeed provide the dreams or visions that people need to see in order for the island's grand plan to be furthered.

THOSE WHO SEEK THE DEAD

In addition to characters who have waking dreams or visions, there are those who seek the dead and wholeheartedly believe in their existence. Charlotte Malkin, for example, claims to see the dead. She also had connections with Libby and Mr. Eko shortly before Oceanic 815's departure. Eko argues with Charlotte when she tells him she bears a message from Yemi ("The 23rd Psalm," 2.10). He believes the girl is trying to entrap him and wants nothing to do with her. Libby, who watches this encounter, intercedes, possibly believing that young Charlotte might be in danger from the angry Eko. Charlotte seems to have a psychic gift, although her father, a "professional" psychic, confesses to Eko that he is a fraud who conducts research on his clients, rather than reveals information from supernatural sources. Whether the senior Malkin has the gift of foresight or simply bilks clients is unclear, but Charlotte seems a sincere young woman.

She, like other characters, including Charlie, cheat death at least once. Before Charlie's death by drowning, he suffers several near misses, the most important being hanging. When Jack brings back Charlie from the dead ("All the Best Cowboys Have Daddy Issues," 1.11), the young man seems inexplicably well for someone who was clinically dead for several minutes. That Charlie survives seems a miracle, but perhaps he was merely being prepared to be a messenger from the afterlife to the living. Unlike Charlie, Charlotte Malkin survives her drowning and comes back to life on an autopsy table ("The 23rd Psalm," 2.10). Life and death, for many of these characters, are indelibly intertwined.

Another "seer" is Desmond. He also survives a near-death experience during the hatch's implosion. Conversely, he might've died but been brought back by the island. It seems strange that an implosion making such a large crater—and destroying Desmond's clothing—would leave the man unscathed except for a newfound ability to see "flashes" of the future. However, his ability to see the future may be part of a larger plan set in motion by Mrs. Hawking, or even Charles Widmore. (We don't yet know if Desmond's flashes of the future continue after his rescue.) Because Desmond is a time traveler who can't control his back-and-forth trips and glimpses of potential futures, his visions seem less spiritual or supernatural than the result of a scientific breakthrough in time-travel experimentation.

One more seer/seeker of the dead, Miles Straume, talks with the dead as part of his profession. Before coming to the island, he makes his living by "exorcising" spirits that the living no longer want in their lives ("Confirmed Dead," 4.2) and uses information from the dead to his financial advantage. On the island, we see him talking with Naomi's body. Although we can't hear their conversation, dead Naomi obviously tells him the truth about the way she died. That revelation convinces Miles that Kate has been telling him the truth about events leading to Naomi's death.

Miles also looks at Claire strangely during the long walk toward the beach after New Otherton is attacked ("Something Nice Back Home," 4.10). Miles "feels" something wrong and finds the shallow graves where Karl and Rousseau were hastily buried. He stares so intently at Claire that her new protector, Sawyer, warns him not to look at her again. Only after Claire abandons Aaron and follows her father to Jacob's cabin do we wonder whether Miles saw Claire as one of the dead.

SPECIAL OR INSANE?

Each character who "sees" someone who, to other people, isn't there is often deemed "insane" or "crazy," a term which Hurley in particular despises. *Lost* posits that these encounters might be real or they might be induced by an altered mental state. Locke talks with Boone, who shows him glimpses of the future, only after he takes a hallucinogenic drug during a vision quest ("Further Instructions," 3.3). Jack takes clonazepam to quell his anxiety and soon after sees his dad ("Something Nice Back Home," 4.10). Religious Charlie, according to the consensus of his fellow castaways, may be saying Hail Mary's to heroin once again; after all, he maintains a convenient stash of Virgin Mary statues full of heroin, even though he swears he's sober. During this time his "dream" of Biblically-garbed Hurley, Claire, and his (likely) deceased mother tell him to save Aaron ("Fire + Water," 2.12). Mr. Eko suffers the after-effects of a polar bear attack and the hatch's implosion when he begins to talk with Yemi ("The Cost of Living," 3.5). When stressed out, Hurley often sees people no one else (or only other "crazy" people) can see: Dave, identified as Hurley's "imaginary" friend from the mental institution, shows up on the island when the big man tries to give up junk food ("Dave," 2.18); now-dead Charlie shows up when Hurley has trouble coping with his return home as one of the Oceanic 6 ("The Beginning of the End," 4.1).

Nevertheless, these characters often are some of the most "special" (or "chosen") people on the island. Locke becomes important to the Others as Ben's potential rival, and even Ben worries that Locke hears, and later sees, Jacob ("The Man Behind the Curtain," 3.20). Without any intention, or even knowledge, of Jacob's cabin, Hurley seems to be summoned; no matter where he turns, he sees the cabin in front of him ("The Beginning of the End," 4.1). Ben recognizes that only Hurley may be able to find the cabin again; even Locke doesn't know where it is and may be losing his special connection with the island ("The Shape of Things to Come," 4.9).

Lost makes us wonder if we're the ones truly lost from the "reality" of the time/space continuum. After all, Walt's special psychic abilities have been scientifically tested by the Others; he learns how to use their equipment to project himself into another place in order to give his friends secret messages to help them survive, often against the Others' wishes. Whether the Others, Jacob, or other so-far-unknown forces implant visions in the willing to believe (such as Locke and Charlie) or use Smoky as a shapeshifter to mislead (such as Eko and possibly Jack), audiences still have the option of accepting the possibility of messages beyond the grave. Whether we accept the notion that the undead can live again and information from another dimension/afterlife can be sent as frequently as text messages, Lindelof's and Cuse's land of the dead is a crazy good plot device.

CHAPTER FIVE

THE SIGNIFICANCE OF PLACE

Although filming scenes most often on Oahu, *Lost* prides itself on its global locations. Anywhere in the world is fair game, and the "feel" of events and situations changes with the location. In addition to *Lost*'s chameleon quality, the series also benefits from lush tropical scenery and the many beautiful beach and jungle locales. Although *Lost* as a series is native to Hawaii, the international cast of characters and increasingly global intrigue make it one of the most "multinational" series ever filmed in one area. Unlike other dramas that span the globe, like *24*, *Lost* must accurately replicate dozens of very different real locations, from the past or in the present, during a single season. In Season Four, for example, *Lost* took us to Iraq, Tunisia, Scotland and England (U.K.), Germany, South Korea, China, Bali, the Bahamas, and the U.S.—quite a feat for filming taking place on one small island in the Pacific.

Places help make people who they are, and audiences and characters often have preconceptions about others, depending on where they're from. Australia might bring to mind images of vast open spaces, the Sydney Bridge, or kangaroos, for example. Audiences might expect Australians to sound a certain way or use specific slang. For some viewers, Claire might seem "very Australian," although she comes from a city instead of the outback, and her teenaged Goth rebellion (shown in flashbacks during "Par Avion," 3.12) is typical of young women in many Western countries, not just Australia. (Alex is a good example of the island version of teenaged rebellion.) Still, upon learning Claire is Australian, the castaways (and audience) may have cultural expectations for her behavior.

Sometimes a single place name evokes powerful emotional responses, as well as links characters, past and future. When Juliet reminds Sayid that he doesn't need more blood on his hands, she cryptically refers to what he did in Basra ("One of Us," 3.16). The Others' vast files on the castaways, plus Ben's own visits to the region, help them understand exactly what Sayid did. Once one of the most populous cities in Iraq, the powerful port became reduced to rubble during a series of wars, including the Gulf and Iraqi wars. Located on the "Highway of Death," the region suffered multiple bombings during the end of the 1990s; atrocities became commonplace. Whatever Sayid did during the Gulf War (after being coerced by the U.S. military to become an "interrogator") probably wasn't pleasant and most likely is something he tries to bury in his past.

Ben apparently is a frequent visitor in the Middle East. Under the guise of "Dean Moriarty," he checks into a Tunisian hotel on October 24, 2006, between a visit (via time portal) into the Sahara Desert and Nadia's funeral in Tikrit, Iraq.[52] Basra as a location also resonates with that episode's title, "The Shape of Things to Come" (4.9), which shares the title with H.G. Wells' "future history" that features world conferences held in Basra.

Any metropolis contains many distinct neighborhoods and districts, and narrowing the audience's focus to one small area provides a greater sense of place than simply showing a generic alley or apartment. To give viewers details that enhance the story, *Lost* often highlights specific areas of large cities. Christian Shephard is found in a Sydney alley near Queen's Cross ("White Rabbit," 1.5). The area, now known as King's Cross, was renamed in the early 1900s to avoid confusion with Queen Square. (Why *Lost* used the "old" name is unknown.) The King's Cross area is a busy tourist section offering all types of nightlife.

Turning large cities into familiar spaces adds yet another layer of detail to *Lost* and makes it more plausible that characters might run into each other within a neighborhood or near a well-known landmark. In London, Charlie and Liam share a flat in Brixton, an interesting but (once) seedy area. During the late 1990s or early 2000s, when Charlie would have lived there, the area hadn't yet seen a resurgence of clubs and nightlife. In 1996 Brixton became a battleground between residents and police; low employment, high crime, and drug trade were common.

In contrast to the Brixton Underground station close to the flat, a station in a more affluent area becomes the meeting point for Desmond and Charlie ("Flashes Before Your Eyes," 3.8). More affluent still, Charlie's girlfriend Lucy and her father live in Knightsbridge ("Homecoming," 1.15), a fashionable area with upscale shops and museums; Knightsbridge also is home to Desmond's love, Penny Widmore, during his incarceration ("Live Together, Die Alone," 2.23). When she agrees to answer Desmond's phone call on Christmas Eve 2004 (a strange promise made years in advance), Penny lives at 423 Cheyne Walk in London, a historic Chelsea street also favored by pre-Raphaelite painter and poet Dante Gabriel Rossetti, novelist George Eliot, Prime Minister David Lloyd George, and Rolling Stone Mick Jagger ("The Constant," 4.5). Her father likes to shop Sotheby's auctions for special items like a *Black Rock* journal, and his London home isn't a secret from Ben, who likes making a late-night visit to threaten his nemesis ("The Shape of Things to Come," 4.9).

Within Los Angeles, the Oceanic 6 continue to cross paths, too. Jack returns to work at St. Sebastian Hospital but sometimes visits Hurley at the Santa Rosa Mental Health Facility. Hurley agrees to be institutionalized again after a harrowing car chase with police that begins in the La Brea district ("The Beginning of the End," 4.1). Sayid later tells Ben that Nadia died as a result of a hit-and-run at the corner of La Brea and Santa Monica ("The Shape of Things to Come," 4.9). According to Ben, Ishmael Baki, supposedly one of Widmore's operatives, was seen shortly before the accident only three blocks away. Sayid, Kate, Jack, Aaron, Ben, Locke, and Hurley have pre- and post-island connections in Southern California. Linking so many characters within a vast urban sprawl further emphasizes that these people are inextricably bound to each other.

What makes a city special or unique also adds to a sense of place, not only for the characters but for the audience taking a virtual tour during different characters' backstories. *Lost* slips in clues to local culture in New York, London, Manchester, Glasgow, and Phuket:

- Michael wants to show Walt great architecture, including New York's Flat Iron Building ("…In Translation," 1.17), which inspired him to become an artist. This triangular landmark was an engineering feat in 1902; its steel skeleton, unusual at the time, allowed it to become one of the city's tallest buildings. Although Michael returns to New York City, he confesses his murderous ways to Walt, who refuses to have anything to do with him ("Meet Kevin Johnson," 4.8). Instead of showing Walt the sights, Michael has an enlightening conversation in the Hotel Earle's penthouse with Tom Friendly, who loves the perks (including a handsome young lover) of off-island living. (The renamed Washington Square Hotel in the West Village once was home to Bob Dylan in the 1960s.)

- When Charlie and Naomi share Mancunian memories, he explains that DriveShaft's first gig took place in the Night and Day Bar ("Greatest Hits," 3.21). The real Night and Day Café on Oldham Street features a variety of bands. (Its current schedule is posted at www.nightnday.org.)

- Desmond's former fiancé doesn't believe that he experienced a spiritual epiphany, which causes him to leave her at the altar; his only "religious experience," she claims, was when "Celtic won the Cup" ("Catch-22," 3.17). This detail establishes Desmond in Glasgow, when previous backstories only referred in general to his Scottish past and refers to the Celtics' 1995 Scottish Cup. By 1996, Des trains with the Royal Scots Regiment at Camp Millar, north of Glasgow. Scenes of basic training in the pouring rain reinforce the stereotype of Scotland as a very wet nation ("The Constant," 4.5).

- Jack's visit to Phuket showcases diversity of place: a beach hut, a city restaurant, a street festival, and a tattoo parlor. Each setting shows a different side of the area, from tranquil beachside to colorful, pulsing streetscape. These little details bring place and character into clearer focus.

Language also helps audiences understand place. Jack doesn't understand the Thai boy selling him drinks on the beach; a U.S. audience, like Jack, probably won't understand the language without subtitles (not provided in this scene) ("Stranger in a Strange Land," 3.9). Throughout this episode Jack seems very much out of place, truly a stranger in what to him is a strange land. The customs of the people he encounters underscore his and locals' different expectations of each other and, ultimately, their inability to reconcile these differences.

A sense of place is incredibly important to *Lost's* characters on a very personal level, too. One of the castaways' most important early questions is "Where are we?" quickly followed by "How do we go home?" The answers have shifted during the first four seasons—108 days since the crash at the time the Oceanic 6 arrive in Hawaii—and "home" proves not be an ideal destination. When Jack's and Kate's flashforwards to Los Angeles take viewers off-island, the juxtaposition of the Southern California metropolis with the previous scene's remote tropical island make the city seem strange and foreign ("Through the Looking Glass," 3.22–3.23). The modern "jungle" provides more heartaches than happy reunions, making the island potentially the "better" home and leading us to consider the irony of the Season Four finale's title, "There's No Place Like Home" (4.12–4.13). "Home" may turn out, for Hurley, to be a mental institution instead of the family mansion or, for emotionally isolated Sun, an exclusive Seoul high-rise "prison." Wealth and celebrity fail to bring happiness to the Oceanic 6 when they try to return to their past lives or carve new, independent identities.

Marking boundaries and establishing "home turf" are important even on an uncharted island. Identifying their territory helps the castaways establish what they deem is theirs, who they are, where they need to go—or avoid, or where other people might be. Sayid first leaves the group not only to ostracize himself from their society but to map the perimeter of the island ("Solitary," 1.9). Rousseau hides from the Others and creates deadly boundaries to mark her territory (e.g., "Solitary," 1.9; "Everybody Hates Hugo," 2.4; "One of Them," 2.14; "Catch-22," 3.17). Everyone seems to want or have a map— Sayid finds Rousseau's and, with Shannon's help, tries to decode it ("Whatever the Case May Be," 1.12); Locke discovers the map on the hatch blast door and tries to re-create it ("Lockdown," 2.17; "?" 2.21); the Nigerian drug runners' plane contains maps ("Deus ex Machina," 2.19); Sayid, Locke, and Kate take Mikhail Bakunin hostage and follow his map to the Others' encampment ("Enter 77," 3.11). During Season Four, Ben provides a map so Rousseau can take Alex to safety in the temple ("Meet Kevin Johnson," 4.8). Directed by a dream in which long-dead DHARMA devotee Horace Goodspeed tells Locke to find him, John locates the body in a mass grave and removes a map stored in Goodspeed's pocket; it conveniently shows Locke how to find Jacob's cabin ("Cabin Fever," 4.11).

Compasses and instructions, sometimes from mystical sources, also play a prominent role: Locke gives Sayid his compass, but North isn't where it should be ("Whatever the Case May Be," 1.12); Locke believes that words carved on Mr. Eko's "Jesus stick" will guide him where the Others hold Jack, Kate, and Sawyer ("I Do," 3.6); Desmond leads Hurley, Charlie, and Jin on a "camping trip" guided by images of the future he sees flashing before his eyes ("Catch-22," 3.17). Most cryptically, the elusive Jacob tells Locke to "move the island" ("Cabin Fever, 4.11), a command that Ben fortuitously knows how to obey. He turns the "frozen donkey wheel" (Lindelof's and Cuse's nickname for the top-secret finale script and the episode's time-and-space shifter) to alter the island's location ("There's No Place Like Home," 4.13).

Being lost from one place, as well as oneself, and traveling to another location, literally or metaphorically, are key elements to understanding *Lost*. People gain peace of mind by knowing where they are and how they "belong" physically with the rest of the world. Culturally, too, they establish expectations of how to behave and what is "normal" based on where they are.

Other characters—and the audience—are surprised when a character exceeds cultural expectations. Jin gradually overcomes a language barrier to become a more integral part of the English-speaking community; speaking Korean is the most obvious sign of his coming from a different culture and frames the way he interacts with others. When Michael meets Jin on the freighter, he seems shocked to learn that Jin has become remarkably fluent in English during the brief time since Michael left the island ("Meet Kevin Johnson," 4.8). Charlotte, born in Essex, brought up in Bransgrove, and university educated at Kent and Oxford ("Confirmed Dead," 4.2), adheres to many viewers' preconceptions of a reserved British woman. Even her interest in archeological digs in Tunisia can be explained in light of a long history of British archeologists excavating their Empire. What is more surprising is Charlotte's "outside the box" ability to speak Korean ("Something Nice Back Home," 4.10). Where people come from often sets up their expectations about other people and their homelands.

HOMETOWNS AND SPECIAL PLACES

Through flashbacks, viewers learn a great deal about where the castaways live during crucial moments in their lives. Hometowns and native countries give audiences a better idea of the cultural expectations and experiences that made the castaways who they are today. Some places are not hometowns but gain personal significance because they are associated with a pivotal moment or special event in a character's life. The following table summarizes places important to current or former island dwellers.

PEOPLE AND PLACES

Name	Important Place	Significance	Episode
Kate Austen	Cedar Rapids, IA	Her birthplace is in Cedar Rapids, and she periodically returns home.	"What Kate Did" (2.9)
	Washington	She says her father taught her to track.	"All the Best Cowboys Have Daddy Issues" (1.11)
	South Korea	Her "father" is stationed there when Kate is conceived.	"What Kate Did" (2.9)
	Taos, NM	She robs a bank to retrieve a model airplane.	"Whatever the Case May Be" (1.12)
	Miami, FL	She marries Kevin.	"I Do" (3.6)
	Tallahassee, FL	She tries to buy a ticket there when she's captured by the marshal.	"What Kate Did" (2.9)
	Harrison Valley, PA	Kate's mug shot is taken by the police.	"Tabula Rasa" (1.3)

Name	Important Place	Significance	Episode
	Canada	She tells her employer that she's Canadian.	"Tabula Rasa" (1.3)
	Bali	She says she wants to travel there.	"What Kate Did" (2.9)
	Australia	The marshal captures her.	"Whatever the Case May Be" (1.12)
	Honolulu, HI	As one of the Oceanic 6, she meets the press at a military facility west of Honolulu.	"There's No Place Like Home" (4.13)
	Los Angeles, CA	She lives there after being rescued from the island and agrees to remain in California.	"Through the Looking Glass" (3.23); "Eggtown" (4.4)
Juliet Burke	Miami, FL	She researches genetics and fertility at Miami Central University; sister Rachel lives there.	"Not in Portland" (3.7)
	Portland, OR	She begins a job with Mittelos Bioscience, "outside Portland."	"One of Us" (3.16)
Boone Carlyle	Los Angeles, CA	His birthplace is assumed but not specifically mentioned.	
	New York, NY	He lives there briefly while working for his mother.	"Abandoned" (2.6)

Name	Important Place	Significance	Episode
	Sydney, Australia	He travels there to help Shannon with a problem boyfriend.	"Hearts and Minds" (1.13)
Ana Lucia Cortez	Los Angeles, CA	Her birthplace is assumed but not specifically mentioned; she works as a police officer in LA.	"The Other 48 Days" (2.7)
	Sydney, Australia	She travels there as a companion to Christian Shephard.	"Two for the Road" (2.20)
Michael Dawson	New York, NY	Michael was born in the city. He lives there after he returns from the island.	"Special" (1.14); "Meet Kevin Johnson" (4.8)
	Sydney, Australia	He retrieves motherless Walt from Sydney.	"Special" (1.14)
Mr. Eko	Nigeria	He was born in this country.	"The 23rd Psalm" (2.10)
	London, England	Masquerading as a priest, he takes Yemi's place in order to study (and get out of Nigeria).	"?" (2.21)
	Sydney, Australia	He travels there to investigate the possibility of a miracle.	"?" (2.21)

Name	Important Place	Significance	Episode
Daniel Faraday	Queen's College, Oxford University, Oxford, England	Daniel teaches physics and conducts research. He meets Desmond and shows him one of his time-travel experiments.	"The Constant" (4.5)
	Essex, MA	He and his caretaker watch news reports of the discovery of Oceanic 815.	"Confirmed Dead" (4.2)
Nikki Fernandez	Los Angeles, CA	She is the star of the TV series, Exposé.	"Exposé" (3.14)
	Brazil	She becomes a guest on a Brazilian TV show, where she meets future boyfriend and partner-in-crime Paulo.	"Exposé" (3.14)
James Ford (Sawyer)	Jasper, AL	Sawyer was born there and lived there at least through the time his mother had an affair with "Tom Sawyer."	"The Brig" (3.19)
	Knoxville, TN	The boy sends letter to "Sawyer" about his parents' death.	"Confidence Man" (1.8)
	Tennessee	He tells a shrimp vendor he's from Tennessee.	"Outlaws" (1.16)
	Tampa, FL	He grouses about the ill-fated "Tampa job."	"Confidence Man" (1.8)

Name	Important Place	Significance	Episode
	Tallahassee, FL	He receives a bad case of "sunburn."	"Lockdown" (2.17)
	Sioux City, IA	He tells Cassidy to meet him at the Sage Flower Motel there.	"The Long Con" (2.13)
	Sydney, Australia	He follows a tip to find "Sawyer" but kills an innocent man.	"Outlaws" (1.16)
Rose Henderson	Bronx, NY	She says she lives there (but it is unknown if this is her birthplace).	"Pilot" (1.1)
	Niagara Falls, NY	She becomes engaged to Bernard, although she confides in him that she's dying.	"S.O.S." (2.19)
	Australia	Bernard brings her to Australia to consult with the healer Isaac.	"S.O.S." (2.19)
Desmond Hume	Glasgow, Scotland	He stands up his fiancé Ruth at their wedding.	"Catch-22" (3.17)
	Carlisle, Scotland	Penny's family lives there.	"Catch-22" (3.17)
	Camp Millar, Scotland	Desmond goes through basic training for the Royal Scots Regiment.	"The Constant" (4.5)
	Queen's College, Oxford University, Oxford, England	He visits Daniel Faraday to learn more about time travel.	"The Constant" (4.5)

Name	Important Place	Significance	Episode
	London, England	He (briefly) lives there with Penny; later he has time-travel experiences to London. In 1996 he visits Penny to tell her that he'll call her in 2004.	"Flashes Before Your Eyes" (3.8); "The Constant" (4.5)
Sayid Jarrah	Tikrit, Iraq	Sayid is born there. He returns home to bury his wife, Nadia, and joins forces with Ben Linus.	"Pilot" (1.1); "The Shape of Things to Come" (4.9)
	Cairo, Egypt	He attends University of Cairo and meets his future "terrorist" roommate.	"The Greater Good" (1.21)
	Basra, Iraq	He may have committed atrocities—Juliet alludes to what he did there.	"One of Us" (3.16)
	Paris, France	He works as a chef but is captured by the husband of a woman he tortured in Iraq.	"Enter 77" (1.11)
	London, England	ASIA and CIA agents detain him at Heathrow Airport and persuade him to infiltrate a terrorist cell in Australia.	"The Greater Good" (1.21)

Name	Important Place	Significance	Episode
	Sydney, Australia	He infiltrates a terrorist cell and betrays his college roommate to the authorities.	"The Greater Good" (1.21)
	Honolulu, HI	As one of the Oceanic 6, he meets the press at a military base west of Honolulu.	"There's No Place Like Home" (4.13)
	Berlin, Germany	He briefly enjoys a romantic relationship with Elsa, initially to gather information about her employer in order to kill him.	"The Economist" (4.3)
Jin Kwon	Namhae, South Korea	Jin is born in this village.	"…And Found" (2.5)
	Seoul, South Korea	He works as a doorman, meets Sun and marries her, and works for Mr. Paik.	"…And Found" (2.5); "…In Translation" (1.17); "The Glass Ballerina" (3.2)
	China	On behalf of Mr. Paik, he takes a baby gift to an important client.	"Ji Yeon" (4.7)
	Los Angeles, CA	He plans to escape Paik's influence and start a new life with Sun there.	"Exodus" (1.24)
	Sydney, Australia	He delivers a package to Paik's associate.	"Exodus" (1.24)

Name	Important Place	Significance	Episode
Sun Kwon	Seoul, South Korea	This is Sun's birthplace and where she attends Seoul National University and meets and marries Jin. Upon her return from the island, she buys controlling interest in her father's company and gives birth to a daughter at Choogdong Hospital.	"…And Found" (2.5); "…In Translation" (1.17); "The Glass Ballerina" (3.2); "There's No Place Like Home" (4.12); "Ji Yeon" (4.7)
	Sydney, Australia	She plans to disappear from the airport.	"Exodus" (1.24)
	Honolulu, HI	As one of the Oceanic 6, she meets the press at a military base west of Honolulu.	"There's No Place Like Home" (4.13)
Libby	Newport Beach, CA	Her boat, the Elizabeth, is registered out of Newport Beach.	"Live Together, Die Alone" (2.23)
	Sydney, Australia	It is unknown why she is there, but she is on Oceanic 815 and confronts Eko at the airport.	"?" (2.21)
	New York, NY	"Ghost" Libby may be real or a drug-induced figment of Michael's mind when he awakens in hospital after a car crash/ suicide attempt.	"Meet Kevin Johnson" (4.8)

Name	Important Place	Significance	Episode
	Fiji	"Kevin" joins the crew of the freighter *Kahana*.	"Meet Kevin Johnson" (4.8)
Ben Linus	Outside Portland, OR	His early birth during his parents' hiking trip leads to his mother's death.	"The Man Behind the Curtain" (3.20)
	Tunisia	Ben teleports into the Sahara Desert. He soon checks into a hotel in Tozeur.	"The Shape of Things to Come" (4.9)
	Tikrit, Iraq	He recruits Sayid as an assassin.	"The Shape of Things to Come" (4.9)
	London, England	He confronts Charles Widmore in his bedroom, and they up the ante in their high-stakes "game." Widmore wants to take back "his" island; Ben plans to kill Penny.	"The Shape of Things to Come" (4.9)
Frank Lapidus	Edenberg, Bahamas	After Frank sees news reports of the discovery of Oceanic 815, he calls the airlines to disagree with the pilot's identification.	"Confirmed Dead" (4.2)
Charlotte Staples Lewis	Essex, England	Charlotte is born there.	"Confirmed Dead" (4.2)

Name	Important Place	Significance	Episode
	Bransgrove, England	She grows up in this town.	"Confirmed Dead" (4.2)
	Kent, England	She completes her undergraduate degree work at university.	"Confirmed Dead" (4.2)
	Oxford University, Oxford, England	She completes her doctoral work.	"Confirmed Dead" (4.2)
	Medenine, Tunisia	She visits an archeo-logical dig and finds a DHARMA Initiative tag near polar bear bones.	"Confirmed Dead" (4.2)
Claire Littleton	Sydney, Australia	This is her birthplace and hometown prior to the crash.	"Raised by Another" (1.10); "Par Avion" (3.12)
	Los Angeles, CA	She plans to give up her baby for adoption there.	"Raised by Another" (1.10)
Walt Lloyd	New York, NY	Walt is born in New York. He lives with his grandmother after his release from the island.	"Special" (1.14); "Meet Kevin Johnson" (4.8)
	Amsterdam, Netherlands	Susan Lloyd takes him there as a baby, when she relocates with a new job.	"Special" (1.14)
	Rome, Italy	Susan Lloyd moves again with her job, taking Walt with her.	"Adrift" (2.2)

Name	Important Place	Significance	Episode
	Sydney, Australia	Susan Lloyd settles with her husband and Walt in Sydney.	"Special" (1.14)
John Locke	Los Angeles, CA	His birthplace is assumed but not specifically mentioned.	
	Portland, OR	Mittelos Bioscience operates a summer science camp to which teenaged Locke, a science fair winner, is invited.	"Cabin Fever" (4.11)
	Possibly Iowa	He lives in a commune for a few months (presumed site).	"Further Instructions" (3.3)
	Tustin, CA	He works as a regional manager for a box company.	"Walkabout" (1.4)
	Mexico	After pushing John out a window, Anthony Cooper escapes to Mexico.	"The Man from Tallahassee" (3.13)
	Melbourne, Australia	He tries to go on a walkabout.	"Walkabout" (1.4)
	Sydney, Australia	He leaves Australia in a wheelchair for the return flight to the U.S.	"Exodus" (1.24)

Name	Important Place	Significance	Episode
	Tallahassee, FL	His father is "taken" from I-10 outside Tallahassee to the box on the island, presumably so John can deal with his daddy issues once and for all.	"The Man from Tallahassee" (3.13)
Bernard Nadler	New York, NY	He meets Rose (presumably he lives in NYC).	"S.O.S." (2.19)
	Niagara Falls, NY	He proposes to Rose.	"S.O.S." (2.19)
	Australia	He takes Rose to Australia in the hope that she'll be cured by Isaac.	"S.O.S." (2.19)
Charlie Pace	Manchester, England	His birthplace is Manchester. DriveShaft first performs at the Night and Day Bar there.	"The Moth" (1.7); "Greatest Hits" (3.21)
	Clitheroe, Lancashire, England	DriveShaft breaks down on the road outside Clitheroe, where they are scheduled to play; Charlie first hears DriveShaft on the radio.	"Greatest Hits" (3.21)
	Dresden	DriveShaft was touring there when niece Megan was born.	"The Moth" (1.7); "Fire + Water" (2.12)
	Finland	DriveShaft completed two tours of Finland.	"The Moth" (1.7)

Name	Important Place	Significance	Episode
	London, England	Liam and Charlie live there during DriveShaft's last days. Charlie later lives there alone and steals from the women he dates. He also plays for money on the city's streets.	"Fire + Water" (2.12); Homecoming" (1.15); "Greatest Hits" (3.21)
	Los Angeles, CA	He plans to return and restart his musical career.	"Born to Run" (1.22)
	Sydney, Australia	He visits Liam to entice him to return to DriveShaft.	"The Moth" (1.7)
Paulo	Brazil	He is born somewhere in Brazil and works as a chef.	"Exposé" (3.14)
	Los Angeles, CA	He plans to relocate and live with girlfriend and accomplice Nikki.	"Exposé" (3.14)
Hugo Reyes (Hurley)	Los Angeles, CA	Hurley is born in LA and lives there throughout his young adulthood. Apparently he opens a Mr. Cluck's franchise there. He returns home to the family mansion, but within months is again a resident at the Santa Rosa Mental Health Facility.	"Numbers" (1.18); "Tricia Tanaka Is Dead" (3.10); "The Beginning of the End" (4.1); "There's No Place Like Home" (4.12)
	Santa Monica, CA	He fishes with his grandfather off the pier.	"Numbers" (1.18)

Name	Important Place	Significance	Episode
	Tustin, CA	He owns a box company there.	"Everybody Hates Hugo" (2.4)
	Las Vegas, NV	His father travels there after abandoning the family.	"Tricia Tanaka Is Dead" (3.10)
	Kalgoorlie, Australia	He visits Sam Toomey's widow to learn about the curse.	"Numbers" (1.18)
	Sydney, Australia	He oversleeps on the day he's flying home to LA.	"Exodus" (1.24)
	Honolulu, HI	As one of the Oceanic 6, he meets the press at a military base west of Honolulu.	"There's No Place Like Home" (4.13)
Ethan Rom	Ontario, Canada	He tells census-taker Hurley that he's from Ontario.	"Raised by Another" (1.10)
	Miami, FL	He lives down the hall from Juliet's sister Rachel.	"Not in Portland" (3.7)
	Portland, OR (or not)	He works with Richard Alpert to bring Juliet "outside Portland" to work with Mittelos Bioscience.	"Left Behind" (3.15)
Danielle Rousseau	Possibly France	She speaks French, but her origins are unknown.	

Name	Important Place	Significance	Episode
	Tahiti	Her research team left from Tahiti.	"Solitary" (1.9)
Shannon Rutherford	Los Angeles, CA	Her birthplace is assumed but not specifically mentioned. She lives there with her father and stepmother; her father dies there.	"Abandoned" (2.6)
	New York, NY	She receives a dance scholarship and hopes to live with or near Boone.	"Abandoned" (2.6)
	Paris, France	She works as a nanny while studying in France for a year.	"Whatever the Case May Be" (1.12); "Abandoned" (2.6)
	Sydney, Australia	She lives with a lover and plans to scam Boone out of money.	"Hearts and Minds" (1.13)
Jack Shephard	Los Angeles, CA	His birthplace is assumed but not specifically mentioned. He becomes a surgeon there and returns home after being rescued, for a time living with Kate and Aaron.	"The Hunting Party" (2.11); "Through the Looking Glass" (3.22); "Eggtown" (4.4); "There's No Place Like Home" (4.12)
	New York, NY	He attends Columbia University Medical School.	"A Tale of Two Cities" (3.1)

Name	Important Place	Significance	Episode
	Phuket, Thailand	He gets tattoos revealing his true nature.	"Stranger in a Strange Land" (3.9)
	Sydney, Australia	He searches for his father, only to learn that he's died in an alley.	"White Rabbit" (1.5)
	Honolulu, HI	As one of the Oceanic 6, he meets the press at a military base west of Honolulu.	"There's No Place Like Home" (4.13)
Miles Straume	Englewood, CA	Miles "exorcises" the spirit of Mrs. Gardner's grandson from her home.	"Confirmed Dead" (4.2)
Charles Widmore	Glasgow, Scotland	Charles meets Desmond upon his release from prison.	"Flashes Before Your Eyes" (3.8)
	London, England	He bids on a journal from the *Black Rock*. Later he has a late-night chat with Ben, who breaks in to his hotel residence.	"The Constant" (4.5); "The Shape of Things to Come" (4.9)
	Thailand	He "buys" bodies to fill the fuselage of an Oceanic airliner presumed to be Oceanic 815.	"Meet Kevin Johnson" (4.8)
	Fiji	His freighter *Kahana* sails from Fiji in an attempt to locate the island.	"Meet Kevin Johnson" (4.8)

In particular, Kate, Sawyer, and Jin seem more closely bound to their early origins. Kate says she's Canadian ("Tabula Rasa," 1.3) but her father taught her how to track in the Washington forests ("All the Best Cowboys Have Daddy Issues," 1.11). Of course, she's also created several aliases, too, so knowing exactly what is truth or fiction may be difficult. Much of Kate's early life seems to take place in Iowa, however, where Midwestern values often seem at odds with Kate's outlook on life.

Iowa has a "heartland" reputation of family values and solid rural living. Although in an increasingly urban, high-tech age the "Midwestern myth" of wholesome, God-fearing people living in harmony with nature often conflicts with reality, *Lost* strips the veneer off this lifestyle; Kate and Sawyer, as well as the people in their lives, aren't as well adjusted, happy, or family oriented as the stereotype would suggest. Cities like Cedar Rapids, reportedly Kate's hometown ("Born to Run," 1.22; "What Kate Did," 2.9), promote events throughout the year designed to bring the family together. Burning dear old dad in the family home isn't socially acceptable behavior.

Cedar Rapids is the City of Five Seasons. Its website illustrates the city's value of appreciating nature as crucial to a happy life: "taking the time to appreciate everyday beauty extends life, almost like an extra season is added to every year. This fifth season affords us time to enjoy all other seasons, and to enjoy life."[53] This type of outdoor appreciation seems appropriate to Kate. Her on-island ability to shinny up trees, hike across rough terrain, and rough it suggest an early preference for being outdoors. She likely developed these tomboyish talents to be more like her adored father, Sgt. Austen, who knows how to survive in enemy territory.

However, the small-town world of diners and farms also likely makes Kate realize just how much her life with mother and "step"-father differed from the ideal close-knit, loving Midwestern family. Although Kate seems to have learned about the Catholic Church somewhere along the line ("Left Behind," 3.15) and knows a lot about sainted female martyrs, her sense of justice became twisted. To give her mother a better life, Kate takes it upon herself to kill her mother's abusive husband, not understanding just how much she loves him and why she can't forgive her for murdering him.

Kate's Midwestern roots tie her to traditional American family values while pointing out just how off-kilter her family life has been. Armed with outdoor survival skills and an understanding of small-town life, before her post-crash life in Los Angeles, Kate seems a good match for Sawyer, who comes from a similar working class background.

After her trial ("Eggtown," 4.4), however, Kate settles into life as a financially comfortable suburban mom. When live-in love Jack proposes, Kate seems to have the "perfect family" denied her as a child. She becomes determined to maintain a stable, loving home for "son" Aaron. Jack's increasing suspicion of Kate's activities while he's at work causes a rift in the relationship, forcing Kate to banish Jack from her and Aaron's life ("There's No Place Like Home," 4.12–4.13). Despite Kate's real childhood lacking wholesome, Midwestern family values, she has clear ideas of what the ideal family should be. The more she adapts to Jack's suburban lifestyle, the further she moves from common ground with good ol' boy Sawyer.

A letter to the original "Sawyer" bears a Knoxville, Tennessee, postmark from the U.S. Bicentennial in 1976 ("Confidence Man," 1.8). Although James (Sawyer) Ford may not have lived in the city, he tells others that he's from Tennessee ("Outlaws," 2.16). His survival skill level (i.e., inability to clean fish or track game) suggests that he may have watched television and read books instead of spending a lot of time outdoors ("Stranger in a Strange Land," 3.9). He provides a glimpse of his early life in "The Brig" (3.19), when he finally confronts Locke's father, "Tom Sawyer," whom he blames for his parents' deaths; he reminds the traveling con man of the woman he seduced in Alabama. Whether Alabama or Tennessee receives James Ford's allegiance, he clearly sees himself as a Southerner who can slather on the charm and suggestively deepen his drawl when the need arises.

Sawyer's Southern gentleman persona comes forth when Claire and Aaron need a protector. He tries to warn Claire before New Otherton is attacked ("The Shape of Things to Come," 4.9) and watches over her and Aaron as long as possible, even caring for the baby after Claire disappears into the jungle ("Cabin Fever," 4.11). Like Kate the product of a dysfunctional family, Sawyer reveals the positive side of the gold ol' boy charmer with his need to protect women and children.

Jin's hometown fishing village, Namhae, South Korea, prepared him for an isolated island life ("...And Found," 2.5). As the son of a fisherman, he quickly returns to the once-familiar jobs of creating nets, knowing where and how to fish, and cleaning the catch. Although his desire to have a more affluent life led him into the darker side of business, on the island he seems content to have the type of life he once left behind. Ironically, Sun is leading the life her mother always feared for her daughter—being the wife of a fisherman ("Catch-22," 3.17)—but this lifestyle brings her and Jin closer together. When Sun, sans Jin, reclaims her wealthy cosmopolitan life in Seoul ("There's No Place Like Home," 4.13; "Ji

Yeon," 4.7), she ironically becomes isolated. Of the other Oceanic survivors, only Hurley visits, and Sun quickly estranges herself from her parents. Life in a fishing village, even on a mysterious island, turns out to be the more emotionally comfortable home for Sun.

Common Destinations

During *Lost's* four seasons, references have been made to every continent: Asia (Afghanistan, China, Iraq, South Korea, Thailand [Siam], Tunisia), Africa (Egypt, Mozambique, Nigeria, Uganda), Antarctica, Australia/Pacific (Australia, Bali, Fiji, Madagascar, [the fictitious] Mumbata, Sumba, Tahiti), Europe (Finland, France, Germany, Italy, Portugal, U.K. [England, Scotland], Ukraine [former USSR]), North America and Atlantic (U.S., Canada, Mexico, Bahamas), and South America (Brazil). Almost everyone who lives or lived on the island came from somewhere else; this is a well-traveled group.

For all the diversity on *Lost*, with characters coming from around the globe and representing different regions and cultures even within the same country of origin, the world does seem to be a very small place. Many characters lived in or visited the same cities as the people with whom they end up sharing an island. Some common destinations include Sydney, Los Angeles, New York, Miami, Paris, and London.

Sydney, of course, is the common denominator for the survivors of Oceanic 815. Although Claire leaves home when she boards the flight, everyone else's business has been completed, although not satisfactorily. Most characters are nearing closure for some critical point in their lives and hovering on the brink of a new direction: Claire plans to give up her baby for adoption; Jack's immediate concern is his father's funeral; Jin wants to escape his father-in-law's clutches and disappear with Sun; Charlie must find a new job now that DriveShaft officially is dead; Hurley must live with the curse of the numbers or give away his money; Shannon has to start over yet again in Los Angeles; Locke must finally come to grips with the limitations of his wheelchair; Walt and Michael begin to establish their relationship; Kate has lost her freedom; Paulo and Sawyer kill men, but only Paulo believes he'll now have a better life. Sydney, with its disappointments and problems, is what these people leave behind, but they have no idea where their new beginning is about to take place.

Los Angeles and nearby cities Tustin, Newport Beach, Englewood, and Santa Monica also figure prominently in backstories, especially for the Oceanic 6, Ana Lucia, Boone, and Shannon. These characters have different socioeconomic backgrounds, and their backstories include diverse backdrops. Hurley initially works for and then owns a Mr. Cluck fast-food restaurant. As one of the Oceanic 6, he comes home to the family mansion but has trouble coping with his post-island life and returns to the Santa Rosa Mental Health Facility, where he spends time chatting with dead friend Charlie ("The Beginning of the End," 4.1). Jack's backstories feature everything from hospitals to upper-class homes to schoolyards to AA meetings, all around the city. After his rescue from the island, he returns to work at St. Sebastian Hospital and shares a home with Kate, who is confined to California as part of her court judgment ("Eggtown," 4.4). Sayid and Nadia attend Hurley's welcome home/birthday bash before they marry and live in the area ("There's No Place Like Home," 4.13). After Nadia is killed in a car accident, Sayid fails to settle down again ("The Shape of Things to Come," 4.9). Locke's resume includes stints in a toy store, an office, and in the field as a home inspector. His funeral at the Hoff/Drawler

Funeral Home attracts both Jack and Ben ("There's No Place Like Home," 4.13). Police officer Ana Lucia wants to patrol rougher neighborhoods than her partner and mother select for her post-recovery return to the job ("Collision," 2.8). Hurley meets her former partner during his interrogation after a car chase; the officer asks Hurley if he knew Ana Lucia ("The Beginning of the End," 4.1). Boone and Shannon share a wealthy upbringing, although Shannon's fortunes change with her father's death. The variety of locations representing Los Angeles provides a better picture of a city as complex as the lives of these characters.

Miami is another city well-populated by future island dwellers. Kate and Juliet both lived there, though Kate's Miami life seems far removed from Juliet's. Kevin's Dade County patrol car provides a tip-off that the couple lives somewhere in the city ("I Do," 3.6). Juliet and Edmund Burke work at the fictitious Miami Central University ("Not in Portland," 3.7), and Juliet's sister Rachel lives in a "generic" apartment (with Ethan Rom just down the hall). Only the headline of the September 22, 2004, *Miami Journal* (not the city's *Miami Herald*) specifically lists this location ("One of Us," 3.16).

Paris is temporary home to Sayid, who pretends to be a Syrian sous chef until his true identity is discovered by an Iraqi couple ("Enter 77," 3.11). For a year Shannon lives in Paris, where she learns French from the family for whom she is a nanny ("Whatever the Case May Be," 1.12; "Abandoned," 2.6). Again, the location seems more generic in the choice of restaurants and homes, rather than specifically Parisian. Like Sydney, Paris doesn't hold many pleasant memories for these characters, who eventually move on once more.

London becomes a popular home base for several characters. Charlie and Liam settle there as DriveShaft's popularity dwindles;

eventually Liam leaves Charlie behind to fend for himself in a rundown flat ("Fire + Water," 2.12). Busker Charlie meets Desmond on a London street ("Flashes Before Your Eyes," 3.8) and, when a downpour interrupts his performance one afternoon, ends up saving Nadia from a mugger ("Greatest Hits," 3.21). Although Desmond isn't especially pleased with his London flat, Penny leaves her upscale Knightsbridge home to move in with him—a "history" that changes outcomes as Desmond changes his future ("Flashes Before Your Eyes," 3.8). After their breakup, Penny returns to a much more upscale Cheyne Park neighborhood ("The Constant," 4.5). Mr. Eko's life as a priest truly begins in London, where he takes Yemi's place to study ("?" 2.22). Sun travels to London to confront Charles Widmore and make him a potential ally ("There's No Place Like Home," 4.13).

Lost allows the audience to travel around the globe with characters and takes care to infuse enough local culture that international viewers accept the way non-U.S. locations are presented on screen. As with other aspects of telling the story, global geography celebrates cultural diversity while reminding characters and viewers that no matter our place of origin, we are all connected.

GEOGRAPHIC CONNECTIONS

Lost is well known for its labyrinthine connections among characters, whose backstories resemble an increasingly dense web of pre-crash experiences that bind them together. Place, however, unites some character pairs more than others and in more than passing ways—multiple places in common provide an extra layer of connection.

Kate and Sawyer, for example, not only share similarities in working class, down-home, troubled family backgrounds, but they also have been in the same places. That may not sound strange for large cities like Los Angeles or Sydney, which are home bases or flight-departure points for many *Lost* characters; however, smaller cities like Cedar Rapids or Sioux City, IA, might be more of a stretch in credibility. Nevertheless, *Lost* shows Sawyer being served breakfast by Kate's mother in a diner ("The Long Con," 2.13). Sawyer tells lover/mark Cassidy to wait for him at Sioux City's Sage Flower Motel, but he has no intention of meeting her there. Cassidy, however, soon meets Kate, who returns home in an attempt to talk with her mother. Cassidy and Kate form a working partnership of two women outside the law, not completely trusting but understanding each other. Ironically, Kate suggests that Cassidy turn in the man who impregnated her, conned her out of her money, then left her ("Left Behind," 3.15).

Sawyer and Kate also share common destinations in Florida: Tallahassee and Tampa. Sawyer reveals to Jack his less-than-discriminating love life, which brought him a bad case of "sunburn" during his stay in Tallahassee ("Lockdown," 2.17). Kate's attempt to buy a ticket to Tallahassee is thwarted when the marshal takes her into custody ("What Kate Did," 2.9). (Locke's father, the "Man from Tallahassee" [3.13], is the original Sawyer, creating another Tallahassee connection for James "Sawyer" Ford.) He angrily refers to the botched "Tampa job" in a confrontation with his former partner ("Confidence Man," 1.8). Could Sawyer or his partner be the fugitive Kate's (Monica's) husband Kevin tracks to Tampa ("I Do," 3.6)?[54]

Although Kate and Sawyer (so far) don't seem to have been in the same place at the same time before the crash, they do have some common connecting points and people. Because Iowa and Florida aren't geographically close, *Lost* may be making a point about their being "destined" to be together, although Sawyer doesn't turn up in Kate's flashforwards in Seasons Three and Four.

Sayid and Shannon are another pair of lovers who share cities, even if they don't run into each other before their first fateful meeting at the Sydney airport. Shannon works as a nanny in Paris, becoming her employer's lover before the year is out ("Whatever the Case May Be," 1.12; "Abandoned," 2.6). Sayid takes on a false identity while working as a chef in a Parisian restaurant, but he is found out by the husband of a woman Sayid once tortured ("Enter 77," 3.11). Shannon later moves to Sydney but again winds up in a dead-end affair ("Hearts and Minds," 1.13); Sayid is brought to Sydney to infiltrate and stop a terrorist group ("The Greater Good," 1.21). Although Paris and Sydney are large cities with many foreign guests and residents, more than coincidence seems to have brought these two together.

Desmond shares pre-island connections—or maybe multiple timelines—with several people who later inhabit the *Lost* island. A time-confusing backstory sequence in "Flashes Before Your Eyes" (3.8) shows Desmond's and Charlie's brief meeting in London, where Desmond recognizes Charlie while he plays guitar for money outside a tube station. He also remembers meeting Jack in Los Angeles ("Man of Science, Man of Faith," 2.1) and had an almost immediate—and profitable—run-in with Libby moments after he arrived in LA ("Live Together, Die Alone," 2.23). In 1996, he visits Daniel Faraday at Oxford University while on a quest to learn more about time travel ("The Constant," 4.5). (Oxford is also a connecting point for Charlotte and Daniel. He taught physics there, and she earned her doctorate in a different discipline.)

Lost prides itself on bringing together characters in unlikely places (e.g., Christian Shephard is father both to Jack [Los

Angeles] and Claire [Sydney]), but some encounters are simply humorous or less consequential. Sawyer, for example, literally runs into Christian Shephard as he opens a car door ("Two for the Road," 2.20). Places that keep popping up in backstories, however, may indicate more significant links between characters.

In keeping with its reputation for providing a wide range of perspectives with its always-changing cast of international characters, *Lost* emphasizes the idea that people must "live together or die alone" by setting storylines in geographically separated locations. The series does more than simply label a character as Scottish or Korean; it provides cultural details and visual documentation of each character's background and experiences in a specific locale. *Lost* builds its characters' (and the series') credibility by choosing visually stimulating images that provide clues to the plot while taking the audience on a virtual tour of the world.

HAWAII AS A CHARACTER

Unlike most U.S. television series, which are filmed primarily in Los Angeles and, more often than not, in a studio, *Lost* makes the most of its Hawaiian location. Oahu, masquerading as a difficult-to-find island (or two), offers just about every possibility for "global" locations—whether in a residential area, on the beach, in warehouses, on airfields, around the business district, as well as in studios geared to television production. With the right location and careful set dressing, *Lost*'s crew can create the appearance of a Thai street festival, a London neighborhood, rural Iowa, a Nigerian village, the Sahara Desert, or the Sydney airport. The red-and-white crew parking signs alert the curious that *Lost* is being filmed nearby, but locals familiar with seeing *Lost* filmed on location are almost blasé about seeing the caravan of trucks pull into their neighborhoods or close off a section of beach.

Although residents pride themselves on being friendly but maintaining distance from "their" celebrities, *Lost*'s increased popularity sometimes poses problems for the cast and crew, who want to keep the series' secrets quiet and also value their privacy. In January 2007 the production estimated at least a half-million-dollar loss in delayed filming caused by Matthew (Jack) Fox's and Dominic (Charlie) Monaghan's fans trying to get on set.[55] Because *Lost* often films in public areas, word of where the crews are filming each week spreads quickly in the community and via the Internet. Friendly but persuasive guards do a good job of keeping ardent fans away from scenes being filmed, but interest in the series is high.

Stories about paparazzi horrify the locals nearly as much they do the actors. Residents of Oahu seem appalled at that type of behavior; their encounters with the actors have been, for the most part, pleasant, low key, and off-set. Almost everyone has some type of *Lost* story: tour guide Malia exchanged hellos with Dominic Monaghan at Piha Point one afternoon; university teacher LeiLani spotted Terry O'Quinn (Locke) at a North Shore beach, and some of the school's buildings stood in for Tikrit during Nadia's funeral; Waikiki bus driver Monica and her husband chatted with Daniel Dae Kim (Jin) and Jorge Garcia (Hurley) at a Thai restaurant; the counter man at Giovanni's shrimp truck, near North Shore, mentioned that Jorge Garcia sometimes stops there on his way to work—and cast members had signed the truck (a local tradition of filling every available space on the shrimp truck with signatures and favorable comments about the food). *Lost* has become a fixture on Oahu, and with the rising popularity of cinematic tourism, fans who visit Hawaii want to see where their favorite characters live and die.

Any trip to Oahu is worthwhile for its breathtaking scenery and diversity within a very drivable distance. Mountains compete with black, white, or brown sand beaches; busy Honolulu is the opposite of smaller towns around the rest of the island. Sections of Wailua, complete with red dirt and hundred-year-old former sugar mill, stand in for Nigeria. Hurley's family, as well as Kate, "live" in Kahala. The rocky shores and long stretches of beaches toward the North Shore, where *Lost* set up temporary camps during the first four seasons, truly seem like deserted oases in a crowded world. Fans who want to "get *Lost*" on the island really are only limited by the number of days they want to spend tracking down locations from the first four seasons, and they'll find at least a few former film locations in almost any direction they travel.

Because space limits our photos in this chapter, we have included a tantalizing few (different from those in the book's first edition). These pictures might help fans decide where and what they want to visit during a Hawaiian holiday. Another good site for virtual traveling is www.lostvirtualtour.com, a fan site that gathers tips from residents about "sightings." It may not be foolproof, but it explains what to see at the location and how the scene was filmed there. Recent magazines about Hawaii also feature former shooting locations.[56]

The Kualoa Ranch, a short drive outside Honolulu, has been the location of many *Lost* scenes. Because the ranch is on privately owned land, only the ranch's ATV and horseback tours, and Ed Kos' Hummer tours, can travel into the *Lost* valley. Kualoa Ranch's valleys and hills, as well as the nearby Tropical Farms and Macadamia Nut Farm (also known as Moli'i Gardens) and fish pond (the perfect place to sink a sub), have provided backdrops for numerous television series and films, including *Jurassic Park* and *Pearl Harbor*.

During Season Two, *Lost* crew members turned a building at Moli'i Gardens into a Nigerian bar. A forked tree nearby became the ideal spot to perch the wreckage of Yemi's plane. Season Three scenes shot on the ranch, for example, involved the Others' submarine, the deadly sonic fence, a Korean fishing village, the castaways' graveyard, and the tree where the mysterious parachutist lands. Hurley and Charlie took their joyride in the DHARMA Initiative's van on Kualoa property. Season Four features bunkers as well as jungle locations. Kualoa Ranch properties provide a wealth of filming options within a few miles spanning coastal waters and jungle. More *Lost* locations are added to the tour as the ranch receives permission to let fans know exactly which scenes were shot at different locations. (See www.kualoaranch.com for more information about tours and a history of the property.)

The "Nigerian" bar visited by warlord Eko ("The 23rd Psalm," 2.10)

Fish Pond dock, most famously seen in "The Man from Tallahassee" (3.13)

However fans decide to divide their time or interests in finding *Lost* locations, there is something for everyone. Just a reminder: Many scenes are filmed on private property, including near-beach and residential areas or homes. Although beaches are public space, the tree line becomes the border of private property.

OUTSIDE HONOLULU

Honolulu and the Waikiki Beach area provide lots for tourists to do and see, but those who want a better sense of Oahu and a true feeling of how it feels to be "*Lost*" also need to travel outside the city and around the island. Close to North Shore, Police Beach, better known to residents of Oahu as Papa'iloa, is easily recognizable as the castaways' campground in Seasons Two through Four; almost every possible camera angle has been used along the beach, among the rocks, and through the trees. A walk around the beach, for example, quickly leads to a lightly wooded area, where the castaways run from the monster during its early appearances. The grove can be seen from the path near Hale'iwa Beach Park's parking lot, but the site itself is on private land.

Filming in such public spaces provides benefits for *Lost* cinematic tourists. During the writers' strike in January 2008, fans visiting the beach could clearly see the castaways' camp. Although the huts were wrapped in plastic to preserve them from visitors and the weather, the camp looked much as it does on TV, although it seemed eerily quiet with only surf sounds in the background. Near the encampment stands Mr. Eko's church, also the site of Locke's vision quest.

Police (or Papa'iloa) Beach

On the other side of the island, the *Honolulu Advertiser*'s production facilities in Kapolei occasionally become Mittelos Bioscience, although the location clearly is "Not in Portland" (3.7). The gates leading to the front entrance were featured during Juliet's farewell to her sister.

Castaway camp, January 2008

Mr. Eko's church

Because *Lost* locations encompass just about every part of the island, a day trip can easily include some *Lost* highlights and allow time to enjoy the beaches along the way.

Around Honolulu

Fans with limited time or those staying in Waikiki may want to visit a section of Honolulu's Chinatown and the nearby business district to check out the former filming sites there. A good place to start is Nuuanu Avenue, home to two Irish pubs: Murphy's and O'Toole's, which are across the street from each other. O'Toole's has provided the setting for several episodes, including Desmond's Season Three backstory ("Flashes Before Your Eyes," 3.8). Although he hears the jukebox playing "Make Your Own Kind of Music," O'Toole's patrons more often watch television above the bar—the *Lost* crew brought in the jukebox. However, fans can sit at Desmond's table. Charlie or Locke fans may prefer to visit Murphy's, where Locke meets his father for a drink ("Lockdown," 2.17). Charlie chats up soon-to-be-girlfriend Lucy and her friends ("Homecoming," 2.8), while putting into play his and drug-supplier Tommy's scam. The alley outside also became a focal point for scenes between Charlie and Tommy. *Lost* creatively uses geographically close sites to represent widely divergent places. Within a few blocks of these pubs, fans might recognize the bank Kate "robbed" of a miniature airplane, the gate where Desmond stopped to read a military-recruitment poster, and the alley where Rose and Bernard first meet in Boston.

A nearby Honolulu landmark, the First Hawaiian Center, is the tallest building in Hawaii and home to a museum's art gallery as well as corporations' headquarters. To *Lost* fans, however, the inside is more easily recognized than the famous exterior. Pregnant Sun slowly walks up the staircase leading to her father's office (or the first floor of contemporary museum exhibits) in Season Four's "There's No Place Like Home" (4.12). The wall at the top of the staircase is part of Mr. Paik's office (also shown in "The Glass Ballerina," 3.2). The downtown area includes many other former

Lost shooting locations within easy driving distance of the business district, Chinatown, or Aloha Tower.

Mr. Paik's (soon to be Sun's?) office

Visitors with a little more time should check out the Honolulu Convention Center. The interior is often dressed to resemble different sections of the Sydney airport, and the escalators have been shown in the background of several airport-based scenes, as well as featured in Locke's vision ("Further Instructions," 3.2). Just around the corner is the Ala Wai Canal. Sun and Jin meet while walking along the canal ("…And Found," 2.5), and Michael says goodbye to toddler Walt while seated at one of the benches along the walkway ("Adrift," 2.2).

Lost frequently features Honolulu churches, and two of the most photographed are St. Andrews Priory and Parke Chapel, which stand next to each other on Queen Emma Square. In addition to the churches' interiors, the covered walkway outside the chapel has been prominently featured in several episodes. Charlie finds Liam waiting for him in the chapel ("The Moth," 1.7), and the two continue discussing DriveShaft as they stroll through the walkway from the chapel. Crossing the courtyard in front of the arched walkway, Desmond carries cases of wine to Penny's van ("Catch-22," 3.17), although an appropriately rural backdrop is blue- or green-screened behind Penny to hide the churches' parking lot. The churches become the monastery, home to Mariah Vineyards. Also along this famous walkway, Desmond accosts Daniel Faraday after his physics class at Oxford University ("The Constant," 4.5). Next door, St. Andrews Priory also serves as "Priest" Eko's London sanctuary ("?" 2.22).

Walkway leading to Parke Chapel

St. Andrews Priory

(Parke Chapel to the right, with the walkways between the buildings)

A tour of Honolulu, with its beautiful architecture and blend of traditional Hawaiian culture with Western and Eastern influences, should be a priority for *Lost* fans. Not only will they find locations "as seen on TV," but even a quick tour of the city leads to a deeper appreciation for the diversity and cultural history of Oahu.

THE ART OF SELECTING LOCATIONS AND DRESSING SETS

Lost does an excellent job of selecting locations and then dressing the sets and creating the right mood so that, for example, downtown Honolulu becomes London, Seoul, Los Angeles, or Sydney. What may be surprising to fans is just how many ordinary buildings—homes, churches, supermarkets, hotels, high-rise offices—can take on a very different atmosphere with the right decoration and camera angles. Honolulu's rich culture offers a wide range of architectural styles, historic and modern buildings, and restaurants of varied cuisines; the island offers streetscapes, beaches for sunrises or sunsets, rugged peaks, and lush jungle. There are vast opportunities to transform these different styles into the location the script calls for, and, when all else fails, interiors can be shot in studio.

Lost often has to capture the exotic and the quirky in order to provide audiences with a visual experience unlike most viewers' everyday reality; Hawaii, Oahu in particular, offers the ambiance and variety needed to tell such a complex story. If *Lost* was only filmed in Los Angeles, the experience for viewers and the richness of the cinematography would be very different. In 2006, producer Jean Higgins emphasized that "*Lost is* Hawaii, pure and simple… You don't have these looks on the mainland."[57] Although the island "disappears" during the Season Four finale, *Lost* likely will return to it in Seasons Five and Six, much to the relief of fans and residents who enjoy the tropical locale as part of the story. *Lost*'s location, sets, and careful attention to the details within them take fans to other times and places and bring audiences into the story.

Dedication to detail is a trait of production designer Zack Grobler and location manager Jim Triplett. They spend hours before each episode finding just the right locations and then creating the visual feast that renders each setting realistic and memorable; "creating the perfect atmosphere is the most important part of the show that viewers seldom observe."[58] Triplett's many years in Hawaii pay off for *Lost*; he knows where to find likely locations for just about anyplace the characters need to be.

Filming *Lost* is an expensive proposition, and each year renews the question of whether the series should move permanently to the mainland for less expensive per-episode costs. If cost issues someday cause the series to retreat to Los Angeles for good, fans, Oahu, and *Lost* will end up losing. For now, however, characters still plan on being *Lost* on the island, even if their flashforward futures are on the mainland or very different, highly cosmopolitan islands.

GIVING BACK TO THE COMMUNITY

The *Lost* cast and producers often try to give back to the community by signing autographs for fundraisers, discussing film and television on panels at film festivals, and attending local events. In September 2005, the cast lined up to sign autographs and pose for pictures to raise money for Hurricane Katrina victims.[59] The state's film festival keeps growing in popularity each year, and *Lost* cast members usually participate in a panel or two.[60] For the first few years of production, hosting a season's first new episode at Sunset on the Beach in Waikiki was another way to say thank you to the many people involved even peripherally with *Lost*. Fans lined up to meet the actors, and cast, crew, and fans then viewed the premiere (a few days before the episode was broadcast nationally) on a gigantic screen on the beach. Although the writers' strike (and thus the return of many *Lost* cast members to the mainland) meant that the Season Four premiere was canceled, fans hope that future seasons will see the return of this event. These activities not only promote the series and actors but help foster events important to the community.

The series' creators and producers also help promote their profession by providing on-set internships for students at the University of Hawaii—Manoa's Academy for Creative Media. In this way, *Lost* paves the way for the next generation to work with visual media.[61] *Lost* has become a part of Hawaii just as much as it has become home to the cast and crew and, at least virtually, fans.

CHAPTER SIX

PLAYING GAMES

Lost fans love to play games, just like the castaways or their island "hosts." Like Locke, some viewers prefer the tried-and-true, such as backgammon or board games like Mousetrap or Operation. These strategy games are slower paced but require lots of thought and, to win the board games, patience and dexterity, all traits that Locke apparently has cultivated over the years. The more physical types, like Sawyer, enjoy a rousing game of ping pong, although poker is a suitable alternative for those quiet afternoons on the beach. Ben likes role-playing games with some unexpected mental twists—a real life D&D, even if the "dragon" doesn't like sonic fences. In this spirit, several toymakers and gamers have developed a wide range of products, all centering on *Lost*'s propensity for intrigue, danger, and mystery—online role-playing games (RPGs), a videogame, "strategy" board games, and puzzles.

Beginning in 2006, multiple companies working in various niches of the game industry began to release products marketed to *Lost*'s savvy, Internet-loving fandom. More games, including the much-anticipated videogame, are promised in the near future. The following games indicate only a part of the evolving, increasingly numerous adventures that fans living off the island can play (especially during long hiatuses between new seasons).

A Puzzling Mystery

TDC Games, the maker of four *Lost* puzzles, posted a spoiler warning: "Do not assemble any puzzle unless you want exclusive new insight into TV's most puzzling hit drama."[62] Former *Lost* writer Javier Grillo-Marxuach "wrote" the puzzles, providing that authentic touch for TDC's product. Anyone who has put one together knows how challenging it can be; many pieces look remarkably similar, and the pattern often is hard to discern—just like *Lost*. (One of us spent an entire holiday assembling Puzzle #1: The Hatch, whose picture turned out to reveal, well, not as many secrets as anticipated but did include attractive photos of Desmond and Charlie.) Each 1,000-piece puzzle, the last released early in October 2006, emphasizes a group or theme within *Lost*: #1: The Hatch, #2: The Others, #3: The Numbers, #4: Before the Crash (illustrating connections among characters). Fans ideally solve all four to find greater meaning from the collection than individual puzzles.

These puzzles give an interesting twist to an old format and are highly appropriate to *Lost*. Puzzles are time consuming to piece together in order to see the "big picture," an apt metaphor for *Lost*. Damon Lindelof and Carlton Cuse often refer to the remainder of the series (Seasons Four through Six) as filling in the frame with pieces to solve the puzzling mystery; the questions have been posed, and the remaining episodes provide the answers. As with *Lost*, puzzle fans may think they have a section figured out only to discover that the pieces don't quite fit as expected. In a press release, TDC Vice President Sandra Bergeson promised that "[a]ssembling the puzzles is just the first step. Just when you think you've uncovered the big secret, you have only just begun."[63]

Following a rumor, fans at About.com's *Lost* site suggested using a black light to look at the completed puzzles for more information,[64] only to learn that the back of each puzzle has glow-in-the-dark information similar to that found on the hatch's blast-door map. Each puzzle provides more of the message, which then must be decoded by piecing together individual letters from directions to chapters and lines within *The Turn of the Screw*, a novel seen in "Orientation" (2.3).

The problem with providing a series of puzzles promising "secrets" is that the series quickly (in relative terms) outpaces whatever is revealed in the puzzles' imagery. Because *Lost* fans regularly network and share just about everything (spoilers be damned) on the Internet, keeping the "big picture" a secret also is challenging. Not long after the puzzles were released, fans shared photos to help others work the puzzles or simply see what they revealed.[65]

Even when the final message was deciphered—which did, as rumored, require fans to work all four puzzles and decode a complex message in glow-in-the-dark letters on the back—script supervisor Gregg Nations noted that the information was created by people stuck for long periods in the hatch; perhaps their mental state or limited knowledge clouded any clues they could provide.[66] Thus, any "secrets" provided by the puzzles might be highly suspect. By the conclusion of Season Three, the information provided by the puzzles seems rather inconsequential; many fans have previously speculated what the puzzles reveal as "canon." Like all *Lost* information, that gleaned from puzzles has a short shelf life in the ever-changing "big picture" of the series, but playing along—and sharing clues with like-minded fans who enjoy cracking the code—provides hours of enjoyment.

Those fans who missed the "game" in progress still can enjoy the puzzles' cool factor by figuring out the clues themselves, alone or with the guidance of sites revealing how to find the hidden message. The puzzles are simply interesting to solve and see, and several viewers have created puzzle-posters by gluing a back to the completed picture. Perhaps Puzzle #4 is the best "poster" in the bunch, because it boasts photos of all major cast members and several recurring characters, showing the many links among the castaways who boarded Oceanic 815.

THE *LOST* STRATEGY

A role-playing board game, which debuted in October 2006, provides as many twists as the series. The man behind the game, Keith Tralins, has a long history of creating video games, and the *Lost* board game (his first venture in this format) requires players to develop strategy as complex as anything found online or as the series itself. Tralin's company, MegaGigaOmniCorp, worked with Cardinal Industries to create the game. All characters, equipment, and locations come from Seasons One and Two.

Fans have compared the *Lost* game to chess and Magic, but Tralins thinks a better analogy is Talisman, a favorite during his university days: "I didn't care if it took three days to play with all the expansions, it was just so awesome to play it and pull an all-nighter...I wanted to recreate that feeling, which is the same feeling I get when I watch *Lost*."[67] A long-time fan of the series, Tralins created an early online *Lost* game, which has since been replaced. His familiarity with games, plus his interest in *Lost* and previous experience creating a game based on J.J. Abrams' pre-*Lost* hit, *Alias*, made him a natural choice for developing a multi-layered "survival" scenario.

Playing the game might best be compared to a combination of two episode titles: "Live Together, Die Alone" and "Every Man for Himself." Some fans prefer the strategy of working as a group to solve challenges, whereas others try to outwit everyone else. Regardless of players' choice of strategy, the game allows only one "winner," much like *Survivor*. The game provides players with multiple variations on the "*Lost* story" and requires a steep learning curve. Although early fan reviews were positive, the game's reliance on elements like Fate, character, equipment, location cards, characters' power levels, and a lengthy rule set can be daunting to first-time players.

Again, Tralins and fans come to the rescue with handy FAQ lists, forums to discuss rules and game play, a downloadable rule book, and a walkthrough for new players at the board game's website.[68] The game's positive reviews and inclusion on 2006 holiday lists, such as *People*'s gift guide, gave it immediate attention. Although little new has been added since late 2006, such a strategy-reliant game, involving multiple players, should have greater longevity than puzzles or even strictly "by-the-episode" mobile or videogames. Plus, fans have to love a game with cards labeled Internal Bleeding and Channeling the Dead.

VIDEO AND MOBILE GAMES

Fans waited a long time for Ubisoft Montreal's *Lost* videogame, entitled *Lost: Via Domus*, which Lindelof assured gamers was "very impressive." The game took over a year for post-production before its early 2008 release.[69] As Joystiq questioned in its report shortly after the podcast, "is developer Ubisoft Montreal focusing more time and effort on delivering a title whose graphics are on par with our expectations for the newest generation of console?"[70] Late in July 2007, Ubisoft issued a press release with more details about the game. Players become Oceanic 815 crash survivors who interact with the series' characters; gamers must "confront [their] dark past, seek redemption and ultimately find a way home."[71] A thirty-second trailer of the game was released at Comic Con 2007. Opening on a dark screen, the audible sound of whispering fills the watcher's ears—followed by shots of Sawyer reading on the beach, Jack carrying a torch, and Locke puzzling over the hatch computer. The realistic graphics and tidbits from the text of the series (DHARMA logos, the mural from the hatch, and the sounds of the monster in the background) promise a game loaded with content that every *Lost* fan can spend hours pouring over.

When the game hit the market, fans rushed to purchase and play, most with high expectations for the long-awaited new release. The game opens with the Oceanic 815 crash. Realistic action, sound, and graphics invite the players to immerse themselves in the *Lost* island's surroundings. After the crash, the lead character, called the "Photojournalist," awakes (with a camera view of his hazel eye opening) to realize he has amnesia. He's charged with figuring out the mystery of his past by taking snapshots with a camera of flashbacks.

While the game took an age to develop and was eagerly purchased by *Lost* fans, many later complained about the brief duration of the game. For its high U.S. sticker price ($60) and an average time-to-beat of 6 hours, it's easy to see why fans were less than satisfied with the long awaited *Lost* video game.

Gameloft offers a mobile game that allows players first to help save people in the aftermath of the crash (Level 1, shown on

the demo at www.gameloft.com/lost-mobile-game/demo/demo_
us.html) and, at higher levels of play, explore the beach, jungle,
hatch, *Black Rock*, and other typical island locations. *Lost*: The
Mobile Game, announced in 2006 and made available in early
2007, features lots of scenarios from Seasons One and Two.[72]
Gamers role play as Jack as they go about typical survival tasks
ranging from setting up camp to avoiding the island's monsters.
Gameloft promises that "the island is calling," and fans owning
most brand name mobile phones (a list is provided at the game site)
can answer the call to adventure.

Gameloft partnered with Touchstone and ABC to develop
products for both *Lost* and *Desperate Housewives*, promising a series
of mobile games beginning in 2007. Michael Guillemot, Gameloft's
president, recognizes the potential market: "We are excited to develop
and deliver games based on these shows to over 1 billion mobile users
worldwide."[73] This move, along with ABC's plan to continue offering
mobisodes and downloads of regular-length episodes via mobile
phones, helps *Lost* corner a huge part of the fan marketplace; more
"viewers" are watching episodes through media other than weekly
television broadcasts. Making *Lost* available in a variety of formats,
from episodes to games, shows that the series' creators clearly know
how to play the marketing game.

In late May 2007, just as Season Three ended, Gameloft
introduced a version of its mobile game for iPod, with an upgrade
in visuals. Instead of the phone version's castaway drawings and
written dialogue, the iPod version relies on cast photos and
their TV dialogue to make the game that much more "real." A
strength—or weakness, depending on the fan—is the game's strict
adherence to TV canon. One review notes that the structure
makes a player "more of a puppeteer than a gamer, putting hero

Jack through the paces dictated by show scribes,"[74] but the game, developed by *Lost*'s writers, does offer more details to supplement episodes re-enacted in the game. Although gamers not familiar with *Lost* will be "spoiled" to the series' plot, die-hard *Lost* fans are the more likely players, and knowledge of the episodes' plot twists can actually help gamers survive on the virtual island.

CHAPTER SEVEN

BEHIND THE SCENES

LOST ACTORS

Adewale Akinnuoye-Agbaje (1967–). *Lost* character: Mister Eko. **You might recognize him as** Simon Adebisi in *Oz* and from roles in such movies as *Get Rich or Die Tryin'*, *The Bourne Identity*, *The Mummy Returns*, *Ace Ventura: When Nature Calls*, and *Congo*.

Sam Anderson. *Lost* character: Bernard Nadler. **You might recognize him as** Holling Manners in *Angel* or from numerous roles in movies (*Critters 2*, *The Puppet Masters*, *Airplane 2*) and TV series (*CSI: NY*, *Cold Case*, *Medium*, *ER*, *Boston Legal*, *CSI*, *Boomtown*, *Everybody Loves Raymond*, *The X-Files*, *The Adventures of Brisco County, Jr.*, *L.A. Law*, *Growing Pains*, *Dallas*, *Magnum, PI*, *Hill Street Blues*).

Naveen Andrews (1969–). *Lost* character: Sayid Jarrah. **You might recognize him from** such movies as *The Brave One*, *Grindhouse*, *Bride & Prejudice*, *Rollerball*, *Mighty Joe Young*, *The English Patient*, *London Kills Me*.

Anthony Azizi (1973–). *Lost* character: Omar. **You might recognize him from** such TV series as *Veronica Mars*, *Without a Trace*, *Sleeper Cell*, *Criminal Minds*, *Desperate Housewives*, *Commander* *in Chief, 24, The West Wing, NYPD Blue, Threat Matrix, Gilmore Girls, The Shield*, and *JAG*.

Blake Bashoff (1981–). *Lost* character: Karl. **You might recognize him from** a recurring role on *Judging Amy*.

Zoe Bell (1978–). *Lost* character: Regina. **You might recognize her as** a busy stunt double (in *Kill Bill* and other films) and from such movies as *Grindhouse*.

Ron Bottitta (1960–). *Lost* character: Leonard Simms. **You might recognize him from** a variety of movies (*Pirates of the Caribbean: Dead Man's Chest, In Good Company*) and TV series (*Jericho, E-Ring, Alias, The Shield, Boston Public*).

Julie Bowen (1970–). *Lost* character: Sarah Shephard. **You might recognize her from** roles in such movies as *American Werewolf in Paris, Happy Gilmore, Multiplicity*, and TV series like *Boston Legal, Jake in Progress, Ed, Dawson's Creek, ER*.

Michael Bowen (1953–). *Lost* character: Danny Pickett. **You might recognize him from** roles in movies like *Cabin Fever II, Walking Tall, Kill Bill II, Magnolia*, and *Jackie Brown* and such TV series as *Bones, CSI, The X-Files, Walker, Texas Ranger, Nash Bridges, JAG, NYPD Blue, ER*, and *The Adventures of Brisco County, Jr.*

Grant Bowler (1968–). *Lost* character: Captain Gault. **You might recognize the Australian actor from** such TV series as *Outrageous Fortune* (a New Zealand crime family drama) and *Farscape*.

Clancy Brown (1959–). *Lost* character: Kelvin Inman. **You might recognize him as** the sadistic prison guard in *The Shawshank Redemption* and Brother Justin Crowe in HBO's *Carnivale*. Has also done voice work in scores of films and TV series.

L. Scott Caldwell (1944–). *Lost* character: Rose Henderson. **You might recognize her from** roles in such movies as *Gridiron*

Gang, Devil in a Blue Dress, Dutch, and on such TV series as *Ghost Whisperer, Cold Case, ER, Nip/Tuck, The Practice, Judging Amy, Chicago Hope, JAG, Murder One, Hunter, L.A. Law, The Cosby Show.*

Nestor Carbonell (1967–). *Lost* character: Richard Alpert. **You might recognize him from** the TV series *Cane, The Tick, and Suddenly Susan;* from movies such as *The Dark Knight;* and from voice work on *Kim Possible.*

François Chau (1959–). Cambodian born. *Lost* character: Dr. Marvin Candle. **You might recognize him from** roles in such movies as *Lethal Weapon 4* and on such TV series as *Numb3rs, Grey's Anatomy, 24, Alias, Nash Bridges,* and *The Adventures of Brisco County, Jr.*

Byron Chung. *Lost* character: Mr. Paik. **You might recognize him from** several appearances (as different characters) in *M*A*S*H.*

Brett Cullen (1956–). *Lost* character: Goodwin. **You might recognize him from** recurring roles in *Ugly Betty, The West Wing, Friday Night Lights,* and *Desperate Housewives.*

Henry Ian Cusick (1967–). Peruvian born. *Lost* character: Desmond David Hume. **You might recognize him from** roles in *24, Waking the Dead, The Book Group, Casualty,* and *Taggart.*

Alan Dale (1947–). New Zealand born. *Lost* character: Mr. Widmore. **You might recognize him as** Bradford Meade on *Ugly Betty,* Caleb Nichol on *The O.C.,* and VP James Prescott on Day 3 of *24.*

Jeremy Davies (1969–). *Lost* character: Daniel Faraday. **You might recognize him as** Charles Manson in the made-for-TV movie *Helter Skelter,* from such TV series as *Dream On, Melrose Place, The Wonder Years,* and films like *Saving Private Ryan, Rescue Dawn, Twister, Dogville, Nell, Solaris,* and *Spanking the Monkey.*

Emilie de Ravin (1981–). Australian born. *Lost* character: Claire Littleton. **You might recognize her from** a recurring role in *Roswell* and for playing the female lead in *The Hills Have Eyes*.

Kim Dickens (1965–). *Lost* character: Cassidy Phillips. **You might recognize her as** Joannie Stubbs in *Deadwood*.

Andrew Divoff (1955–). Venezuelan-born. *Lost* character: Mikhail Bakunin. **You might recognize him from** scores of television and film roles, usually as a villain.

Starletta DuPois. *Lost* character: Michael's Mom. **You might recognize her from** such TV series as *Chicago Hope, Crossing Jordan, Doogie Howser, Falcon Crest, Hill Street Blues, Knots Landing, The Steve Harvey Show, The Jeffersons, The Equalizer, Little House on the Prairie*, and *St. Elsewhere* and movies like *A Raisin in the Sun* (for TV), *Big Momma's House, Hollywood Shuffle, Family Reunion, The Notebook, Waiting to Exhale*, and *Pee-Wee's Big Adventure*.

Kevin Durand (1974–). *Lost* character: Martin Keamy. **You might recognize the Canadian-born actor from** the TV series *CSI: Miami, Without a Trace, The Dead Zone, Kyle XY, Threshold, CSI: Crime Scene Investigation, Dead Like Me, Dark Angel, Stargate SG-1, ER, Shark* and the movies *3:10 to Yuma, Wild Hogs, The Butterfly Effect, Walking Tall, Scooby Doo 2, Mystery, Alaska*, and *Austin Powers: The Spy Who Shagged Me*.

Michael Emerson (1954–). *Lost* character: Benjamin Linus. **You might recognize him from** his Emmy winning role (for Outstanding Guest Actor in a Drama Series) as William Hinks in *The Practice* and for appearances in a wide variety of films (including a memorable part in *Saw*) and television series.

Jeff Fahey (1952–). *Lost* character: Frank Lapidus. **You might recognize him from** the TV series *Nash Bridges, Crossing Jordan, Criminal Minds, The Cleaner, American Dreams, Alfred Hitchcock*

Presents, and *One Life to Live*, and the movies *Grindhouse*, *Wyatt Earp*, *The Lawnmower Man*, *White Hunter*, *Black Heart*, and *Silverado*.

Nathan Fillion (1971–). *Lost* character: Kevin Callis. **You might recognize him as** Captain Mal Reynolds in *Firefly* (and the film *Serenity*) and Caleb in *Buffy the Vampire Slayer*. Has also played a recurring role on *Desperate Housewives* and the male lead in such films as *Slither*, *Waitress*, and *White Noise 2*.

Fionnula Flannigan (1941–). Irish born. *Lost* character: Mrs. Hawking. **You might recognize her as** Mrs. Bertha Mills in *The Others* and as Harriet Shaw Weaver in *James Joyce's Women*.

Matthew Fox (1966–). *Lost* character: Jack Shephard. **You might recognize him as** Charlie Salinger in *Party of Five*. Recently starred in the movies *We Are Marshall*, *Vantage Point*, and *Speed Racer*.

Mira Furlan (1955–). *Lost* character: Danielle Rousseau. **You might recognize her as** Delenn in *Babylon 5*.

Andrea Gabriel (1978–). *Lost* character: Noor "Nadia" Abed Jazeem. **You might recognize her from** roles in *Law & Order*, *JAG*, and *Criminal Minds*.

M. C. Gainey (1948–). *Lost* character: Tom Friendly. **You might recognize him as** a busy character actor in both film and television, best known perhaps for his performance as inept deputy Roscoe Coltrane in the big screen version of *Dukes of Hazard*.

Billy Ray Gallion. *Lost* character: Randy Nations. **You might recognize him from** minor roles in *The X-Files* and *Charmed*.

Jorge Garcia (1973–). *Lost* character: Hugo (Hurley) Reyes. **You might recognize him from** his recurring role as Hector Lopez on *Becker* and as a pot dealer on *Curb Your Enthusiasm*.

April Grace (1962–). *Lost* character: Bea Klugh. **You might recognize her as** Detective Toni Williams in *Joan of Arcadia* and recurring roles in *Chicago Hope* and *Star Trek: The Next Generation*.

Maggie Grace (1983–). *Lost* character: Shannon Rutherford. **You might recognize him from** such movies as *The Fog* and in such TV series as *Cold Case*, *Oliver Beene*, and *CSI: Miami*.

Evan Handler (1961–). *Lost* character: Dave. **You might recognize him from** his role as Harry Goldenblatt in *Sex and the City* and as Charlie Runkle in *Californication*.

Josh Holloway (1969–). *Lost* character: Sawyer (James Ford). **You might recognize him from** minor roles in several movies and such TV series as *NCIS*, *CSI*, *Angel*, and *Walker, Texas Ranger*.

Neil Hopkins (1977–). *Lost* character: Liam Pace. He has appeared in a variety of films and television series.

Lilian Hurst (1949–). *Lost* character: Carmen Reyes. **You might recognize her from** recurring roles as Celia in *Dharma and Greg* and on *The Nine* and *The Comeback* and scores of other film and television appearances.

Nick Jameson (1935–). *Lost* character: Richard Malkin. **You might recognize him from** *24*, in which he plays Russian President Yuri Suvarov and from scores of television and movie roles.

Kimberley Joseph (1973–). Canadian born. *Lost* character: Cindy Chandler. **You might recognize her from** recurring roles on *Cold Feet* and *All Saints*.

Malcolm David Kelley (1992–). *Lost* character: Walt Lloyd. **You might recognize him as** the young *Antwone Fisher* and from several TV appearances.

Daniel Dae Kim (1968–). *Lost* character: Jin Kwon. **You might recognize him as** Gavin Park in *Angel* and from recurring roles in *24* and *ER*.

Yunjin Kim (1973–). *Lost* character: Sun Kwon. Most of her previous screen roles were in her native Korea.

Swoozie Kurtz (1944–). *Lost* character: Emily Locke. **You might recognize her as** many movie characters, as Alexandra 'Alex' Reed Halsey Barker in *Sister*, and a recurring role in *Huff*. She also plays Lily in *Pushing Daisies*.

Tony Lee. *Lost* character: Jae Lee. **You might recognize him from** numerous television and film roles.

Fredric Lehne. *Lost* character: US Marshal Edward Mars. **You might recognize him from** scores of movie parts and recurring roles in such TV series as *Mancuso, FBI*, and *Dallas*.

Ken Leung (1970–). *Lost* character: Miles Straume. **You might recognize him from** the TV series *The Sopranos, Law & Order*, and *Oz* and the movies *X-Men: The Last Stand, Inside Man, The Squid and the Whale, Saw, Red Dragon, Vanilla Sky, AI, Spy Game, Rush Hour*, and *Welcome to the Dollhouse*.

Evangeline Lilly (1979–). *Lost* character: Kate Austen. **You might recognize her from** small roles in *Smallville* and *Tru Calling*.

Paula Malcolmson. *Lost* character: Colleen Pickett. **You might recognize her as** Trixie in *Deadwood* and in *John from Cincinnati*.

William Mapother (1965–). *Lost* character: Ethan Rom. **You might recognize him as** the abusive, murderous ex-husband in *In the Bedroom* and roles in *Threshold, Mission: Impossible II*, and *The Grudge*.

Cheech Marin (1946–). *Lost* character: David Reyes. **You might recognize him as** half of the stoner comic duo of Cheech & Chong, as Joe Dominguez in *Nash Bridges*, in a recurring role in *Judging Amy*, and for many movie appearances.

Adetokumboh M'Cormack. *Lost* character: Yemi. **You might recognize him from** a recurring role in the final season of *Gilmore Girls*.

Elizabeth Mitchell (1970–). *Lost* character: Juliet Burke. **You might recognize her from** performances in movies like *Frequency* and recurring roles in *ER*, *The Lyon's Dean*, and *Time of Your Life*.

Dominic Monaghan (1976–). German born. *Lost* character: Charlie Pace. **You might recognize him as** the hobbit Merry in *The Lord of the Rings* trilogy.

Rebecca Mader (1979–). *Lost* character: Charlotte Lewis. **You might the recognize the British actress from** the TV series *Justice*, *Mr. and Mrs. Smith*, *One Life to Live*, *The Guiding Light*, *All My Children*, *Third Watch*, and the movies *The Devil Wears Prada* and *Hitch*.

Terry O'Quinn (1952–). *Lost* character: John Locke. **You might recognize him as** the eponymous *Stepfather* and from recurring roles in *The X-Files*, *Millennium*, and *Alias*.

Robert Patrick (1958–). *Lost* character: Hibbs. **You might recognize him as** the liquid metal terminator in *Terminator 2*, Agent John Doggett in the final season of *The X-Files*, and Davey Scatino in *The Sopranos*.

Harold Perrineau (1963–). *Lost* character: Michael Dawson. **You might recognize him from** *Matrix Reloaded* and *Matrix Revolutions* and recurring roles in *Oz* and *I'll Fly Away*.

Jeff Perry (1955–). *Lost* character: Frank Duckett. **You might recognize him from** his continuing role as Harvey Leek on *Nash Bridges* and as Meredith Grey's father in *Grey's Anatomy*.

Tania Raymonde (1988–). *Lost* character: Alexandra Rousseau. **You might recognize her from** a recurring role on *Malcolm in the Middle*.

Lance Reddick. *Lost* character: Matthew Abaddon. **You might recognize him from** the TV series *The Wire*, *Fringe*, *Numb3rs*, *CSI: Miami*, *Law & Order*, *Law & Order: Criminal Intent*,

Law & Order: Special Victims Unit, Oz, The Corner, West Wing, and *New York Undercover,* and such movies as *Dirty Work, Don't Say a Word,* and *The Siege.*

Michelle Rodriguez (1978–). *Lost* character: Ana Lucia Cortez. **You might recognize her from** key roles in movies like *Girlfight, S.W.A.T., Resident Evil,* and *Blue Crush.*

Daniel Roebuck (1965–). *Lost* character: Leslie Arzt. **You might recognize him from** a recurring role as cop-gone-bad Rick Bettina in *Nash Bridges* as well as scores of movie and TV appearances.

Katey Sagal (1954–). *Lost* character: Helen. **You might recognize her from** roles as Peg Bundy in *Married With Children* and Cate Hennessy in *8 Simple Rules.*

Kiele Sanchez (1977–). *Lost* character: Nikki Fernandez. **You might recognize her from** recurring roles in the TV series *Related* and *Married to the Kellys.*

Rodrigo Santoro (1975–). Brazilian-born. *Lost* character: Paolo. **You might recognize him from** parts in movies like *300, Charlie's Angels: Full Throttle,* and *Love Actually,* and those Baz Luhrman-directed Chanel No. 5 ads with Nicole Kidman. A major soap-opera star in his native land.

Ian Somerhalder (1978–). *Lost* character: Boone Carlyle. **You might recognize him from** a role in the movie *Pulse.*

Tamara Taylor. *Lost* character: Susan Lloyd-Porter. **You might recognize her from** her role as Dr. Camille Saroyan in *Bones* and as the teacher in the opening sequence of *Serenity.*

John Terry. *Lost* character: Christian Shephard. **You might recognize him from** recurring roles on *24, Las Vegas,* and *ER.*

Marsha Thomason (1976–). British-born. *Lost* Character: Naomi. **You might recognize her as** Nessa Holt on *Las Vegas.*

Kevin Tighe (1944–). *Lost* character: Anthony Cooper. **You might recognize him from** scores of movie performances and recurring roles in such TV series as *Murder One* and *Emergency!*

Cynthia Watros (1968–). *Lost* character: Libby. **You might recognize her from** roles on the soaps *Guiding Light* and *Another World* and *The Drew Carey Show*.

Sonya Walger (1974–). *Lost* character: Penelope Widmore. **You might recognize her from** recurring roles in *Mind of the Married Man*, *Sleeper Cell*, *CSI: NY*, *Coupling*, *Tell Me You Love Me*, and *Terminator: The Sarah Connor Chronicles*.

Robin Weigert (1969–). *Lost* character: Rachel. **You might recognize her as** Calamity Jane in *Deadwood* and the TV series *Life*.

LOST WRITERS

J.J. Abrams (1966–). *Lost* **episodes written/co-written:** "Pilot (I)," "Pilot (II)," "A Tale of Two Cities." In addition to authoring/co-authoring such films as *Taking Care of Business, Regarding Henry, Forever Young, Gone Fishin'*, and *Armageddon* **has also written episodes of** *Alias* and *Felicity*.

Carlton Cuse (1959–). *Lost* **episodes written/co-written:** "Hearts & Minds," "Deus Ex Machina," "Exodus (I)," "Exodus (II)," "…And Found," "The Other 48 Days," "The 23rd Psalm," "One of Them," "Lockdown," "?," "Live Together, Die Alone, Part 1," "Live Together, Die Alone, Part 2," "Further Instructions," "I Do," "Not in Portland," "Enter 77," "One of Us," "The Brig," "Through the Looking Glass," "The Beginning of the End," "The Constant," "There's No Place Like Home (Parts I and II)." **Has also written episodes of** *Nash Bridges, The Adventures of Brisco County, Jr., Crime Story*.

Leonard Dick. *Lost* **episodes written/co-written:** "…In Translation," "The Greater Good," "Adrift," "The Long Con," "S.O.S.," "Collision." **Has also written episodes of** *House, Tarzan, Relic Hunter, Sister, Sister, Mad TV.*

Paul Dini (1957–). *Lost* **episodes written/co-written:** "The Moth." **Has also written episodes for such cartoon series as:** *Justice League, Batman Beyond, Tiny Toon Adventures,* and *Transformers.*

Brent Fletcher. Previously a stuntman and occasional actor. *Lost* **episodes written/co-written:** "Numbers." **Has also co-authored an episode of** *Angel.*

David Fury (1959–). *Lost* **episodes written/co-written:** "Walkabout," "Solitary," "Special." **Has also written episodes of** *24, Angel, Buffy the Vampire Slayer, Pinky and the Brain, Dream On.*

Drew Goddard (1975–). *Lost* **episodes written/co-written:** "Outlaws," "The Glass Ballerina," "Flashes Before Your Eyes," "The Man from Tallahassee," "One of Us," "The Man Behind the Curtain," "Meet Kevin Johnson," "The Shape of Things to Come." **Has also written episodes of** *Alias, Angel,* and *Buffy the Vampire Slayer,* and the movie *Cloverfield.*

Javier Grillo-Marxuach (1969–). *Lost* **episodes written/ co-written:** "House of the Rising Sun," "All the Best Cowboys Have Daddy Issues," "…In Translation," "Born to Run," "Orientation," "Collision." **Has also written episodes of** *Medium, Jake 2.0, Boomstown, Dead Zone, Law & Order: Special Victims Unit, Charmed, Pretender.*

Adam Horowitz. *Lost* **episodes written/co-written:** "Born to Run," "Everybody Hates Hugo," "Fire + Water," "Dave," "Three Minutes," "Every Man for Himself," "Trisha Tanaka Is Dead," "Exposé," "D.O.C," "Greatest Hits," "The Economist,"

"Something Nice Back Home." **Has also written episodes of** *One Tree Hill*, *Birds of Prey*, *Felicity*, and *Popular*.

Jennifer Johnson. *Lost* **episodes written/co-written:** "The Moth," "Whatever the Case May Be." **Has also written episodes of** *Cold Case*, *The Guardian*, and *Providence*.

Christina M. Kim. *Lost* **episodes written/co-written:** "The Whole Truth," "Two for the Road," "Per Avion." Her *Lost* scripts were her first.

Edward Kitsis. *Lost* **episodes written/co-written:** "Born to Run," "Everybody Hates Hugo," "Fire + Water," "Dave," "Three Minutes," "Every Man for Himself," "Trisha Tanaka Is Dead," "Exposé," "D.O.C," "Greatest Hits," "The Economist," "Something Nice Back Home." **Has also written episodes of** *Birds of Prey*, *Felicity*, and *Popular*.

Dawn Lambertsen-Kelly. *Lost* **episodes written/co-written:** "Maternity Leave." Her *Lost* script was her first.

Damon Lindelof (1973–). *Lost* **episodes written/co-written:** "Pilot (I)," "Pilot (II)," "Tabula Rasa," "Confidence Man," "Whatever the Case May Be," "Homecoming," "Deus Ex Machina," "Exodus (I)," "Exodus (II)," "Man of Science, Man of Faith," "...And Found," "The Other 48 Days," "The 23rd Psalm," "One of Them," "Lockdown," "?," "Live Together, Die Alone, Part 1," "Live Together, Die Alone, Part 2," "A Tale of Two Cities," "I Do," "Flashes Before Your Eyes," "Enter 77," "Left Behind," "The Brig," "Through the Looking Glass," "The Beginning of the End," "The Constant," "There's No Place Like Home (I and II)." **Has also written episodes of** *Crossing Jordan*, *Nash Bridges*.

Lynne E. Litt. *Lost* **episodes written/co-written:** "Raised by Another." **Has also written episodes of** *Crossing Jordan*, *Tarzan*, *The Practice*, *Gideon's Crossing*, *Law & Order*, *Nash Bridges*.

Steven Maeda. *Lost* **episodes written/co-written:** "Adrift," "What Kate Did," "The Long Con," "S.O.S." **Has also written episodes of** *Day Break*, *CSI Miami*, *The X-Files*, and *Harsh Realm*.

Greggory Nations. *Lost* **episodes written/co-written:** "Eggtown." **Has also written episodes of** *The District*.

Monica Owusu-Breen. *Lost* **episodes written/co-written:** "The Cost of Living." **Has also written episodes of** *Alias*, *Brothers & Sisters*, and *Charmed*.

Kyle Pennington. *Lost* **episodes written/co-written:** "Cabin Fever." His *Lost* script was his first.

Jeff Pinkner. *Lost* **episodes written/co-written:** ""The Glass Ballerina," "Not in Portland," "The Man from Tallahassee," "Catch-22." **Has also written episodes of** *Alias*, *Profiler*, *Ally McBeal*, and *Early Edition*.

Matt Ragghianti. *Lost* **episodes written/co-written:** "Maternity Leave." His *Lost* script was his first.

Jordan Rosenberg. *Lost* **episodes written/co-written:** "Per Avion." His *Lost* script was his first.

Liz Sarnoff. *Lost* **episodes written/co-written:** "Abandoned," "The Hunting Party," "Further Instructions," "Stranger in a Strange Land," "Left Behind," "The Man Behind the Curtain," "Eggtown," "Meet Kevin Johnson," "Cabin Fever." **Has also written episodes of** *Deadwood*, *Crossing Jordan*, and *NYPD Blue*.

Alison Schapker. *Lost* **episodes written/co-written:** "The Cost of Living." **Has also written episodes of** *Alias* and *Charmed*.

Janet Tamaro. *Lost* **episodes written/co-written:** "Do No Harm." **Has also written episodes of** *Bones*, *Sleeper Cell*, *CSI: NY*, *Law & Order: Special Victims Unit*.

Christian Taylor. *Lost* **episodes written/co-written:** "White Rabbit." **Has also written episodes of** *Miracles* and *Six Feet Under*.

Brian K. Vaughan. Prolific graphic novelist (*Ave Maria*, *Doctor Strange*, *Ex Machina*, *The Last Man*, *Pride of Baghdad*, *Runaways*). *Lost* **episodes written/co-written:** "Catch-22" (his first television script), "Meet Kevin Johnson," "The Shape of Things to Come."

Craig Wright. *Lost* **episodes written/co-written:** "Orientation," "What Kate Did." **Has also written episodes of** *Dirty Sexy Money*, *Brothers & Sisters*, and *Six Feet Under*.

Lost Directors

J.J. Abrams (1966–). *Lost* **episodes directed:** "Pilot (I)," "Pilot (II)," "A Tale of Two Cities." **Has also directed episodes of** *The Office*, *Alias*, *Felicity*.

Daniel Attias. *Lost* **episodes directed:** "Numbers." **Has also directed episodes of** over forty televisions series including *Big Love*, *House*, *The Wire*, *Deadwood*, *Entourage*, *Six Feet Under*, *Alias*, *Huff*, *Boston Legal*, *CSI: Miami*, *The Sopranos*, *Buffy the Vampire Slayer*, *Ally McBeal*, *Party of Five*, *Northern Exposure*, *Beverly Hills 90210*, *The Adventures of Brisco County, Jr.*, *Miami Vice*.

Paris Barclay (1956–). *Lost* **episodes directed:** "Stranger in a Strange Land." **Has also directed episodes of** over thirty television series including *CSI*, *Cold Case*, *House*, *Numb3rs*, *The Shield*, *Law & Order*, *Huff*, *West Wing*, *ER*, *NYPD Blue*, *Sliders*, *Diagnosis Murder*.

Matt Earl Beesley. *Lost* **episodes directed:** "The 23rd Psalm." **Has also directed episodes of** ten television series including *Jerico*, *CSI: Miami*, *Criminal Minds*, *Law & Order: Special Victims Unit*, *Prison Break*, *CSI*.

Jack Bender. *Lost* **episodes directed:** "Tabula Rasa," "Walkabout," "The Moth," "Whatever the Case May Be," "Outlaws," "Exodus (I)," "Exodus (II)," "Man of Science, Man of Faith," "Orientation," "Fire + Water," "Maternity Leave," "Dave," "Live Together, Die Alone, Part 1," "Live Together, Die Alone, Part 2," "A Tale of Two Cities," "The Cost of Living," "Flashes Before Your Eyes," "The Man from Tallahassee," "One of Us," "Through the Looking Glass," "The Beginning of the End," "The Economist," "The Constant," "The Shape of Things to Come," "There's No Place Like Home (I and II)." **Has also directed episodes of** *The Sopranos*, *Carnivale*, *Joan of Arcadia*, *Judging Amy*, *Ally McBeal*, *Felicity*, *Profiler*, *Beverly Hills 90210*, *The Paper Chase*.

Adam Davidson (1964–). *Lost* **episodes directed:** "Abandoned." **Has also directed episodes of** over twenty television series including *Shark*, *Rome*, *Big Love*, *Dexter*, *Criminal Minds*, *Grey's Anatomy*, *Deadwood*, *Six Feet Under*, *Jake 2.0*, *Monk*, *Law & Order*.

Roxann Dawson (1958–). Formerly an actress (*Baywatch*, *Star Trek-Voyager*, *Matlock*). *Lost* **episodes directed:** "The Long Con." **Has also directed episodes of** thirteen television series, including *Crossing Jordan*, *Cold Case*, *Enterprise*, *Charmed*.

Paul A. Edwards. Former camera operator and cinematographer. *Lost* **episodes directed:** "What Kate Did," "Two for the Road," "The Glass Ballerina," "Per Avion," "Cabin Fever." **Has also directed an episode of** *Heroes*.

Tucker Gates. *Lost* **episodes directed:** "Confidence Man," "…In Translation," "Born to Run," "I Do." **Has also directed episodes of** over forty five televisions shows including *The*

Office, *Weeds*, *Alias*, *Carnivale*, *Huff*, *Boston Legal*, *CSI*, *CSI: Miami*, *American Dreams*, *Roswell*, *Angel*, *Buffy the Vampire Slayer*, *Providence*, *Nash Bridges*, *The X-Files*, *The Commish*, *Wiseguy*, *21 Jump Street*.

Karen Gaviola. *Lost* **episodes directed:** "The Whole Truth," "Left Behind." **Has also directed episodes of** *CSI: Miami*, *Prison Break*, *Bones*, *Alias*, *Crossing Jordan*, *Cold Case*, *NYPD Blue*.

Marita Grabiak. *Lost* **episodes directed:** "Raised by Another." **Has also directed episodes of** *Eureka*, *Surface*, *One Tree Hill*, *Law & Order: Special Victims Unit*, *Alias*, *Battlestar Galactica*, *Wonderfalls*, *Gilmore Girls*, *Smallville*, *Angel*, *Buffy the Vampire Slayer*, *Firely*, *ER*.

David Grossman. *Lost* **episodes directed:** "The Greater Good." **Has also directed episodes of** over forty television series including *Desperate Housewives*, *Monk*, *Malcolm in the Middle*, *CSI*, *Dead Like Me*, *CSI: Miami*, *Buffy the Vampire Slayer*, *Angel*, *Ally McBeal*, *Timecop*, *Roswell*, *Lois and Clark*, *Hercules: The Legendary Journeys*, *Mantis*, *Weird Science*.

Rod Holcomb. Veteran television director, at work since the 1970s. *Lost* **episodes directed:** "Hearts and Minds." In addition to numerous made-for-television movies **has also directed episodes of such series as** *Numb3rs*, *Invasion*, *ER*, *China Beach*, *Wiseguy*, *Scarecrow and Mrs. King*, *The A-Team*, *Hill Street Blue*, *Battlestar Galactica* (the original), *6 Million Dollar Man*, *Quincy*, *M.E.*

Kevin Hooks (1958–). Son of actor Robert Hooks and an occasional actor himself (*White Shadow*, *Sounder*). *Lost* **episodes directed:** "White Rabbit," "Homecoming." **Has also directed episodes of** *Prison Break*, *24*, *Ghost Wisperer*, *Alias*, *Cold Case*, *NYPD Blue*, *Without a Trace*, *ER*, *Profiler*, *Homicide*, *V*, *St. Elsewhere*. Directed feature film *Passenger 57* (1992).

Eric Laneuville (1952–). *Lost* **episodes directed:** "The Other 48 Days," "S.O.S.," "Trisha Tanaka Is Dead," "The Brig," "The Other Woman." **Has also directed episodes of** over forty shows including *Ghost Whisperer, Prison Break, Invasion, Everybody Hates Chris, Medium, Gilmore Girls, My Wife and Kids, Monk, ER, NYPD Blue, Midnight Caller, Quantum Leap, L.A. Law, St. Elsewhere.*

Robert Mandel. *Lost* **episodes directed:** "Deus Ex Machina." **Has also directed episodes of** *Prison Break, The District, Nash Bridges, The Practice, The X-Files,* and several made-for-TV movies.

Bobby Roth (1950–). *Lost* **episodes directed:** "The Man Behind the Curtain." **Has also directed episodes of** *Numb3rs, Prison Break, Commander-in-Chief, Boomtown,* and many other series in a 20+ year career.

Deran Sarafian (1968–). *Lost* **episodes directed:** "?." **Has also directed episodes of** over twenty television series including *House, Night Stalker, CSI: NY, CSI, CSI: Miami, Cold Case, Without a Trace, Buffy the Vampire Slayer* and several forgettable films.

Alan Taylor (1965–). *Lost* **episodes directed:** "Everybody Hates Hugo." **Has also directed episodes of** numerous HBO series like *The Sopranos, Big Love, Rome, Deadwoood, Carnivale, Sex and the City, Six Feet Under* as well as other series like *West Wing* and *Homicide.*

Frederick E.O. Toye (1967–). *Lost* **episodes directed:** "D.O.C." **Has also directed episodes of** *Ghost Whisperer, Alias* (12 episodes), *4400,* and *Invasion.*

Stephen Williams. *Lost* **episodes directed:** "All the Best Cowboys Have Daddy Issues," "Do No Harm," "Adrift," "...And Found," "Collision," "The Hunting Party," "One of Them," "Lockdown," "Three Minutes," "Further Instructions,"

"Every Man for Himself," "Not in Portland," "Enter 77," "Exposé," "Catch-22," "Confirmed Dead," "Eggtown," "Ji Yeon," "Something Nice Back Home," "There's No Place Like Home (I)." **Has also directed episodes of** *Crossing Jordan, Las Vegas, Ed, Dark Angel, Kevin Hill.*

Greg Yaitanes (1970-). *Lost* **episodes directed:** "Solitary," "Special." **Has also directed episodes of** *Grey's Anatomy, Prison Break, House, Bones, Nip/Tuck, The Closer, CSI: Miami, CSI: New York, Cold Case, Nash Bridges.* Also directed the feature film *Hard Justice.*

Michael Zinberg. *Lost* **episodes directed:** "House of the Rising Sun." **Has also directed episodes of** over fifty television series including *Gilmore Girls, The Practice, NCIS, Crossing Jordan, Everybody Loves Raymond, Boston Public, Charmed, Pretender, JAG, The Commish, Quantum Leap, L.A. Law, Cheers, Lou Grant, WKRP in Cincinnati, The Bob Newhart Show.*

CHAPTER EIGHT

TOP 10 LISTS

TOP 10 MOVIES AND TELEVISION SERIES FOR *LOST* FANS

- *Alias*
- *Jurassic Park*
- *Lost Horizon* or *Brigadoon*
- *Nash Bridges*
- *The Prisoner*
- *Survivor*
- *Twilight Zone*
- *Twin Peaks*
- *The Wizard of Oz*
- *The X-Files*

TOP 10 *LOST* WEBSITES

- Thetailsection.com
- www.lost-media.com
- abc.go.com/primetime/lost
- TheFuselage.com
- www.thelostblog.com

- The Wikis: **en.wikipedia.org/wiki/Lost_(TV_series)**, **www.lostpedia.com/wiki** **lost.wikia.com**
- **thelostexperience.com** (and any upcoming websites created by the owners of thetailsection.com)
- **www.lost-tv.com** (only for transcripts now, not updated as often as it used to be)
- **http://spoilerslost.blogspot.com/—DarkUFO's** site was involved in the controversy in May 2007 about spoilers being leaked. DarkUFO asked for a vote before posting (highly accurate) details of the finale, then posted them under a cut—unlike other sites that simply blurted the details without placing the spoilers under cuts. This is an interesting, frequently updated site, and probably should be somewhere in our list.
- **http://www.loststudies.com/—The Society for the Study of** *Lost*. A must-visit site for intellectual and in-depth looks at the deeper significance of *Lost* themes in a peer-reviewed online journal.

TOP 10 IMAGES ON *LOST*

1. **The "DHARMA Initiative" Symbol—the Baghua:** The Tao eight-sided symbol has made its appearance throughout the text of *Lost*, representing the unity of the DHARMA Initiative. The main logo is the basic octagon shape of the Baghua with "DHARMA" written at its center. We first see the logo during the "Orientation" film, but it also appears on disk seven of the Season Two box disk set, in the ARG,

on the front of the van in "Trisha Tankaka Is Dead" (3.16) and on countless jumpsuits.

2. **The Swan Station Logo:** The Swan station logo is a baghua with an interestingly shaped swan. The Swan—home to the hatch computer and island hangout for the second and third season for the crash survivors is easily one of the most recognized logos.

3. **The Hatch Mural:** Seen in both the hatch and at Claire's father's baby's house (Tom), the detailed hatch painting was actually done by *Lost*'s own Jack Bender. The hatch mural features a myriad of images that foreshadowed events that would later happen in the series, including the number "108," a plane crash, the taking of Walt by the Others, and Mr. Eko.

4. **The Hieroglyphs:** The hieroglyphs, defined by Damon Lindelof in both the July 31, 2007 podcast and a Comic Con 2007 as meaning "the underworld," appeared when the hatch countdown timer reached less than zero. The five symbols appear on either a black background in red script or vice versa.

5. **The Hatch "Countdown" Computer:** Reset every 108 minutes, the countdown clock serves as eerie reminder of the fate of the world—and ultimate destruction of the hatch.

6. **Mr Eko's Stick:** The so-called "Jesus Stick" (labeled by Charlie) is what Eko uses to carve important scripture passage, including the 23rd psalm, Acts 4.2, and perhaps most importantly John 3:05, a message to John Locke.

7. **The Blast Door Map:** When Locke is locked down with a closed blast door, he sees an illuminated map that contains notations in English, latin, symbols, and mathematical

equations. Several of the abbreviations contained on the map were later revealed in the jigsaw puzzle game.

8. **The Smoke Monster:** The smoke monster has housed in its mists countless images, including Yemi and scenes of the Catholic church and village Eko once belonged to, and the "heart of the island" for John Locke.

9. **The Virgin Mary Statues:** Since the first season, the Virgin Mary statues have played an important part in the plot of *Lost*. The beatific virgin mother houses pure grade-A heroin—both Charlie's temptation and the cause of Yemi's death.

10. **Charlie's Fingers:** When Charlie tapes his fingers and writes "LATE" and "FATE" on the white tape, the audience is left to puzzle at the symbolic meanings behind these visual clues.

Top 10 *Lost* Episodes

Favorite Episodes

#	Porter	Lavery	Robson
1	"Through the Looking Glass"—Excellent story involving all cast members, a "game changer" for the rest of the series (the flash-forwards to LA), foreshadowing of the castaways' future rescue from the island. This episode sets	"Flashes Before Your Eyes" and "The Constant"—In a series known for blowing our minds, these two episodes (which I am counting as one episode since they both deal with the Desmond/Penny pre-Island	"Through the Looking Glass"—The thrills! The chills! The action! After the closing scene (and when I started breathing again) I was firmly convinced that *Lost* was by far the best show on television.

#	Porter	Lavery	Robson
1 (cont.)	up all kinds of character interactions for future episodes, brings back Walt—who apparently brings back Locke from the (near)dead, kills one of the original castaways, kills several Others and shakes up the Others' society—its action packed, well acted, and very cool. To date, this is my favorite finale and one of the best hours of television ever.	story) might be the most boggling. The moment where Mrs. Hawking explains to Desmond why he can't marry Penelope might be my favorite in the series so far. Both directed by Bender (who helmed seven of my top ten) and written by Lindelof with *Buffy* alum Drew Goddard ("Flashes") and Darlton ("The Constant").	
2	"There's No Place Like Home"—Three hours for the price of one episode—what a deal! Great Sawyer moments (shirtless or not), the long-awaited Desmond-Penny reunion, the loss of Michael and (perhaps) Jin, Sun's meeting with Charles Widmore (thus potentially setting her up as a world-class "player"), Locke in a coffin, and	"Through the Looking Glass"—Lived up to and surpassed all our expectations. Directed (again) by Bender and written by Darlton, this is the episode that saved the series for many fans.	"Orientation"—I personally watched this episode at least ten times, and it helped to fuel my speculations for a full two seasons. "Orientation" is brilliant on many levels: one, it's a tip of the hat by Cuse and Lindelof for the repeated re-watching that most *Lost* fans can admit to; secondly, we got more information about the illustrious

#	Porter	Lavery	Robson
2 (cont.)	a disappearing island! (And those were just the previews.)		DHARMA initiative, was introduced to Dr. Marvin Candle, and found out there's more than just one hatch on the island. What more can an audience ask for in one *Lost* episode?
3	"Pilot"—High-quality production, riveting pace. This episode hooked me immediately on the series. This is not your typical series opener.	"Pilot"—J.J. Abrams' major contribution to the series he would abandon, the most expensive pilot ever was worth every penny.	"The 23rd Psalm"—Who knew that silent-for-40-days, carry-a-big-Jesus-stick, Catholic priest Eko was a Nigerian drug running warlord? Not I, and certainly not anyone else who wasn't spoiled silly for this shocker of an episode. Eko was—and remains—one of my favorite characters, and this episode only intensified my love for this complex and amazing character.
4	"Numbers"— Wicked fun, well-written, humor and pathos in the same episode. It sets up the	"The Man Behind the Curtain"— Finally, Ben's backstory, and with it the truth (or some of it)	"Further Instructions"— Locke + Sweat Lodge + Boone = A trippy good time. And a good time it

#	Porter	Lavery	Robson
4 (cont.)	mythology of the Numbers, and it's about Hurley—always a plus for me.	about DHARMA. The episode that also gave us our first glimpse of Jacob.	was. This episode seemed surreal, off-the-charts weird, and full of hidden secret messages that I felt sure I was supposed to decipher.
5	"Flashes Before Your Eyes"/"The Constant"—tie—"FBYE" introduces the possibility of time travel, sets up the prophesy for Charlie's story arc, is a referential episode for later episodes—including "Catch-22" and "Greatest Hits," and further develops Desmond as an integral character. "Constant" completes the time-travel part of Desmond's story and lets us eavesdrop on Des' fateful Christmas Eve 2004 phone call. I love a good love story, and the Desmond-Penny romance is about as close as *Lost* comes to a happy not-quite-ending.	"Live Together, Die Alone"—Another Bender-directed episode, this season finale made us wonder (we still do) if *Lost* is not in part a variation on *The Odyssey*, with Desmond (the episode is his back-story) as Odysseus and Penelope as, well, Penelope. Another Darlton-authored masterpiece.	"Greatest Hits"—I cried so hard—and for so long—that I didn't think I'd stop. *Lost* has never been a show to provoke that sort of emotion in me, so when I got literally carried away with emotion during "Greatest Hits" it seemed best to just go along with it. A beautifully orchestrated tale of self-sacrifice and giving—RIP Charlie.

#	Porter	Lavery	Robson
6	"Greatest Hits"—This is Charlie's finest hour, and although I'm a Charlie fan and not as objective about him as I could be, the episode shows just how much this character has matured and makes his upcoming sacrifice heartbreaking. Plus, Dominic Monaghan's work is outstanding. Although the backstory isn't as strong as it could've been, the emotion in real time more than makes up for it.	"Man of Science, Man of Faith"—The pre-title sequence alone made this one of the greatest episodes, the one in which we met Desmond (obviously one of my favorite characters). Surprise: written by Lindelof, directed by Bender.	"One of Them"—I'll admit it—I'm a sucker for torture, and when we wanted to believe that "Henry Gale" was evil, Sayid confirmed our suspicions. I remember chanting at the television "Kill him! Kill him!" which is exactly what the writers wanted us to do—and why this episode was so powerful.
7	"The Beginning of the End"—I love Hurley, and although it pains me to see him back at Santa Rosa (after a glorious car chase), I'm glad he can chat with old friends. (One of my favorite fan avatars of Charlie proclaims "Over my hot reanimated corpse." I concur	"The Man from Tallahassee"—In this Bender-directed episode (co-authored by Jeff Pinkner and Goddard) we finally learned how John Locke ended up in a wheel chair. Riveting.	Numbers"—How can this episode not be in a top-ten list? "Numbers" upped the ante for *Lost* fans and made viewing more of an adventure, a game that we could immerse ourselves in completely. And it gave us the much needed comic relief of the cursed

#	Porter	Lavery	Robson
7 (cont.)	with the sentiment.) Back on the island, the freighter folk arrive, and the castaways have to decide if they should go or stay. This episode gives Charlie fans some closure while opening up the story in lots of new directions in two timeframes. Even if the Season Four opener truly is the beginning of the end, I'm eager to see where we're going.		Hurley, adding depth and dimension to a character we already loved.
8	"Exodus"—This episode sets up plenty of plot points for Season Two—hatch opened, Walt kidnapped, uncertain fate of Sawyer, Jin, and Michael on the raft. The interesting "add-on" scene shows Hurley getting to the airport—some well-needed ironic comedy to end the season.	"Not in Portland"—The "arlton" half of Darlton, Cuse, and Pinkner wrote this Juliet-intensive tale, which I found powerful and haunting. After watching it, I felt like I had been hit by a bus.	"Fire + Water"—Charlie's hallucinations of John the Baptist and Claire as Mary were only part of why I loved this episode. As a huge fan of religious scholarship, I was delighted by the attention to detail in this episode, from a biblical sense to an adoption of Charlie as prophet—complete with corvine hood, denigration, and

#	Porter	Lavery	Robson
8 (cont.)			his subsequent ostracision from the camp. Definitely a top-ten episode.
9	"The Other 48 Days"—An interesting look at the story from a different perspective, and an excellent re-enactment of crash from the island's perspective. Although I tired of the Tailies as a separate group, I appreciate the tie-ins from previous episodes and yet another way to interpret events we thought we understood.	"Walkabout"—Though I was fascinated with *Lost* from the first minute, this was the episode that made me a true believer, written by another *Buffy* alum, David Fury, and directed, of course, by Bender.	"Hearts and Minds"—OK, so I was convinced after episode two of season one that Boone and Shannon were "more" than brother and sister. There was just something too intimate about Boone's attachment with her. This episode gave me the ultimate payoff in my speculation and fulfilled my soap-opera like needs for something naughty.
10	"A Tale of Two Cities"—Surprise! The Others live in suburbia. If only we hadn't seen their torture chamber quite so closely after this promising start. With two seasons of hindsight, I like the New Otherton scenes even	"The Other 48 Days"—A definitely-in-the-minority "Ana-L" fan, I loved this virtuoso piece of television narrative.	"Exodus"—I had to include this as one unit. There's so much going on in this episode that you can't help but sit on the edge of your seat and wonder what is going to happen next. We meet the Others and find they are a seafaring

#	Porter	Lavery	Robson
10 (cont.)	better—Ben is creepier and Juliet at a pivotal point in her career with Mittelos Bioscience.		folk. The raft gets blown to high heaven, Danielle steals Claire's baby, and Kate, Jack, and Locke descend into the hatch. This was a perfect season finale—one that kept our thoughts on the show all summer long, full of anticipation for what was to come.

BIBLIOGRAPHY

Adams, Richard. *Watership Down.* New York: Macmillan, 1972.

Alias. J.J. Abrams. ABC. Episode 3.4. "The Awful Truth."

Amillerphoto. Post. "Geronimo Jackson…New Future Theory." May 15, 2006. The Fuselage.

Arneson, Erik. "*Lost*—The Game: Interview with the Designer." About.com. http://boardgames.about.com/od/lostboardgame/a/designer_intvw.htm.

"Backstage with DriveShaft." *Lost.* The Complete First Season DVD, 2005.

Baum, L. Frank. *The Wizard of Oz.* New York: Tor Classics, 1993.

Bierce, Ambrose. *Collected Writings.* Ed. Clifton Fadiman. New York: Citadel Press, 1946.

___. "An Occurrence at Owl Creek Bridge."

___. "The Damn Thing."

___. "A Psychological Shipwreck."

Bloom, Harold. *The Anxiety of Influence: A Theory of Poetry.* New York: Oxford U P, 1973.

___. *A Map of Misreading.* New York: Oxford U P, 1985.

Blume, Judy. *Are You There, God? It's Me, Margaret.*

Bramwell, Tom. "News. Ubisoft Details *Lost* Game." Eurogamer. July 27, 2007. http://www.eurogamer.net/article.php?article_id=80424.

Brian. "Lost Puzzles." Posts. Nov.-Dec. 2006. About.com. http://lost.wpadmin.about.com/?comments_popup=7378.

Buchanan, Levi. "*Lost* for iPod Review." Wireless-IGN. June 17, 2007. http://wireless.ign.com/articles/797/797374p1.html.

Bullock, Alan and Oliver Stallybrass, eds. *The Harper Dictionary of Modern Thought.* New York: Harper and Row, 1977.

Cairns, Bryan. "From Shore to Score." *Lost*, May/June 2007, 42.

Card, Orson Scott, ed. *Getting Lost: Survival, Baggage and Starting Over in J. J. Abrams'* Lost. Dallas: BenBella, 2006.

"cardiopulmonary resuscitation." WordNet® 3.0. Princeton University. 29 Jul. 2007. Dictionary.com. http://dictionary. reference.com/browse/cardiopulmonary resuscitation.

Carroll, Lewis. *Alice's Adventures in Wonderland.* Norton Critical Edition. Ed. Donald J. Gray. New York: W.W. Norton, 1971.

Carter, Bill. *Desperate Networks.* New York: Broadway Books, 2006.

Cedar Rapids. City of Five Seasons. http://www.cedar-rapids. org/community/fifthseason.asp.

Chatwin, Bruce. *The Songlines.* New York: Penguin, 1987.

Crichton, Michael. *Jurassic Park.* New York: Knopf, 1990.

Cuder, Amanda. "Tuning Into the Keys of 'Lost.'" *Connecticut Post*, June 22, 2007. http://www.connpost.com/leisure/ ci_6170895.

DarkUFO. July 27, 2007. http://spoilerslost.blogspot.com/ 2007/07/comic-con-2007-spoiler-summary.html.

Defoe, Daniel. *Robinson Crusoe.* Ed. Michael Shinagel. Norton Critical Edition. New York: W.W. Norton, 1975.

Dickens, Charles. *Our Mutual Friend.* London: Wordsworth Classics, 1995.

DJ Dan. The Lost Experience. Second podcast. Sept. 24, 2006.

"Dominic Monaghan Discusses Charlie's Fate—and What's Next." Interview with Kristin Veitch. Eonline. May 23, 2007. http://www.eonline.com/uberblog/b3704_Exclusive__ Dominic_Monaghan_Discusses_Charlie_s_Fate_amp_ amp__8212_And_What_s_Next.html.

Dostoevsky, Feodor. *The Brothers Karamazov.* Trans. Constance Garnett. New York: NAL, 1957.

DriveShaft. MySpace. http://www.myspace.com/driveshaft.

"electromagnetism." The American Heritage® Science Dictionary. Houghton Mifflin Company. 30 Jul. 2007. Dictionary.com. http://dictionary.reference.com/browse/ electromagnetism.

Fish, Stanley E. *Is There a Text in This Class? The Authority of Interpretive Communities.* Cambridge: Harvard U P, 1980.

Fox, Matthew. *The Tonight Show with Jay Leno.* NBC. May 8, 2007.

Gameloft. *Lost:* The Mobile Game. http://www.gameloft.com/ lost-mobile-game/.

"Gameloft Secures Mobile Gaming Rights to Hit ABC/ Touchstone Television Series *Lost* and *Desperate Housewives.*" Business Wire. Aug. 14, 2006. http://findarticles.com/p/ articles/mi_m0EIN/is_2006_August_14/ai_n16620641.

"Geronimo Jackson." Lost Wiki. http://lostwiki.abc.com/page/ Geronimo+Jackson.

Giacchino, Michael. Official *Lost* video podcast. April 11, 2007. http://Abc.go.com.

Gilgamesh. Trans. N.K. Sandars. New York: Penguin, 1972.

Golding, William. *Lord of the Flies.* Casebook Edition. Ed. James R. Baker and Arthur P. Ziegler, Jr. New York: Putnam's, 1954.

Greene, Brian. *The Elegant Universe: Superstrings, Hidden Dimensions, and the Quest for the Ultimate Theory.* New York: Vintage, 2003.

Hawking, Stephen. *A Brief History of Time: From the Big Bang to Back Holes.* New York: Bantam Books, 1988.

Heller, Joseph. *Catch-22.* New York: Dell, 1961.

Henfield, Sally. "Charlie's Lost It." *This Is Lancashire.* May 2007. http://www.thisislancashire.co.uk/news/headlines/display. var.1415430.0.charlies_lost_it.php.

"Hieronymus." *Lost* Screencaps and Easter Eggs. http://losteast-ereggs.blogspot.com/2007/02/hieronymus.html.

Hilton, James. *Lost Horizon.* New York: Pocket Books, 1939.

Homer. *The Odyssey.* Norton Critical Edition. Ed. and trans. Albert Cook. New York: W.W. Norton, 1974.

Iheartdriveshaft. http://iheartdriveshaft.blogspot.com.

Iser, Wolfgang. "The Repertoire." *Critical Theory Since 1965.* Ed. Hazard Adams and Leroy Searle. Gainesville: University Press of Florida, 1986: 358-80.

James, Henry. *The Turn of the Screw.*

Jensen, Jeff. "*Lost* Findings." *Entertainment Weekly*, 3 March 2006. http://www.ew.com/ew/article/commentary/ 0,6115,1162044_3_0_,00.html.

—. "*Lost* in Transition." *Entertainment Weekley*, April 20, 2007, 10-11.

—. *Entertainment Weekly* column on *Lost.* http://www.ew.com.

"Jigsaw Puzzles." Lostpedia. http://lostpedia.com/wiki/Jigsaw_ puzzles#Secret_writing_on_back_side.

Joy, Nick. "*Lost* Season One. Review." Music from the Movies. http://www.musicfromthemovies.com/review.asp?ID=6255.

Kahn, Janine. Navel Gazing. July 27, 2007. http://blogs. ocweekly.com/navelgazing/san-diego-comic-con-2007/ comiccon-2007-the-lost-panel/.

King, Stephen. *Carrie*. New York: Doubleday, 1974.

—. *The Dark Tower: The Gunslinger*. Revised and Expanded Edition. New York: Viking, 2003.

—. "*Lost*'s Soul." *Entertainment Weekly* 9 September 2005: 150.

—. *The Stand*. New York: Gramercy Books, 1978.

Kitsis, Edward, and Adam Horowitz. *Lost*. Complete Second Season DVD, 2006.

L'Engle, Madeline. *A Wrinkle in Time*. New York: Dell, 1963.

Lavery, David. "The Island's Greatest Mystery: Is *Lost* Science Fiction?" *The Essential Science Fiction TV Reader*. Edited by J. P. Telotte. Lexington: U P of Kentucky, 2008.

—. "*Lost* and Long Term Television Narrative." *Third Person*. Edited Pat Harrigan and Noah Wardrip-Fruin Cambridge: Massachusetts Institute of Technology Press, 2008.

Lem, Stanislaw. *Solaris*. *Solaris*. Trans. Joanna Kilmartin and Steve Cox. NY: Berkley Medallion, 1971.

Letson, Russell F. "Heinlein, Robert Anson (1907-1988)." *The New Encyclopedia of Science Fiction*. Ed James Gunn. New York: Viking, 1988: 220-222.

Levinson, Paul. "Infinite Regress" Blog: *Lost*. http://paul-levinson.blogspot.com/search/label/Lost.

Lost. The Board Game. http://www.lostboardgame.com/home. html.

"*Lost* Fans Baffled Over Jigsaw Puzzles." 24-7PressRelease. com. http://24-7pressrelease.com/pdf /2006/10/04/press_release_19003.pdf.

"*Lost* Groupies Halt Filming." *PR Inside.* Jan. 15, 2007. http://www.pr-inside.com/rss/lost-groupies-halt-filming-r40101.htm.

MagnaCarta.net. http://magnacarta.net.

Miller, Ross. "*Lost* Video Game Confirmed for PS3, Xbox 360, and PC." *Joystiq,* April 17, 2007. http://www.joystiq.com/2007/04/17/lost-video-game-confirmed-for-ps3-xbox-360-and-pc/.

Mittell, Jason. "*Lost* in an Alternative Reality." *Flow* Volume 4, No. 7 (2006). http://jot.communication.utexas.edu/flow/?jot=view&id=1927.

Monaghan, Dominic. *Lost* Bonus. Watch with Kristin. The Vine. Eonline. March 2007. http://www.eonline.com/thevine/player.jsp?channelID=search&mediaID=19694.

More, Sir Thomas. *Utopia.* Norton Critical Edition. Trans. and Ed. Robert M. Adams. New York: W.W. Norton, 1975.

Mortensen, Viggo, and Buckethead. *pandemoniuminamerica.* CD. Percival Press and Viggo Mortensen, 2003.

Nabokov, Vladimir. *Laughter in the Dark.*

Nations, Gregg. "Re: Jigsaw Puzzles." The Fuselage. Feb. 28, 2007. http://www.thefuselage.com/Threaded/showthread.php?p=1404039.

Nelson, Willie. "Are You Sure." Cowboy Lyrics.com. http://www.cowboylyrics.com/lyrics/nelson-willie/are-you-sure-10278.html.

Nichols, Katherine. "Location, Location, Location." *Honolulu Star-Bulletin*, Feb. 4, 2007. http://starbulletin.com/2007/02/04/features/story01.html.

—. "'Lost' Home." *Honolulu Star-Bulletin*. May 21, 2006. http://starbulletin.com/2006/05/21/features/story01.html.

—. "'Lost' Stars Take Interactive a Step Further." *Honolulu Star-Bulletin*. Oct. 22, 2006. http://starbulletin.com/2006/10/22/features/story02.html.

Notes from the Underbelly. Barrie Sonnenfeld and Kim and Eric Tannenbaum. ABC. Pilot episode. April 12, 2007.

O'Brien, Flann. *The Third Polceman*. Normal, IL: Dalkey Archive Press, 1999.

Occono. Post. "Geronimo Jackson...New Future Theory." June 2, 2006. The Fuselage. http://www.thefuselage.com/Threaded/showthread.php?t=49221.

The Office. Ricky Gervais, Stephen Merchant, and Greg Daniels. NBC. Episode 3.19. "The Negotiation." April 5, 2007.

Official *Lost* Convention. June 2005. Burbank, CA. Creation Entertainment.

Official *Lost* podcast. Jan. 9, 2006. http://Abc.go.com.

Ozawa, Ryan Kawailani. "*Lost* on Location." *Hawaii*, June 2007, 16-17.

Percy, Walker. *Lancelot*. New York: Farrar, 1977.

Popular Culture Association. "History of the Popular Culture Movement." http://www.h-net.org/~pcaaca/pca/pcahistory.htm.

Porter, Lynnette and David Lavery. *Unlocking the Meaning of Lost: An Unauthorized Guide*. Naperville, IL: Sourcebooks, 2006, 2007.

Rand, Ayn. *Fountainhead*.

Salem, Rob. "Is *Fringe* the Next *Lost?*" *The Toronto Star* 15 July 2008: http://www.thestar.com/entertainment/Television/article/460219.

Schweiger, Daniel. "Music Review: *Lost* Original Television Soundtrack." *iF*, June 19, 2006. http://www.ifmagazine.com/review.asp?article=1296.

Second Tour of Finland. http://www.driveshaftband.com.

Shull, Dean. Fanfare Films. Personal email. Feb. 20, 2007.

Songs of the Celtic Football Club. Green and White Anthems. CD. Glasgow Celtic Football Club, 2000.

Stafford, Nikki. *Finding Lost*; *The Unofficial Guide.* Toronto: ECW Press, 2006, 2007.

Stam, Robert. *Film Theory: An Introduction.* Malden, MA: Blackwell, 2000.

Steinbeck, John. *Of Mice and Men.* New York: Bantam Books, 1981.

TDC Games. http://www.tdcgames.com/lostpuzzles.htm.

Troup, Gary. *Bad Twin.* New York: Hyperion, 2006.

Turner, Jenny. Personal email. April 18, 2007.

"UH Students Win 'Lost' Internships." *Pacific Business News.* Jan. 22, 2007. http://www.bizjournals.com/pacific/stories/2007/01/22/daily49.html.

Vaz, Mark Cotta. *The Lost Chronicles.* New York: Hyperion, 2005.

Notes

1. Personal email. February 20, 2007. Dean Shull and Fanfare Films are in the process of finishing the documentary, which includes a series of interviews with fans and people affiliated with *Lost*.

2. Personal email. Feb. 20, 2007.

3. Our use of the term "ancestor text" is indebted to literary critic and bestselling author Harold Bloom, who has argued that every great writer (and, by extension, every work of the imagination) must struggle to escape from the influence of the writers (and works) that came before. In order to be original, the newcomer must simultaneously borrow from "ancestor texts" and depart from them in order to become unique and innovative.

4. http://en.wikipedia.org/w/index.php?title=The_Fountainhead&oldid=120801813.

5. http://tesla.liketelevision.com/liketelevision/tuner.php?channel=139&format=movie&theme=guide.

6. http://www.lostpedia.com/wiki/VALIS.

7. See Porter and Lavery (2006), 177–178.

8. Oday, Alan, and Hatfield, Bobby. "Rock and Roll Heaven." *Retrospective 1963–1974*. Righteous Brothers.

9. Songs of the Celtic Football Club. Green and White Anthems. CD. Glasgow Celtic FC. 2000.

10 Willie Nelson. "Are You Sure." Cowboy Lyrics.com. http://www.cowboylyrics.com/lyrics/nelson-willie/are-you-sure-10278.html.

11 Aaron Lewis (lyrics) and Fred Durst (composer). "Outside." Staind. Metro Lyrics. http://www.metrolyrics.com/outside-lyrics-staind.html.

12 Sarah McLachlan. "Building a Mystery." SarahMcLachlan.com. http://www.sarahmclachlan.com/discography/lyrics.jsp?song_id=34.

13 Bonobo (Simon Green). "If You Stayed Over."

14 John Farrar. "Xanadu." *Xanadu* soundtrack. 1980. Olivia Newton-John.

15 Buddy Holly. "Everyday." ST Lyrics. http://www.stlyrics.com/lyrics/bigfish/everyday.htm.

16 Hank Cochran. "She's Got You." 1962. Patsy Cline.

17 Edward Kitsis and Adam Horowitz. *Lost*. Season Two DVD. 2006.

18 Official *Lost* Podcast. Abc.go.com. January 9, 2006.

19 The Fuselage. Geronimo Jackson...New Future Theory. Post by Occono. June 2, 2006.

20 The Fuselage. Geronimo Jackson...New Future Theory. Post by Amillerphoto. May 15, 2006. http://www.thefuselage.com/Threaded/showthread.php?t=49221.

21 The *Lost* Experience. DJ Dan. Second podcast. September 24, 2006.

22 Like Charlie, Monaghan writes songs. He and friend Shox from California-based (and Lord of the Rings-fan favorite) World Without Sundays wrote "Photos and Plans," which never made it to the series (as noted in *Lost*: The Complete First Season DVD. Disk 7. Backstage with DriveShaft. 2005). Monaghan

wrote a second song for (3.21) "Greatest Hits" but in a March 2007 interview (*Lost* Bonus. Watch with Kristin. Eonline. The Vine. Video interview with Dominic Monaghan. http://www. eonline.com/thevine/player.jsp?channelID=search&mediaID= 19694) said he was unsure if it would be included. It wasn't. *Lost* isn't Monaghan's first time as a songwriter; he wrote and recorded "Shadow" and "Maybe" for Viggo Mortensen's self-produced 2003 CD *pandemoniuminamerica* (Viggo and Buckethead. Pandemoniuminamerica. CD. Perceval Press and Viggo Mortensen, 2003).

[23] "Watch with Kristin." Interview with Emilie de Ravin. May 8, 2008. http://www.eonline.com/gossip/kristin/detail/index. jsp?uuid=af6fc300-02d4-406b-99d6-ec70ed2ed9ee.

[24] Residents of Clitheroe, Lancashire, resented Charlie's comment that their town is the backside of nowhere. Shortly after "Greatest Hits" was broadcast, *This Is Lancashire* published a rebuttal to note the town's illustrious past with famous rock groups (Sally Henfield, "Charlie's Lost It," http://www.thisislancashire.co.uk/news/headlines/display.var.1415430.0.charlies_lost_it.php). The article stirred lots of local online commentary about Clitheroe and Monaghan's connections with Lancashire, through his Manchester roots and previous TV series *Hetty Wainthropp Investigates*. Even a passing comment on *Lost* generates a lot of discussion.

[25] Bonus. Watch with Kristin. Eonline. The Vine. Video interview with Dominic Monaghan. March 2007. http://www. eonline.com/thevine/player.jsp?channelID=search&mediaID= 19694

26 Amanda Cuder. "Tuning into the Keys of 'Lost' Songs." June 22, 2007. *Connecticut Post.* http://www.connpost.com/leisure/ci_6170895.

27 *Alias.* Season 4, Episode 3. "The Awful Truth."

28 DriveShaft is on MySpace at www.myspace.com/driveshaft; the well-developed fan site Second Tour of Finland's URL is www.driveshaftband.com; the memorial sites can be found at http://remembercharlie.wikidot.com/.

29 The "In Memory" YouTube video was uploaded in December 2007 (http://www.youtube.com/watch?v=OiHB8EMRp3) and by May 2008 had logged more than 13,000 views; the most watched (with more than 31,000 hits to date) is "Goodbye Charlie—Lost," added to YouTube after the Season Three finale.

30 "Watch with Kristin." "Exclusive! Dominic Monaghan Leads a Tour of His Photo Exhibit—and Talks *Lost.*" March 28, 2008. http://www.eonline.com/gossip/kristin/detail/index.jsp?uuid=a15c1c7b-f56e-4dc0-95fd-eb1041076dae.

31 Many fanfiction sites include stories about Charlie's adventures after "Through the Looking Glass" and "The Beginning of the End." Two of the best sites are http://pacejunkie.livejournal.com/19150.html and http://community.livejournal.com/charliepacefic/.

32 Daniel Schweiger. "Review: *Speed Racer* Original Soundtrack." *iF Magazine.* May 15, 2008. http://www.ifmagazine.com/review.asp?article=2528.

33 Bryan Cairns. "From Shore to Score." *Lost* magazine, 10, May/June 2007, p. 42.

34 Interview with Michael Giacchino. Official *Lost* video podcast. April 11, 2007. abc.go.com.

35 Daniel Schweiger. "Music Review: *Lost* Original Television Soundtrack." iF magazine. June 19, 2006. http://www.ifmagazine.com/review.asp?article=1296.

36 Cairns, "From Shore to Score," p. 43.

37 Nick Joy. "*Lost* Season One. Review." Music from the Movies. http://www.musicfromthemovies.com/review.asp?ID=6255.

38 Presentation at the Official *Lost* Convention, June 2005, Burbank, CA, Creation Entertainment.

39 Official *Lost* video podcast, April 11. 2007, abc.go.com.

40 Cairns, "From Shore to Score," p. 42.

41 "Dominic Monaghan Discusses Charlie's Fate—and What's Next." Interview with Kristin Veitch, posted May 23, 2007, http://www.eonline.com/uberblog/watch_with_kristin/b4310_losts_emilie_de_ravin_talks_about_baby.html

42 *MadTV*. Fox. April 26, 2008.

43 Personal interview. Brian D. Bradley. April 8, 2008.

44 *Chuck*. NBC. October 1, 2007.

45 The pilot of *Notes from the Underbelly* features an episode of *Lost* in the background as several couples make love: a young woman trying to become pregnant bemoans the fact that the bedroom doesn't have a television, while her partner runs off without a post-coital cuddle because he wants to watch *Lost;* in other bedrooms, one partner avidly watches the screen while the other strives for greater intimacy (Of course, a good scene *was* playing in the background—a shirtless Jack dives into the ocean to try to save Joanna from drowning.)

46 Popular Culture Association. History of the Popular Culture Movement. http://www.h-net.org/~pcaaca/pca/pcahistory.htm.

47 Jensen, Jeff. "*Lost* in Transition." *Entertainment Weekly*, April 20, 2007, 10-11.

[48] "*Lost*'s Latest Victim." *TV Guide*. April 29, 2008.

[49] Ausiello, Michael. "Exclusive: 'Lost' Resurrects Michelle Rodriguez!" *Entertainment Weekly*, August 25, 2008, http://ausiellofiles.ew.com/2008/08/michelle-rodrig.html.

[50] *Lost:* Missing Pieces webisodes. "So It Begins."November 2007. http://abc.go.com/primetime/lost/missingpieces/index.

[51] Coldplay. "42." *Viva La Vida*. July 2008. Ironically, "42" is, according to the *Hitchhiker's Guide to the Universe*, the meaning of life. It also is one of Hurley's numbers.

[52] Tikrit was hometown not only to Sayid but to former president Saddam Hussein. Many U.S. fans may like Sayid but, like Sawyer, also find it hard to forget that he is Iraqi.

[53] Cedar Rapids. City of Five Seasons. http://www.cedar-rapids.org/community/fifthseason.asp.

[54] Florida also turns up in many casual references. On the freighter, Omar says he hails from Florida ("The Constant," 4.5). Ben explains that some people will believe anything, even that the Virgin Mary appears in mold in Gainesville ("The Other Woman," 4.6). Florida seems to be a popular place with *Lost* characters.

[55] The news item was found online at http://www.pr-inside.com/rss/lost-groupies-halt-filming-r40101.htm, although it also was carried by Honolulu newspapers ("*Lost* Groupies Halt Filming," PR Inside, Jan. 15, 2007).

[56] Ryan Kawailani Ozawa, "*Lost* on Location, *Hawaii*, June 2007, p. 16. The article provides an overview of Oahu locations masquerading as Pittsburgh, Albuquerque, Miami, London, and Seoul.

57 Nichols, Katherine. "'Lost' Home." *Honolulu Star-Bulletin*, May 21, 2006. http://starbulletin.com/2006/05/21/features/story01. html.

58 Nichols, Katherine. "Location, Location, Location." *Honolulu Star-Bulletin*, February 4, 2007. http://starbulletin. com/2007/02/04/features/story01.html.

59 Ryan, Tim. "'Lost' Cast Set to Aid in Disaster." *Honolulu Star-Bulletin*, September 9, 2005. http://starbulletin.com/2005/09/09/ news/story6.html.

60 Nichols, Katherine. "'Lost' Stars Take Interactive a Step Further." *Honolulu Star-Bulletin*, October 22, 2006. http://star-bulletin.com/2006/10/22/features/story02.html.

61 "UH Students Win 'Lost' Internships." *Pacific Business News*. January 22, 2007. http://www.bizjournals.com/pacific/ stories/2007/01/22/htmldaily49.html?from_rss-1.

62 TDC Games. http://www.tdcgames.com/lostpuzzles.htm.

63 "LOST Fans Baffled over Jigsaw Puzzles." 24-7PressRelease. com. http://www.24-7pressrelease.com/pdf/2006/10/04/press_ release_19003.pdf.

64 Comments by Brian. November-December 2006. About.com. "*Lost* Puzzles. http://lost.wpadmin.about.com/?comments_ popup=7378.

65 One of the best sites for spoiler information about the puzzles, including photos of completed puzzles and the decoded messages, is *Lost*pedia's http://lostpedia.com/wiki/Jigsaw_ puzzles#Secret_writing_on_back_side. The website lists all the steps to take to decode the message.

66 Gregg Nations. The Fuselage. Feb. 28, 2007. "Re: Jigsaw Puzzles." http://www.thefuselage.com/Threaded/showthread. php?p=1404039.

[67] Arneson, Erik. "*Lost*—The Game: Interview with the Designer." About.com. http://boardgames.about.com/od/lostboardgame/a/designer_intvw.htm.

[68] *Lost*: The Board Game. http://www.lostboardgame.com/home.html.

[69] As this book goes to print, the currently listed release date is October 1, 2008.

[70] Miller, Ross. "*Lost* Video Game Confirmed for PS3, Xbox 360, and PC." Joystiq. April 17, 2007. http://www.joystiq.com/2007/04/17/lost-video-game-confirmed-for-ps3-xbox-360-and-pc/.

[71] Bramwell, Tom. "News. Ubisoft Details *Lost* Game." Eurogamer. July 27, 2007. http://www.eurogamer.net/article.php?article_id=80424.

[72] *Lost*: The Mobile Game. Gameloft. http://www.gameloft.com/lost-mobile-game/.

[73] "Gameloft Secures Mobile Gaming Rights to Hit ABC/Touchstone Television Series *Lost* and Desperate Housewives." Business Wire. August 14, 2006. http://findarticles.com/p/articles/mi_m0EIN/is_2006_August_14/ai_n16620641.

[74] Buchanan, Levi. "*Lost* for iPod Review." Wireless-IGN. June 17, 2007. http://wireless.ign.com/articles/797/797374p1.html.

INDEX

ABOUT THE AUTHORS

Lynnette Porter is an associate professor at Embry-Riddle Aeronautical University. She has collaborated with David Lavery and Hillary Robson on books about *Lost*, *Heroes*, and *Battlestar Galactica*, as well as contributed chapters and written books about *The Lord of the Rings*. She is frequently a speaker at scholarly and fan conventions internationally. During visits to Oahu in 2007 she took the photographs for this book.

David Lavery holds a chair in film and television at Brunel University in London. The author/co-author/editor/co-editor of scores of essays and twelve books (three with Lynnette Porter and Hillary Robson) on such television series as *Twin Peaks*, *The X-Files*, *The Sopranos*, *Buffy the Vampire Slayer*, *Deadwood*, *Seinfeld*, *My So Called Life*, and *Heroes*, he has lectured on American television around the world.

Hillary Robson is an academic advisor at Middle Tennessee State University and teaches courses in English and University Studies. She has co-authored three books with David Lavery and Lynnette Porter on *Heroes*, *Lost*, and *Battlestar Galactica*, is a co-editor on a forthcoming text on *Grey's Anatomy*, and has contributed to collections on *Alias* and Cult Television. She has given presentations at various conferences in the United States on television and fandom studies.